FROZEN IN TIME

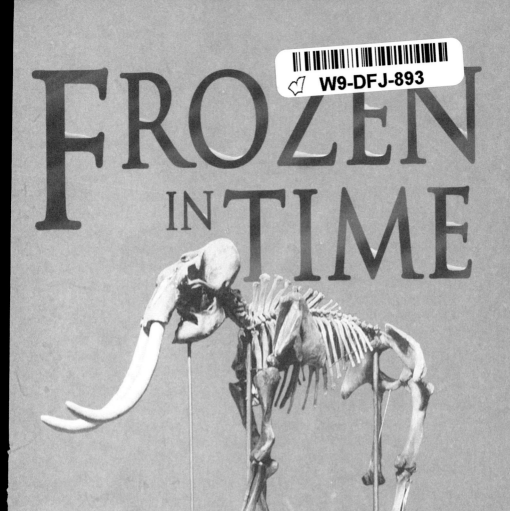

FROZEN IN TIME

BY MICHAEL OARD

MB
Master
Books

ACKNOWLEDGMENTS

I would like to thank all those who have had a part in my thinking about the woolly mammoth and the Ice Age over the years, especially my wife, Beverly, who has not only been an inspiration, but also is the first person I turn to for editing. I am grateful to Answers in Genesis Australia, especially to Don Batten, who devoted considerable time to revising an earlier manuscript. The Institute for Creation Research and Answers in Genesis generously provided many of the illustrations. A number of illustrators, artists, and individuals have significantly enhanced the book. These include David Oard, Mark Wolfe, Ron Hight, Laurel Hemmings, Daniel Lewis, Dan Leitha, Lynn Jolly, Gordon Davison, Alex Lalamov, and Earl and Bonita Snellenberger. Roger Howerton, Brent Spurlock, Judy Lewis, Bryan Miller, and Joanna Swift, editors and artists of Master Books, did an excellent job of giving *Frozen in Time* its final cut and polish.

This book is dedicated to my wife, Beverly, who has not only sacrificed the time I have spent writing this and other books and articles, but also has helped considerably with these projects. I thank the Lord for her gracious spirit and companionship for over 35 years of marriage.

First printing: October 2004

ISBN: 0-89051-418-6
Library of Congress Number: 2004106971

Cover by Bryan Miller

Printed in the United States of America

Please visit our website for other great titles:
www.masterbooks.net

For information regarding author interviews,
please contact the publicity department at (870) 438-5288.

TABLE OF CONTENTS

PREFACE

The bones, tusks, and especially carcasses of millions of woolly mammoths frozen in the tundra of Siberia have excited the imaginations of children and scientists for hundreds of years. Why would the woolly mammoth and many other mammals even want to live in northern Siberia, as well as Alaska and the Yukon Territory? What would they eat in the snowy tundra? Where could they have found enough water to drink? Mammoths are like elephants, which require hundreds of pounds of food and many gallons of water daily. As if the mystery isn't deep enough, it appears that although they lived well for a time, they suddenly went extinct along with dozens of other large mammals and birds from all continents.

When we examine woolly mammoth carcasses, the mysteries multiply. Some carcasses and skeletons have been found in a general standing position. It is known from the character of the blood in the carcasses that three woolly mammoths and two woolly rhinos suffocated. Some carcasses have broken bones. Why should this be? Finally, there is the ever-persistent problem of how millions of woolly mammoths and other mammals are forced into the rock-hard permafrost to remain frozen in time to this day.

It is indeed strange that the mammoth and its cohorts lived in Siberia during the Ice Age but died out at the end of the Ice Age, when living conditions were supposedly improving! Why?

The Ice Age itself is a major mystery. What could have triggered the Ice Age, especially when it occurred not that long ago? In fact, it is the last major geological event on the planet, and yet scientists understand little of its cause. And also intriguing, will we experience another ice age in the near future, as most scientists expect?

If that is not all, there were many huge lakes and rivers in now desert or semi-arid regions of the earth during the Ice Age. Furthermore, it was typical that animals, plants, and other organisms that prefer cold climates lived alongside of organisms that preferred warm climates. These are called disharmonious associations, of which mainstream scientists have no explanation.

Why are there so many mysteries of the recent past? Could it be that mainstream scientists have been looking in the wrong direction for their answers? Is the problem with their assumptions about the past? If they cannot explain such major geological events of the recent past, namely the Ice Age, why should we trust evolutionary/uniformitarian scientists with the solution to events older than the Ice Age?

As an atmospheric scientist, these many questions sparked my interest. After studying meteorology, climatology, and other disciplines of the earth sciences since the 1960s, I developed a theory of the Ice Age based on the Genesis flood (Oard, 1990). This was a unique, fast-acting Ice Age of about 700 years in duration. It is from the background of this unique Ice Age that the answers to the woolly mammoth mysteries find a viable explanation. In other words, I put on my Flood "glasses" to examine the data of science, instead of viewing the world with the "glasses" of slow processes over millions of years, which is the uniformitarian model. I believe the biblical perspective is the key to solving these mysteries, some of which have plagued scientists for over 200 years!

I also found that another key for unlocking these mysteries of the recent past is the short time scale of Scripture from Genesis 1–11. Evolutionary scientists believe one ice age takes 100,000 years and that there were about 30 regularly repeating ice ages in the past few million years. I discovered that by telescoping certain events related to these mysteries, the Ice Age takes only hundreds of years. Time is not a side issue; the short time scale of Scripture is crucial to solving mysteries of the past.

This book will delve into these questions and mysteries. We will first discuss the many mysteries of the woolly mammoths and the Ice Age. Second, we will go into the many theories and ideas that have attempted to explain these mysteries. I will then develop the unique Ice Age from the climatic consequences of the Genesis flood. Fourth, we are then in a position to provide reasonable solutions to the many mammoth problems.

CHAPTER ONE

FROZEN MAMMOTH
CARCASSES IN SIBERIA

Frozen mammoth carcasses found in Siberia have challenged our imagination for centuries. These carcasses sometimes come with skin, hair, and internal organs including the heart (Agenbroad and Nelson, 2002, p. 8). Reports of these discoveries intrigue adults and children alike, for different reasons. One island in the New Siberian Islands, off the Arctic Ocean coast, is described as mostly mammoth bones. Over the years, a lucrative ivory trade developed as thousands of tons of ivory tusks have been unearthed and exported from Siberia. Scientists struggle to understand why these animals lived in Siberia and how they died. Children love stories of frozen carcasses with meat fresh enough to eat.

Many questions arise as a result of these strange discoveries. Why would the woolly mammoth, bison, woolly rhinoceros, and horse be attracted to Siberia? Today, Siberia is a barren, blizzard-scourged wilderness. How could the animals have endured the extremely cold winters? What would they eat? Where would the beasts locate the prodigious quantities of water they require when the land is imprisoned in snow and ice. Even the rivers are covered with several feet of ice every winter. Most puzzling of all is how did the mammoths and their companions die en mass and how could they have become encased in the permafrost?

Over time, various clues about the environment at the time of their death have been discovered and studied. Scientists found partially preserved stomach vegetation

Figure 1.1

in some of the carcasses and so could identify the woolly mammoth's last meal. Solving one mystery just leads to another. They wondered how the stomach contents remained half decayed while the animals froze? This is a problem since it takes a long time to freeze an animal as large as an elephant. A quick freeze came to mind. Birds Eye Frozen Foods Company ran the calculations and came up with a staggering -150°F (-100°C). Once again, the scientists were puzzled. How could such temperatures be reached on earth, especially when apparently they were in a fairly temperate environment before the quick freeze?

Many theories have been postulated. One of the most popular is that the hairy elephants were peacefully grazing on grass and buttercups and were suddenly struck by a huge freezing storm blowing from the Arctic Ocean. Millions of them froze instantly. This kind of quick freeze has never been observed, so some special and imaginative ideas have been proposed. One question seems to always lead to another. This story is based on the Beresovka mammoth that was excavated and shipped back to St. Petersburg, Russia, overland during a heroic expedition led by Otto Herz and E. Pfizenmayer. The expedition started in the late spring of 1901, and ended on February 18, 1902. To transport the mammoth flesh, they had to travel 3,700 miles (6,000 km) by sled during a bitterly cold Siberian fall and winter (Pfizenmayer, 1939).

We will explore these questions in this book and provide another theory based on the Ice Age. This Ice Age answers the questions about the migration and extinction of woolly mammoths and other animals in Siberia. The cause of the Ice Age still remains a mystery for mainstream scientists. So a theory for the Ice Age will be presented based on the Genesis flood as described in the Bible.

WHAT EXACTLY IS A WOOLLY MAMMOTH?

A woolly mammoth *(Mammuthus primigenius)* is essentially a "hairy elephant" with a large shoulder hump, a sloping back, small ears and tail, unique teeth, and a small trunk with two finger-like projections at the tip. They usually have spirally curved tusks up to 11 feet (3.3 m) long. The world-record tusk is 13.5 feet (4.11 m) long and probably weighted around 225 pounds (about 100 kg) (Agenbroad and Nelson, 2002, p. 33). The woolly mammoth was covered with three types of hair: (1) the outer guard hairs that were coarse and just over 3 feet (90 cm) long, (2) an underfur that

Figure 1.2. The Beresovka mammoth.

Figure 1.3. The skull, jaw, and tusks of a woolly mammoth.

was thinner and about 10 to 12 inches (25 to 30 cm) long, and (3) below the underfur a thick layer of wool that was around 1 to 3 inches (2 to 8 cm) long (Agenbroad and Nelson, 2002, p. 42–43). A full-grown mammoth tooth is over a foot long and has a series of parallel enamel ridges. The long hair, small ears, and tiny tail are probably adaptations to a cold climate.

The woolly mammoth is one of two general types of mammoths in the genus *Mammuthus*. The Columbian mammoth is the second type. It is larger than the woolly mammoth, standing about 13 feet (4 m) high, compared to 9 to 11 feet (about 3 m) tall for the woolly mammoth (Agenbroad and Nelson, 2002, p. 40). Both are members of the order Proboscidea in the biological classification system, which includes modern and extinct elephants. There are many disputes over the classification of elephants and mammoths (see appendix 1).

The woolly mammoth has some distinct adaptations to cold, such as thicker fur, than the Columbian mammoth. Did the woolly mammoth develop these adaptations because of the cold, or did the woolly mammoth always have such features and was more favorably disposed to migrate farther north? I would favor the former explanation, but there is no way to know for sure. The reason I favor adaptations to the cold is that such adaptations are built into the genes and chromosomes of many mammals and people today. We adapt to winter temperatures by physiological changes, such as the body producing thicker blood. These changes have nothing to do with evolution but are built into the organism. Certain genes that control other genes are triggered by environmental cues. So, I believe it is the same with the woolly mammoth. The cold likely triggered certain dormant genes that went into action and produced the long hair and other cold-adaptive traits.

ARE THERE MILLIONS OF MAMMOTHS BURIED IN SIBERIA?

Many have claimed that there are millions of mammoths entombed in the permafrost of Siberia. Could this be true or is it a gross exaggeration? Farrand (1961) downsized the estimate to around 50,000 mammoths that died and are buried. It is very difficult to estimate the number of living animals in such a vast, poorly populated territory as Siberia, let alone the number of mammoths that might have died and been buried. Estimates have to be made on how many still lie hidden in the permafrost, which complicates the matter (Ukraintseva, 1993, p. 234). Just how

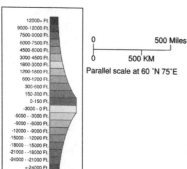

Figure 1.4. Map of Siberia and offshore in the Arctic Ocean, coded for elevation. Note that the northwest is a generally flat plain while there are mountain ranges in the south and east.

many mammoths were buried affects our theories on the environment of Siberia and their extinction.

When writing about the number of mammoth bones, tusks, and carcasses, researchers commonly emphasize the large number of bones that have been found. For instance, Valentina Ukraintseva (1993, p. 224) states that the mammoths from Siberia were *abundant,* based on their *numerous* remains. Dale Guthrie (1990a, p. 67), University of Alaska in Fairbanks, estimates that *hundreds of thousands* of mammal bones have been concentrated along streams in inland Alaska. Of course, a single animal has many bones, but Guthrie's estimate does not include the bones not yet washed out of valley deposits or those that remain buried in the uplands. Irena Dubrovo (1990, p. 3) remarks that there are a *great number* of woolly mammoth remains in Siberia. Explorers have always reported the remains as abundant (Péwé and Hopkins, 1967, p. 266).

The top expert on woolly mammoths in Siberia is Nikolai Vereshchagin, who has spent nearly half a century researching the mammoth fauna. Since 1940, he has identified approximately a million bone fragments from many types of animals found within the permafrost of Eurasia (Vereshchagin, 1995, p. 61). He states that the abundance of remains in Siberia is *remarkable* (Vereshchagin and Baryshnikov, 1982, p. 267). There are *many hundreds of thousands* of large mammals buried in Siberia (Vereshchagin, 1974, p. 3) with *many millions* of bones (Vereshchagin, 1995, p. 62).

Erosion along the Arctic coast varies from 3 to 22 feet (1 to 7 m) a year (Thiede, Kassens, and Timokhov, 2000), spilling an enormous number of woolly mammoth bones from the sea cliffs. In a report in the *Smithsonian* magazine, Stewart (1977, p. 68) refers to an estimate made by Vereshchagin for a section along the Arctic coast between the Yana and Kolyma rivers:

> *Through such causes almost 50,000 mammoth tusks are said to have been found in Siberia between 1660 and 1915, serving an extensive mammoth ivory trade. But this is nothing compared to those still buried, according to Vereshchagin, who calculates that the heavy erosion of the Arctic coast spills thousands of tusks and tens of thousands of buried bones each year into the sea and that along the 600-mile coastal shallows between the Yana and Kolyma [rivers] lie more than half a million tons of mammoth tusks with another 150,000 tons in the bottom of the lakes of the coastal plain.*

If each tusk weighs 100 pounds (45 kg), a reasonable estimate (Agenbroad and Nelson, 2002, p. 33), Vereshchagin's numbers would suggest that five million mammoths are buried in this region! Is he exaggerating? If he is, it probably isn't by much. This area may well contain the highest density of mammoth remains, since the rich New Siberian Islands lie offshore. The coastal zone of the Laptev Sea, which includes the western area of Vereshchagin's estimate is regarded as one of the largest mammoth cemeteries in the world (Thiede, Kassens, and Timokhov, 2000, p. 367).

The number of woolly mammoths is more concentrated in northern Siberia (Howorth, 1880; Digby, 1926, p. 14). Mammoth remains are amazingly abundant on the Lyakhov Islands (Baryshnikov et al., 1999, p. 5) and on the other New Siberian Islands, 140 miles (230 km) north of the mainland (Howorth, 1880; Nordenskiöld, 1883, p. 149, 155). The early report of one of the New Siberian Islands being totally composed of bones is a gross exaggeration. The many bones found on these islands indicates that Siberia and the adjacent continental shelves with their islands was once a vast plain dotted with woolly mammoths and other animals. Vereshchagin and Kuz'mina (1984, p. 219) state:

> *The shelf of the Laptev and East Siberian Seas [along the Arctic continental shelf] in some places . . . is covered with bones of horse, reindeer, bison, musk ox, and mammoth washed up by tidal waters. Occasionally, bones of wolf, brown*

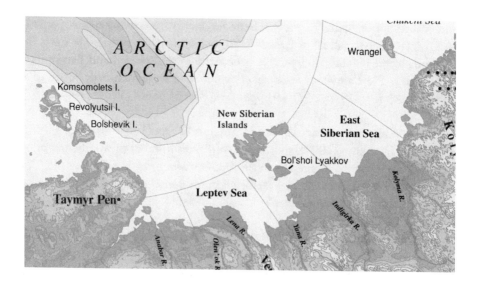

Figure 1.5. North-central Siberia and the New Siberian Islands.

bear, cave lion, and (rarely) woolly rhinoceros, moose, and saiga antelope are also found.

One can see that a wide diversity of animals accompanied the woolly mammoth in Siberia, as well as elsewhere across the Northern Hemisphere. This Ice Age environment has been called the mammoth steppe, which is a vast grassland.

Based on many reports, it appears that estimates of millions of woolly mammoths in the Siberian permafrost are correct. Lister and Bahn (1994, p. 115) note that some scientists put the number at ten million mammoths in the Siberian deep freeze. This makes the question of how they could have possibly found enough food and water in such a cold area even more enigmatic.

Woolly mammoth fossils are not only commonly found in Siberia, but they are also found in unconsolidated sediments all across the mid and high latitudes of the Northern Hemisphere. Sometimes their remains are dredged up from the continental shelves in some locations. Although associated with the Ice Age, they are rarely found in previously glaciated areas. They are mostly found in non-glaciated areas of Siberia. They spread from Siberia into the non-glaciated portions of Alaska and the Yukon by way of the Bering Land Bridge. This land bridge was dry or mostly dry during the Ice Age. From the Yukon, the mammoths migrated through western Alberta by way of the ice-free corridor and spread south throughout the northern United States. The Columbian mammoth is usually found farther south — in the

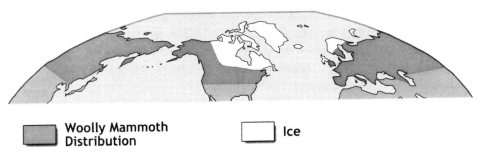

Woolly Mammoth Distribution **Ice**

Figure 1.6. Woolly mammoth carcass distribution in Northern Hemisphere.
(Redrawn by Daniel Lewis with Eurasia; from Khalke, 1999, figure 13.)

southern United States, Mexico, and Central America (Fagen, 1987; Siebe, Schaaf, and Urrutia-Fucugauchi, 1999). The number of woolly mammoth individuals fossilized worldwide probably exceeds 15 million.

CARCASS PUZZLES

As if the existence of frozen carcasses isn't mysterious enough, several aspects of the carcasses are very puzzling.

A number of carcasses, as well as a few skeletons, have been discovered in a general *standing position*. It looks like the animal sank in a bog, but generally Siberian bogs are not deep enough to bury an animal that size. Also, the majority of the sediment surrounding the carcasses is not bog sediment (Howorth, 1887, p. 61, 185; Pfizenmayer, 1939, p. 7). Henry Howorth (1880, p. 551–552) tells us:

> *The same conclusion was arrived at by Brandt, from a consideration of the fact that the bodies and skeletons of Mammoths are sometimes found standing upright, as if they had sunk in that position into the soft ground. This was the case with the specimen found by Ssarytschef, near Alansk . . . with a skeleton found about 1827 near Petersburgh, as reported to Brandt by Pander; a third which was found in the peninsula of the Obi, fifty versts from the mouth of the Yerambei; and a fourth found in the government of Moscow, all of which are discussed by Brandt. . . .*

The Beresovka mammoth was found in a sitting position, although it had slumped down the slope probably in a frozen block before discovery (Pfizenmayer, 1939, p. 86). The unique position of this mammoth indicates that the sliding probably did not change the original position of the mammoth at death. Even the trees were still generally upright in the material that slid down the hill (Guthrie, 1990a, p. 7).

Russian researcher Tolmachoff reported several upright mammoth carcasses in Siberia. One of the carcasses was found in 1839, on the Shangin River, a tributary to the Indigirka River, in an upright position and protruding from a cliff (Tolmachoff, 1929, p. 26). Another upright mammoth was also discovered in a cliff on the New Siberian Islands (Tolmachoff, 1929, p. 32). Tolmachoff (1929, p. 36) himself found parts of the skeleton of a mammoth on the coast of the Arctic Ocean, ". . . protruding out of frozen bluff in a more or less upright position." He mentions in words similar to Howorth's how Brandt was impressed about these upright mammoths:

> Brandt was very much impressed by the fact that remnants of the mammoth, carcasses and skeletons alike, sometimes were found in poses which indicated that the animals had perished standing upright, as though they had bogged (Tolmachoff, 1929, p. 56).

Strangely, scientists investigating three woolly mammoths and two woolly rhinos, including the Beresovka mammoth, found they all died by *suffocation* (Digby, 1926 p. 54; Tolmachoff, 1929; Farrand, 1961, p. 734). For a live animal to die of suffocation, it had to be buried rapidly or drowned.

Several of the carcasses have broken bones. Both of the upper front leg bones and some of the ribs of the Selerikan horse were broken (Guthrie, 1990a, p. 31). It was also missing its head. The Beresovka mammoth had a broken pelvis, ribs, and right foreleg (Digby, 1926; Pfizenmayer, 1939). It takes quite a force to break the bones of a mammoth. The broken bones have inspired the story that the Beresovka mammoth was grazing on grass and buttercups when it accidentally fell into a crevasse in the permafrost. Then it was rapidly covered and suffocated (Pfizenmayer, 1939, p. 90). Buttercups, as well as leaves and grasses, were found in the mouth of the Beresovka mammoth between its teeth and tongue (Pfizenmayer, 1939, p. 39; Guthrie, 1990a, p. 4).

Not only is it difficult to explain the upright burial, but even more challenging is the question of how these many mammoths and other animals ended up inside the permafrost layer. Both carcasses and bones had to be buried quickly, below the summer melt layer of the permafrost, before they rotted. Howorth (1887, p. 95) states the problem this way:

> Now, by no physical process known to us can we understand how soft flesh could thus be buried in ground while it is frozen as hard as flint without disintegrating it. We cannot push an elephant's body into a mass of solid ice or hard frozen gravel and clay without entirely destroying the fine articulations and pounding the whole mass into a jelly, nor would we fail in greatly disturbing the ground in the process.

This is not just Howorth's opinion. Quackenbush (1909, p. 126) reinforces his assessment:

> *But, if flesh was preserved only when protected from air, bodies found entire must have been rapidly and completely covered, and it is not evident how this could have occurred otherwise than by their sinking into some kind of soft or boggy ground.*

Any plausible theory explaining why woolly mammoths inhabited Siberia and how they died must also be able to explain these carcass puzzles, which are shown in table 1.1.

Table 1.1. Mammoth Carcass Puzzles

1) Some carcasses and skeletons were found in a general, standing position

2) Three woolly mammoths and two woolly rhinos suffocated

3) Millions of animals became entombed in rock-hard permafrost

4) Some of the mammals have broken bones

CHAPTER TWO

WHY LIVE IN SIBERIA?

Before I delve into a theory on the demise of the woolly mammoths, some prelimi-nary questions need to be answered. Most importantly, what drew millions of woolly mammoths to the far north where the winters are currently so fiercely cold and the summers so dangerously boggy? And what did they eat while they were there?

THE GREAT SIBERIAN DEATH WISH

In the 1970s, the musk ox was reintroduced to the Taimyr Peninsula, north central Siberia, and Wrangel Island located in the Arctic Ocean (Stuart, 1991, p. 508). If the woolly mammoth and other animals could be brought back to life, possibly by cloning, would they be able to survive in Siberia? Some scientists are even suggesting that cells from a frozen woolly mammoth carcass could possibly be introduced into a female Asian elephant, producing a hybrid.

Siberia is well known for its bitterly cold winters (see map on page 24). Siberian winter temperatures average below zero Fahreinheit (below -18°C). But minimum temperatures commonly descend colder than 40 below (°F or °C) in the winter. The lowest temperature ever recorded in the Northern Hemisphere is -90°F (-68°C) at Verkhoyansk (Knystautas, 1987, p. 27). Large mammals can usually tolerate a fair amount of cold, but could they tolerate the blizzards and extreme wind chills of the winter months? Siberia's cold season lasts nearly nine months of the year.

Interestingly, not many large mammals live in Siberia today. Vereshchagin and Baryshnikov (1984, p. 492) express the opinion of some Russian scientists in regard to woolly mammoths:

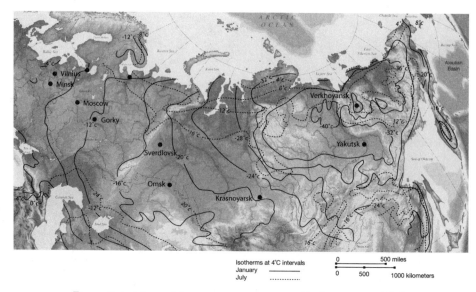

Figure 2.1. Map with average temperatures for January and July.

There would be no place for mammoths in the present arctic tundra of Eurasia with its dense snow driven by the winds.

Mainstream scientists believe that during the Ice Age, winter temperatures were possibly 10 to 20°F (6 to 12°C) colder, making survival even more difficult.

Summers, on the other hand, can be quite warm today due to nearly perpetual sunshine. Digby (1926, p. 195) describes one week he spent in Yakutsk, Siberia. The mercury never dropped below 80°F (27°C), "night" or day! Assuming an animal somehow survived the winter, summers would be comfortable.

Some have thought that the woolly mammoths could easily have migrated into Siberia during the warmer spring and summer. After a summer of fattening on the vegetation, they would then migrate back south during the fall, before the cold of winter hit. Although a few scientists have entertained this possibility (Soffer, 1985), this theory has fatal flaws. The woolly mammoths would have to migrate several thousand miles, before winter, which would severely tax the energy of the mammoths (Guthrie, 1990a, p. 246). A mammoth's legs are heavy and require much more energy to walk than other mammals. Howorth (1887, p. 62–63) further points out that any animals in northeast Siberia would have to migrate even farther. The North Pacific Ocean lies directly to the south of their path. The woolly mammoths would need to travel a few thousand miles farther west, before heading south. Another problem with the migration theory is that spring migration back to northern Siberia makes little sense. There likely would be an adequate food supply in southern Siberia or farther south (G. Haynes, 1991, p. 97). There would be no need to migrate north. Finally, mammoths were pregnant for 22 months, making any kind of yearly migration hazardous. Mammoth expert Gary Haynes (1990, p. 25–26) summarizes the case against mammoth migration:

> Mammoths would not have been capable of making the kind of yearly long-distance return treks that caribou make, because proboscidean feeding requirements would have been too great to allow continual travel and because the smaller herd members, especially weaned calves under twelve years old, would not have been able to feed as well as travel at the same rate as older adults. In addition, since mammoth gestation was at least twenty-two months (and possibly longer) many pregnant females would have had to make an annual migration twice during their pregnancy, placing an intolerable burden on themselves and fetuses in utero.

There is another overpowering reason why summer migration would not be likely. Travel through the summer bogs would be deadly for the mammoths. Siberia is now located in the permafrost zone in which the soil for hundreds of feet (100 m or more) deep is permanently frozen. Every summer the top one to two feet (about ½ m) melts. The ground below remains continually frozen. Melted water from the surface layer pools and forms massive bogs and muskegs. As a result, summer travel is difficult for both man and beast (Digby, 1926, p. 15–16; Vereshchagin and Baryshnikov, 1984, p. 492). Pfizenmayer (1939) describes the tremendous effort it required of his team to travel through Siberia during the summer to the location of the Beresovka mammoth. It took the men until mid-winter to haul out the mammoth. He concludes that the sticky bog mud would decimate large herds of animals. Tolmachoff (1929, p. 57) states that a few inches (about 5 cm) of this sticky mud makes the tundra practically impassable for a man, and that a foot or more of mud would probably trap

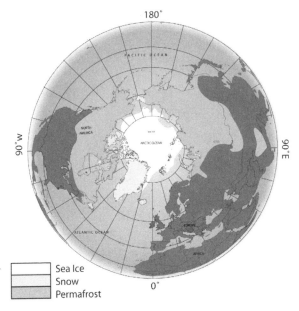

Figure 2.2. Map of permafrost zone for Northern Hemisphere (permafrost areas in general lie to the north of the average annual temperature of -6ºC to -8ºC isotherms).

a mammoth. The woolly mammoth, especially, would have had trouble negotiating marshy ground due to its pillar-like leg structure and stiff-legged locomotion (Farrand, 1961, p. 734). Nor would it have been able to pass over any trench that even slightly exceeded its maximum stride length. Vereshchagin (1974, p. 12) unambiguously proclaims: *"Neither mammoth nor bison could exist in the sort of tundra that exists there [Siberia] today."*

Large mammals such as musk ox, caribou, and moose do live and survive in the high Arctic today. But these herbivorous animals are suited to living on boggy substrate and can eat the type of vegetation that grows in Siberia today. Caribou eat lichens, which they can smell through the snow. They migrate south before the full force of winter hits. Their hooves are well suited for walking on the snow and boggy ground. Moose, with their long legs, can browse in relatively deep snow or in bogs. These herbivores have broadly splayed hooves that decrease the load and help them negotiate swampy muskegs (Guthrie, 1982, p. 310). Regardless of their advantages, the Siberian winter is still harrowing for these mammals: *"Northern ungulates gradually decline in weight and body condition during the winter"* (Guthrie, 1982, p. 320). Mammoths and the many other types of mammals are ill suited for summer conditions in Siberia. What were millions of them doing in Siberia?

STARVING TO DEATH AMIDST ABUNDANCE

Even if somehow the Ice Age mammals survived the cold winters and the boggy summers, they still would need to find food. Siberia has abundant vegetation during the summer. Some scientists believe the mammoth and other animals could have survived on this vegetation. Farrand (1962, p. 451) optimistically states:

> *People who have not been in high arctic areas appear to have little conception of the relatively luxuriant vegetation there — grasses, flowers, shrubs, and dwarf trees. It is amazing what 24 hours of sunshine a day will do!*

There is one daunting problem in Farrand's logic. Practically all these many millions of mammals ate *grass and small shrubs,* but Siberian vegetation today is primarily bog and muskeg vegetation. The current vegetation is *low* in the nutrition necessary for the health of these large animals (Chapin et al., 1995, p. 694). The taiga forest vegetation south of the current tundra is also *non-supportive* for these animals (Sher, 1997, p. 322). The taiga vegetation, plus the woody bark of spruce, dwarf alder, and birch, that grows in Siberia today contain many toxins for mammals (Guthrie and Guthrie, 1990, p. 40). The animals could not survive on this poor fodder. Scientists have labeled this lack of adequate food "the productivity paradox" (Hopkins et al., 1982). In other words, there is hardly any food in Siberia today for all those woolly mammoths and other animals! It is true that there are small patches of grassland, but this is not nearly enough for all the animals that lived there, especially for the large mammals. The woolly mammoth and its cohorts would starve to death amidst the appearance of plenty.

The problem is compounded when one understands the dietary and liquid requirements of a mammoth. A woolly mammoth can be compared to a modern elephant, since they are very similar. A large woolly mammoth would require 400 to 650 pounds (180 to 300 kg) of succulent food daily (Vereshchagin and Baryshnikov, 1982, p. 269). Where is such feed going to come from in Siberia?

Woolly mammoths would also need to drink 35 to 50 gallons (140 to 200 liters) of water daily (Webb, 1992, p. 27). Nearly all of the water in Siberia is frozen during the winter. Some have suggested that the woolly mammoth could have used its tusks to break icicles from cliffs or eat snow to obtain water (Digby, 1926, p. 52; Vereshchagin and Baryshnikov, 1984, p. 490). However, eating snow or ice is not an efficient method of obtaining water. It chills the body. Half the energy consumed by the woolly mammoth during winter would have been used to melt and warm the snow in its stomach (Olivier, 1982, p. 303). Also the *plains* of Siberia do not have many cliffs with icicles.

THE CLIMATE ENIGMA

It is rather obvious at this point that the climate and environment of Siberia had to have been much warmer when the woolly mammoth lived. Yet, paradoxically, they lived during the Ice Age. Computer models of an Ice Age climate vary in quality, but the results are consistent: Siberia had to have been much colder. Arkhipov (1997, p. 54) concludes: *"During glacial and stadial stages, the climate of Siberia was much colder than at present."* A stadial stage is the coldest part of the Ice Age. In their Ice Age climate model, Manabe and Broccoli (1985) calculated temperatures about 20ºF (12ºC) colder than present Siberian winters.

Many such Ice Age computer simulations even develop an ice sheet in Siberia. A good example is the simulation of Dong and Valdes (1995). One of the more interesting general circulation models attempted to develop ice sheets from scratch. It provided the stimulus for ice sheet growth by reducing sunshine around the earth by 6 percent. Paradoxically, the simulation produced a permanent snow cover over Alaska, portions of Siberia, and western Canada, but little over areas where the ice sheets actually developed. This is the *opposite* of where the ice occurred during the Ice Age:

> We now have glaciation, but mainly outside the area where it existed during the last Ice Age (Phillips and Held, 1994, p. 780).

These computer simulations show how easy it is to glaciate Siberia, but something is very wrong. How could the woolly mammoths have survived in Siberia when it supposedly was covered by ice?

Glacial debris indicates that only the *mountains* of Siberia, Alaska, and the Yukon were actually glaciated. The lowlands, where the mammoth bones are found, were *never* glaciated! That would explain how the animals could live in these areas during the Ice Age. But why were these lowlands not glaciated?

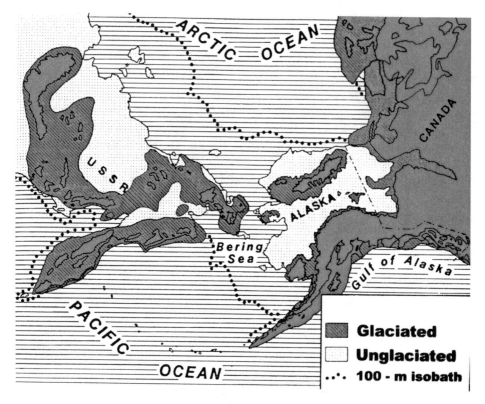

Figure 2.3. Glaciated and unglaciated areas of Siberia, Alaska, and the Yukon during the Ice Age. The shallow continental shelf is shown by the 330-foot (100m) isobath, which is a line of constant depth of the sea.

Some uniformitarian scientists, eager to justify their model, reason that a colder Ice Age climate would have helped the woolly mammoth live in Siberia. Colder temperatures would cause less melting of the permafrost, so the tundra and taiga would have been much less boggy in summer. This situation would certainly help the mammoths negotiate the marshy terrain if it remained frozen. However, a colder climate would cause a shorter growing season with much less food and liquid water. Furthermore, some of the animals could not even endure the cold of today, much less a colder Ice Age.

Once again, what would all the animals eat in such a colder Ice Age? Not much edible vegetation would grow in such a climate. Colder Ice Age temperatures aggravate the productivity paradox. Charles Schweger (1982, p. 219) describes the problem this way:

> *The former presence of larger and more diverse ungulate [hooved mammal] populations in northern regions of periglacial [near a glacier] climate at a time*

when primary productivity presumably was still lower constitutes the paradox. To oversimplify, how does one keep a mammoth alive and well under the seemingly impossible conditions of Ice Age Beringia? [Beringa is eastern Siberia, Alaska, and the Yukon.]

The climate paradox worsens when we look at the animals themselves. Dead bones, of course, do not speak, but they can provide clues to the environment they occupied. The diversity of mammals and their specific ecological requirements strongly suggest an environment quite different from today and far different than the Ice Age climate simulations. The environment of Siberia during the Ice Age has been compared to that of the Serengeti of East Africa (Guthrie, 1982, p. 313; Bocherens et al., 1996, p. 31)!

Based on the fact that practically all these large mammals were *grazers* that ate a wide variety of herbaceous vegetation, mainly grasses, we can recreate the environment of Siberia. These deductions are based on (1) the food preferences of the surviving mammals, (2) the elephant as an analog for the mammoth, (3) the stomach contents of frozen carcasses that contain abundant grasses, and (4) mammoth dung preserved in caves of the southwest United States (Guthrie, 1982, 1990a; G. Haynes, 1991, p. 59). This leads us to conclude that Siberia was a huge grassland during the Ice Age! Dale Guthrie, whom I believe comes closest to understanding the environment of Siberia during the woolly mammoth era, calls Siberia a *mammoth steppe*. A steppe is a semi-arid plain with abundant grass and few trees. There are two main steppes in the world today: (1) the high plains east of the Rocky Mountains in the United States and (2) the north slopes of the central Asian mountains.

Some of the smaller mammals especially reinforce Guthrie's conclusion of a mammoth steppe. The smaller mammal bones found include badgers and ferrets. They occupy short-grass plains, similar to the high plains east of the Rocky Mountains in central North America (Guthrie, 1990a, p. 248–249; Pielou, 1991, p. 151). These animals burrow fairly deep, suggesting a lack of permafrost. A grassland environment is further indicated by a wide distribution of Arctic ground squirrels, which live in open country and require energy-rich seeds and protein-rich herbs (Guthrie, 1982, p. 311).

To sustain this large mix of animals, the grassland must have had a rich variety of plants similar to other grasslands. Guthrie (1982, p. 315) logically concluded that the *plants were also highly diverse* — a diversity that has no modern counterpart in the world today (Wright and Barnosky, 1984; Guthrie, 1984). Small communities of tall bushes and trees punctuated this huge grassland in places. These are found preserved in the permafrost (Tolmachoff, 1929, p. 47; Kaplina and Lozhkin, 1984, p. 147; Anderson, 1985; Sher, 1997, p. 322). Based on the large number of healthy individuals, Guthrie also concludes that Siberia, Alaska, and the Yukon, as well as Europe and western Russia, was *one huge diverse grassland*. The mammoth steppe seemed to cover much of the non-glaciated area of the Northern Hemisphere.

In order for such a diverse grassland to exist, the soil must have been very fertile (Guthrie, 1984, p. 267). The existence of a fertile soil with abundant nutrients is reinforced by the lack of chew marks, called pica, on the Siberian mammal bones (Guthrie, 1990a, p. 215–219). Small animals in many environments today do not obtain enough minerals in their food because the soil cannot provide enough nutrients. So they chew bones of dead animals to obtain missing nutrients.

The growth pattern of the mammals also suggests a fertile grassland (Guthrie, 1982). Most of the mammals have been described as *well-dressed giants*. Horses, woolly rhinoceroses, and woolly mammoths were smaller than their counterparts farther south, but all the other animals were significantly larger than their counterparts today. Moreover, the shaggy ruffs, heavy horns, long tusks, and enormous antlers on many animals are what wildlife managers would recognize as indicators of *high-quality habitat* with little competition and a long growing season (Guthrie, 1982, p. 309). Abundant soil nutrients especially affect the size of both the animal and its social organs (Guthrie, 1984). Bergmann's rule states that the colder the climate the larger the animal. However, others strongly dispute Bergmann's rule and maintain that size is proportional to the quality of feed during the growth season (Geist, 1987; Guthrie, 1984, p. 269, 271). Guthrie (1984, p. 271) demonstrated the size-nutrient association with an experiment on dall sheep in Alaska: they grew bigger with more feed.

To maintain such a large variety of herbaceous vegetation requires a *long growing season with warm soil and rapid spring growth* (Guthrie, 1982, p. 322–324). Such a climate differs greatly from the current environment, where there isn't even a green sprout in northern Siberia until mid-June to early July (Howorth, 1880, p. 553). Steppe climates have a wet spring and a dry late summer and early autumn, the kind

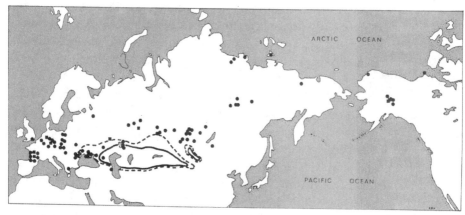

Figure 2.4. Present (solid line), historical (dashed line), and Ice Age (dots) distribution of the saiga antelope.

of climate necessary to maintain a grassland. Consequently, it is reasonable to expect a similar precipitation pattern for Siberia during the mammoth era.

Ninety percent of grass biomass is in the roots below the surface. The plant cannot sprout fresh shoots until the snow melts and the soil warms. Steppe environments are characterized by low soil moisture and light winter snowfall (Berman et al. 1994). This further implies that *winter snows must have been light and melted early*. A mild, relatively dry winter would favor such a spring resurgence.

The presence of several animals that are *intolerant* of deep snow, such as the saiga antelope, bighorn sheep, dall sheep, and wolf, also suggests open range with light winter snowfall (Guthrie, 1990a, p. 201). Bison are quite efficient at scraping away snow with their head and horns, but when the snow exceeds a depth of two feet, they have difficulty obtaining enough food. In central Alaska where many bison remains are found in the permafrost, the snow usually accumulates up to three feet or more. Bison cannot live in central Alaska, except in small, windswept areas (Guthrie, 1990a).

In summary, the ecology of the Siberian animals suggests a much more diverse vegetation with a fertile soil. This further implies a comparatively mild winter with light snowfall and a long growing season. These conditions differ markedly from the modern environment and climate, not to mention uniformitarian computer simulations of the Ice Age climate.

CHAPTER THREE

THE MYSTERY OF
THE ICE AGE

Most scientists believe that woolly mammoths lived during the Ice Age and became extinct near the end of it. To understand what happened to them, we need to understand the Ice Age better. Although it is evident there was an Ice Age, scientists run into a blank wall when they try to provide the cause. They run into mystery after mystery.

Figure 3.1. A terminal or end moraine from Athabasca Glacier, Canada.

WAS THERE REALLY AN ICE AGE?

Looking at the world today, it is hard to imagine that there ever was an Ice Age. It seems inconceivable that ice once covered 30 percent of the land surface of the earth. How do we know there was an Ice Age?

Much of the evidence for an Ice Age comes from the study of modern glaciers. Glaciers today leave mounds of debris called *moraines*.

Figure 3.2. A lateral moraine from Athabasca Glacier, Canada.

Figure 3.3. A striated boulder in ground moraine from Athabasca Glacier, Canada.

Figure 3.4. Striated bedrock from Athabasca Glacier, Canada.

The debris consists of a random assortment of rocks of many sizes within a sand, silt, or even clay matrix. This debris is called *till*. There are three general types of moraines: (1) A terminal or end moraine is a mound of till that is pushed up in the front of a glacier as it moves forward, (2) A lateral moraine is caused by debris that is swept to the sides of the glacier as it moves, and (3) A ground moraine develops under a glacier. Ground moraine generally has a rough, hummocky look.

Within the moraines, we often find scratched or striated rocks. The scratches and grooves are etched on the rocks as rock rubs against rock, or scrapes the bedrock below the glacier. The scratches indicate the direction of the glacier's movement.

We find these same characteristics over large areas on the plains of North America and in the western mountain valleys of the United States as well as parts of Europe, indicating these areas were once covered by glaciers. Clearly, there was an Ice Age. Figure 3.5 displays one of the most distinctive lateral and terminal moraines in the world. It is in the northern Wallowa Mountains of northeast Oregon at about 4,200 feet (1,300 m) above sea level. During the Ice Age, a glacier descended from the Wallowa Mountains north down a valley and out about 2 miles (3 km) onto the small plain near Enterprise, Oregon. The end moraine is rather small, only about 100 feet (30 m) high. The sharp-crested lateral moraines on either side are about 700 feet (210 m) tall near the mountain front. Both moraines form a horseshoe shape that is now occupied by the beautiful Lake Wallowa. The lake occupies an overdeepened valley similar to a fjord. A fjord

Figure 3.5. One of the most distinctive lateral and terminal moraines in the world is in the northern Wallowa Mountains in northeast Oregon.

Figure 3.6. The 700-feet-high (210 m) lateral moraine as shown in figure 3.5.

Figure 3.7. A close-up of the till in the lateral moraine shown in figure 3.6.

is a long, narrow arm of the sea along a coast. It once was a coastal valley that has been deepened by a glacier. The terminal and lateral moraines around Lake Wallula are composed of glacial till, a mixture of rocks of many sizes within a fine-grained matrix.

MID AND HIGH LATITUDES AND TROPICAL MOUNTAINS RECENTLY GLACIATED

By observing the many signs of glaciation, we can piece together where the ice sheets formed. Two large ice sheets covered North America.

Figure 3.8. North American ice sheets.

One is called the Cordilleran Ice Sheet. It dominated the western mountains of Canada and the northwestern United States. The other is called the Laurentide Ice Sheet. It developed over the remainder of Canada and the northern United States (see Figure 3.8). It is still unclear how much of northern Canada was glaciated. An ice-free corridor for the early part of the Ice Age divided the two ice sheets that lay along the east slopes of the Rocky Mountains.

In the United States, the southern edge of the ice sheet extended from northwest Washington State through the northern United States. In the Midwest, the edge is thought to have reached as far south as St. Louis, Missouri, at 38°N latitude. The ice possibly did not extend down to St. Louis. The southern deposits could be remnants from glacial lakes and meltwater features that developed along the edge of the ice sheets. Deposits laid by Ice Age rivers and lakes may have obscured the exact ice sheet boundary in areas where there are no distinct terminal moraines.

There were also two areas that were never glaciated. They lie *inside* the periphery of the Laurentide Ice Sheet. These are called driftless areas. One covers about 15,000 square miles (40,000 sq. km) in southwest Wisconsin and small adjacent areas in southeast Minnesota, northeast Iowa, and northwest Illinois (Hobbs, 1999). The second is located in northeast Montana and south central Saskatchewan and occupies an area of about 6,000 square miles (15,000 sq. km) (Klassen, 1994).

Many large mountainous areas of the western United States had ice caps. These mountains included large parts of the Rocky Mountains, the Cascades of the Pacific Northwest, and the Sierra Nevada Mountains of California. Ice caps covered many smaller mountain ranges, such as the Wallowa Mountains in northeast Oregon, and even the San Francisco Mountains, south of the Grand Canyon of Arizona.

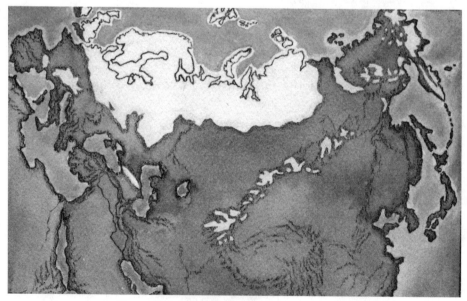

Figure 3.9. The ice sheet in Europe and Asia.

Similar signs of an ice sheet are found in northern Europe and northwest Asia. This ice sheet is called the Scandinavian Ice Sheet. The exact boundaries of this ice sheet in northwest Russia and the shallow ocean north of Norway are still debated (Thiede and Bauch, 1999; Thiede and Mangerud, 1999). Just like in the United States, many of the large mountains of Europe, such as the Alps, Caucasus, and Pyrenees were covered with ice caps.

The Ice Age did not occur just in the Northern Hemisphere. It developed on the mountains of the higher latitudes of the Southern Hemisphere. The mountains of Tasmania, New Zealand, Chile, southern Argentina, and even a small mountainous area of southeast Australia were all glaciated. Most of the ice during the Ice Age in the Southern Hemisphere ended up on Antarctica. The current ice masses on Antarctica, as well as Greenland, remain as a testimony to the great Ice Age.

The tropics were not left out. A cooler climate caused the ice caps that exist today on the highest mountains to be about 3,000 feet (900 m) lower. The volcanic peaks of east central Africa, including Mounts Kilimanjaro, Kenya, and Ruwenzori, and several of the high peaks in the Sahara Desert had ice caps (Rosqvist, 1990). Ice caps also existed on many other tropical mountains that today do not support glaciers. Just like in middle and high latitudes, these tropical mountain ice caps are inferred from till, moraines, scratched rocks, and striated bedrock.

Many of the glacial features are still sharp and only slightly eroded, indicating that the Ice Age was fairly recent. A good example of this is the horseshoe-shaped moraines that extend out from the Wallowa Mountains (figure 3.5). Crickmay (1975, p. 107) remarked on the freshness of many glacial features:

> *The relative weakness of atmospheric influence is shown up strongly in localities that were glaciated in the Pleistocene but have been free of glacial ice for fifteen to twenty thousand years; in that length of time, the atmosphere has done very little toward erasing the glacial striae, though many a stream has cut a canyon 100 meters or more deep.*

The glaciation could easily have been more recent than 15,000 to 20,000 years ago; Crickmay was simply repeating the conventional wisdom. The freshness of glacial features argues for a much younger date. Geologist G. Frederick Wright (1911) noted that little erosion of glacial features has occurred in the state of Wisconsin, and that glacial kames in Europe and North America are also only slightly eroded. In reference to glacial striations on the east coast of Hudson Bay he notes:

> *On Portland promontory, on the east coast of Hudson's [sic] Bay, in latitude 58°, and southward, the high, rocky hills are completely glaciated and bare. The striae are as fresh looking as if the ice had left them only yesterday. When the sun bursts upon these hills after they have been wet by the rain, they glitter and shine like the tinned roofs of the city of Montreal* (Wright, 1911, p. 569).

Striations should be erased rather quickly after exposure. It is unlikely that they would be so distinct after 15,000 to 20,000 years of weathering.

HOW MUCH CLIMATE CHANGE IS REQUIRED
TO CAUSE THE ICE AGE?

For an ice age to develop, some winter snow must last throughout the summer and fall, accumulating each year. Therefore, developing an ice sheet or a glacier over mid- and high-latitude continental areas requires a combination of colder summers and more snow. In most of the areas where the ice built up, winters are already cold enough to sustain the snow and ice, but the summers would cause it to melt.

As snow continues to build up, it turns to ice by two mechanisms. One is by the partial summer melting of snow that percolates downward and then refreezes, forming ice. The second mechanism occurs after the snow becomes deep enough, possibly up to 200 feet (60 m) deep, in a cold environment. The weight of the snow squeezes most of the air out of the snow at the bottom, basically turning it into ice. This is how the snow becomes ice on top of the Antarctic and Greenland ice sheets.

Colder summers and more snow is a tall order. Consider what it would take for an ice sheet to start to develop in Minneapolis, one of the coldest regions in the United States. This area was recently covered by an ice sheet probably around 1,000 feet (300 m) thick not that long ago.

The average summer temperature from June through August in Minneapolis is about 70°F (21°C). For the winter snow not to melt, spring, summer and fall temperatures must remain at least below freezing. This means summer temperatures need to cool by at least 38°F (21°C). However, the intensity of the sunshine causes most of the snow to melt; temperature is a smaller, but still important, factor. Since Minneapolis receives plenty of sunshine during the summer, the average temperature would need to be much lower than freezing for even one inch of snow to remain until the next winter. In high-latitude Antarctica, where the sun is low in summer but the daylight lasts for 24 hours, it has been observed that *net* summer melting along the fringe of the ice sheet occurs at an average temperature of 14°F or -10°C (Pickard, 1984). Although the sun angle at Minneapolis is much higher than the fringes of Antarctica, the nights are longer, so the average summer temperature would likely be similar for net summer melting at Minneapolis. A conservative summer temperature average below which at least a little winter snow would not disappear would be 20°F (-7°C). A drop from the average today of 70°F to 20°F is a whopping 50°F (28°C) change in summer temperature! Of course, a lesser temperature drop would be needed in fall and spring because heat from the sun is less and the seasonal temperatures are naturally cooler.

The above calculations assumed the same amount of snowfall as in the modern climate. If by some mechanism much more snow fell, then not as much summer cooling would be required to keep an inch or more on the ground.

It will be shown later that melting in a dry, cool Ice Age climate (50°F, or 10°C, average summer temperature) near the edge of the ice sheet is about 400 inches (10 m) of ice a year. One inch of ice corresponds to an average of 10 inches of powder snow. So for Minneapolis this would represent 4,000 inches (100 m) of powder snow a year, which is about 100 times their annual average. So, even during a relatively cool summer, the amount of snowfall required is tremendous. Of course, if the average summer temperatures were around 30°F (-1°C), possibly only 20 times the normal snowfall would be necessary.

This highly unusual situation would have to *continue for many years*. What climatic factors would combine to produce a 40°F summer cooling with 20 times the snowfall at Minneapolis for many years? Further complicating the picture, if a mechanism could be found to cause the huge cooling, the atmosphere would have less ability to hold moisture. It would become drier and, therefore, less able to produce the needed snow. This is one of the greatest challenges to any Ice Age theory.

DID ICE INVADE THE UNITED STATES FROM CANADA?

Another possibility is that the ice sheets actually began in the higher terrain of northeast and western Canada and over the mountains of Scandinavia. These areas continue to support glaciers in the very highest terrain today. Since Canada is closer to the North Pole than Minneapolis, not as much summer cooling and snowfall increase would be needed to develop an ice sheet so far north. Scientists believe the ice sheets grew in these northerly areas and over thousands of years inched their way as far south as Minneapolis or even St. Louis, Missouri, in North America. In this way, the scientists think that the encroaching ice sheet from the north caused the needed climate change for the ice sheet to continue to St. Louis.

In Europe, it is suggested that the ice grew over the mountains of Scandinavia and after awhile descended to the lowlands. The ice sheet then continued to grow and inched across the Baltic Sea and into the northern continental part of Europe and northwest Russia.

Is such a vision of the Ice Age possible? Larry Williams (1979) used a computer simulation to try to answer this question. He wanted to find out how much summer cooling and extra snowfall would be needed to maintain a snow cover through one summer in Canada. To help the ice age start, he doubled the normal winter snowfall and lowered summer temperatures by increments of 3°F (2°C). Williams also raised the land surface 400 feet (120 m), blanked out the influence of Hudson Bay, and decreased the intensity of the summer sunshine a little. All these conditions favor an increased summer snow cover. He checked his results against a glacier in northeast Canada to see if his melting equations were correct. His equations were realistic. As he continued to incrementally reduce the temperature by 3°F (2°C), more of the warm-season precipitation fell as snow instead of rain. In his experiments, he finally developed a permanent snow cover northwest and east of Hudson Bay (figure 3.10). He discovered that average summer temperatures in northeast Canada had to drop to

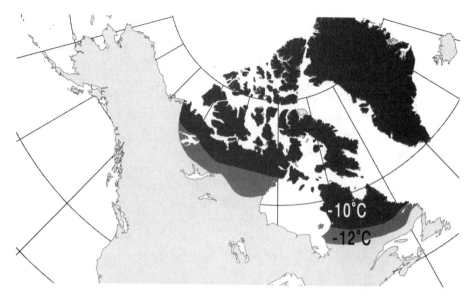

Figure 3.10. Map of Canada showing areas where one inch of snow would still remain from summer melting with temperatures 10 and 12°C (16 and 20°F) cooler than the current summer averages, according to a computer simulation.

30°F (-1°C)! This is a summer cooling of 20°F (12°C) from the average of 50°F (10°C) just for one inch of snow to survive in northeast Canada. Williams concluded that it takes much more summer cooling and snowfall than he previously thought to produce a permanent snow cover in northeast Canada. Once again, we are left with the question of what would cause such a drop in temperature and an increase in snowfall?

And even if the climate could change to glaciate northeast Canada, what further cooling and greater snowfall would cause the ice to spread south to Minneapolis, Minnesota, or St. Louis, Missouri? Even if it managed to inch south, a drastic climate change for Minneapolis is still essential for such an idea. Similar problems are encountered for northern Europe and northwest Asia, as well as in the Southern Hemisphere and the tropical mountains.

SCIENTISTS PERPLEXED

The way some scientists talk, one would get the idea that an ice age can occur easily. Besides the difficulty of an ice age, many other scientists have admitted that the cause of the Ice Age is unknown.

In the mid-1800s, when the Ice Age was first postulated, most scientists could hardly believe such a thing could have happened:

> *It was the idea of vast continental ice-sheets that geologists found hard to believe. . . . The state of the glacial theory about 1850 was more that of an interglacial period than an ice advance. The older geologists as a whole, with the*

exception of Buckland, still seemed to have very little use for the glacial theory and where they had accepted it, did so only with great reluctance and with many reservations (Chorley, Dunn, and Beckinsale, 1964, p. 213, 232).

An ice age seemed too far-fetched; the climate change was too radical for most minds to accept. However, evidence for glaciation was strong. So, eventually, most scientists swallowed hard and acknowledged the possibility.

The next big question was *how?* Scientists have been puzzling over this question ever since the mid-1800s. It is still a major unsolved mystery of science. The August 18–25, 1997, *U.S. News & World Report* had a series of articles on 18 great mysteries of science. One of those mysteries is: "What causes ice ages?" (Watson, 1997) The June 1996, popular science magazine *Earth* reported on a new theory of the Ice Age. Daniel Pendick (1996, p. 22) starts his article off by saying: "If they hadn't actually happened, the Ice Ages would sound like science fiction." In a book about the Lake Missoula flood that swept over eastern Washington, David Alt (2001, p. 180) remarks: "Although theories abound, no one really knows what causes Ice Ages."

Isn't it amazing that after all this time scientists do not know the cause of the Ice Age, which ended not in the remote prehistoric past but recently? Is our climate basically unstable, so that we can be plunged into another ice age soon, wreaking havoc on the nations of the world, as some have suggested? Or was the Ice Age caused by special conditions that are so rare that an ice age will never be repeated?

WET DESERTS DURING THE ICE AGE?

Not only is the cause of the Ice Age a major mystery, but also there are a number of other puzzling features associated with this time.

Deserts or semi-arid regions are common on the earth today. They are especially abundant around 30°S and 30°N because of the dry circulation of the atmosphere in those belts (see figure 3.11). Scientists studying these arid and

Figure 3.11. General circulation of the earth's atmosphere. The downward flowing air at 30° results in drying of the air.

semi-arid areas have made an extraordinary discovery. Many were once wet!

The Great Basin in the southwest
United States includes Nevada, western
Utah, southeast California, and southeast Oregon. All of the rivers in the area
drain internally; no water flows out of
the Great Basin. The Great Salt Lake
is maintained at nearly the same level
by the balance of inflow and evaporation. Many smaller lakes in the Great
Basin have dried up. The basins range
in elevation from Death Valley, 282
feet (86 m) below sea level, to basins
about 4,000 feet (1,200 m) above sea
level. High mountains, many well over
10,000 feet (3,000 m), separate the
low areas. Because the Sierra Nevada
Mountains of California block the

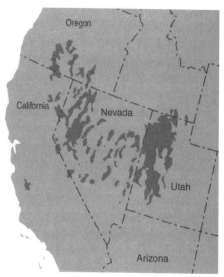

*Figure 3.12. Lakes in the southwestern
United States during the Ice Age.*

moist westerly winds from off the ocean, the Great Basin is semi-arid with blister-
ing summers. Death Valley receives only 2.3 inches (60 mm) of rain a year with
maximum summer temperatures that average 112°F (44°C). In fact, the second
hottest reading in the world, 134°F (56.7°C), occurred in Death Valley (Schmidli,
1991, p. 1).

There is abundant evidence that the Great Basin was once well watered and
verdant. Shorelines from lakes are etched high up on the sides of mountains or hills.
Some of the shorelines are sharp and barely eroded indicating the lake must have
existed for only a short time. Late in the Ice Age, the Great Basin had 120 lakes,
some quite large (figure 3.12). The Great Salt Lake was about six times its current
size and 800 feet (240 m) deeper (Smith and Street-Perrott, 1983). This lake, Lake
Bonneville as it is called, was about the size of Lake Michigan. The shorelines of
ancient Lake Bonneville show very prominently along the surrounding hills. In
northwest Nevada, Lake Lahontan lay in a series of interconnected valleys east of the
Sierra Nevada Mountains. It was the size of Lake Erie. Pyramid Lake, Walker Lake,
and several other saline lakes are all that is left of once mighty Lake Lahontan. Noticeable shorelines along the sides of Death Valley indicate this very hot basin once
possessed a lake about 600 feet (180 m) deep, called Lake Manly (Hooke, 1999). A
series of lakes in southeast California flowed into Death Valley during the Ice Age.
The climate must have been dramatically cooler and wetter during the Ice Age.

The second example is the Sahara Desert. Geologists were astonished to find
fossils of elephants, giraffes, buffaloes, antelopes, rhinoceroses, and other animals
in the desert. Today, this kind of animal diversity is found in the African savannas.

Figure 3.13. Sahara Ice Age art.
(Photo by Corbis)

Fossils of various amphibians, hippopotami, crocodiles, fish, clams, and other aquatic organisms confirm the desert was once a wet environment (Pachur and Kröpelin, 1987; Kröpelin and Soulié-Märsche, 1991). Dwarf crocodiles survived into the 20th century and lived in isolated lakes or pools along several wadis of the high western Sahara (Charlesworth, 1957, p. 1113; Shaw, 1976).

Satellites with radar that can penetrate the shallow sand (McCauley et al., 1982) have observed an old drainage network in the eastern Sahara. This network consisted of large freshwater lakes and several channels the size of the Nile River Valley. Today, the eastern Sahara Desert receives rain at any locality only once every 30 to 50 years! Large drainage networks have also been sighted in other areas of the Sahara (Chorowicz and Fabre, 1997) and the Middle East.

People once lived in the Sahara Desert along with the animals. They have left countless stone tools, pottery, and pictures of animals carved on the rocks (Kröpelin and Soulié-Märsche, 1991; Coulson, 1999). Explorers have even found fishhooks and harpoons! (Shaw, 1976, p. 142). Some of this art is spectacular (figure 3.13). James Wellard (1964, p. 33, 34), Sahara explorer, describes the rock art:

> *The Sahara is a veritable art gallery of prehistoric paintings. . . . The evidence is enough to show that the Sahara was one of the well-populated areas of the prehistoric world. . . . Yet there is his work, in the most inaccessible corners*

of the desert, literally thousands of figures of tropical and aquatic animals, enormous herds of cattle, hunters armed with bows and boomerangs, and even "domestic" scenes of women and children and the circular huts in which they lived.

The wet Sahara and all the lakes that recently occupied desert areas is another one of the many climatic mysteries surrounding the Ice Age. Scientists have speculated that these "pluvial periods," as they call the past abundant rainfall in desert areas, are associated with interglacials, the warm periods between ice ages. We are supposed to be in such an "interglacial" right now. However, if we are in an interglacial, why are our deserts dry? It makes more sense that pluvial periods occurred during a cooler, wetter ice age than what is currently postulated. Regardless, how are these "wet" deserts to be explained?

THE PUZZLE OF COEXISTING WARM AND COLD CLIMATE ANIMALS

Ice Age fossils often display a strange mix of animals that would not be expected to coexist. Remains of animals adapted to the cold are found much farther south than expected. Warmth-loving animals are found as fossils much farther north than they would venture today. Yet, they apparently thrived in the Ice Age environment. This peculiar mixture of animals has been given a special name — *disharmonious associations*.

These disharmonious associations were the *rule* rather than the exception. This mix of cold-tolerant and warm-tolerant animals occurred over the *whole* Northern Hemisphere (Howorth, 1887; Stuart, 1991; Rensberger and Barnosky, 1993, p. 330), including Siberia, Alaska, and the Yukon Territory (Guthrie, 1984, p. 259; Graham and Lundelius, 1984, p. 237). Disharmonious associations are also found in the Southern Hemisphere (Graham and Lundelius, 1984, p. 238).

Disharmonious associations apply not only to large mammals, but also to small mammals, plants, insects, birds, amphibians and reptiles! Graham and Lundelius (1984, p. 224) write:

> *Late Pleistocene communities were characterized by the coexistence of species that today are allopatric [not climatically associated] and presumably ecologically incompatible. . . . Disharmonious associations have been documented for late Pleistocene [Ice Age] floras . . . terrestrial invertebrates . . . lower vertebrates . . . birds . . . and mammals.*

One of the most outstanding examples is the existence of hippopotamus fossils associated with fossils of reindeer, musk oxen, and woolly mammoths found in England, France, and Germany (Nilsson, 1983, p. 223–233; Sutcliffe, 1985, p. 24). Sutcliffe (1985, p. 120) states:

> *Finding conditions so favourable the hippopotamus (today an inhabitant of the equatorial regions) had been able to spread northwards throughout most of England and Wales, up to an altitude of 400 meters [1,300 feet] on the now bleak Yorkshire moors.*

Furthermore, hippo fossils are not rare but rather common in England:

> *Remains of hippopotamuses are known from probably about a hundred localities within England and Wales* (Stuart, 1982, p. 52).

In North America too, *most* late Pleistocene faunas and floras are disharmonious (Graham and Lundelius, 1984, p. 236). Reindeer mingled with warmth-loving animals as far south as Alabama and Georgia. Badgers, black-footed ferrets, ground sloths, camels, and giant beavers that prefer temperate climates are found much farther north in Alaska in association with woolly mammoths and other cold-tolerant animals (Guthrie, 1990b, p. 45; Stuart, 1991, p. 523).

Disharmonious associations have garnered much controversy. Although difficult to explain, most scientists have now accepted that the disharmonious associations during the Ice Age are *real* (Alroy, 1999, p. 107). The reason for the dilemma is that an Ice Age climate is assumed to have been much colder than present-day climates. However, the evidence from the Ice Age fossils instead implies an equable climate with mild winters and cool summers. This climatic deduction from observed fossil evidence is disconcerting, as Kenneth Cole (1995, p. 133) realizes when considering very cold Ice Age computer simulations:

> *Although paleoecologists often conclude that past climates were equable, it is difficult to create equable climates in continental interiors using climate circulation models.*

The explanation of disharmonious association during the Ice Age has resulted in over 150 years of controversy. Cole (1995, p. 131) again writes:

> *One of the longest-running philosophical debates in paleoecological interpretation concerns the importance of mixed, or disharmonious, assemblages which represent past communities with no modern analog. These mixed assemblages challenge our world view. . . . Mixed assemblages are usually explained by invoking past climates more "equable" than that of today.*

Indeed, disharmonious associations do challenge the mainstream Ice Age world view. There does not appear to be any likely solution to this enigma on the horizon.

MASS EXTINCTIONS AT THE END OF THE ICE AGE

It is difficult enough to accept that animals, as well as plants and insects, were disharmonious during the Ice Age. But scientists also are faced with explaining why this mix of animals came to an abrupt end with mass extinctions at the close of the Ice Age — at a time the climate was supposed to be warming and the living area expanding.

Not only did the woolly mammoth die out in Siberia at the end of the Ice Age, it died out everywhere. Tolmachoff (1929, p. 65) summarizes the problem of the disappearance of the woolly mammoth:

> We must explain the extinction of an animal which was living in great numbers, apparently very prosperously, over a large area, in variable physico-geographical conditions to which it was well adapted, and which died out in a very short time, geologically speaking.

One slightly unexpected turn of events has recently occurred. Whereas scientists believed the woolly mammoth became extinct at the very end of the Ice Age, fossils of mammoths have been discovered on Wrangel Island north of Siberia in the Arctic Ocean that have been dated to about 2000 B.C. by carbon-14 (Vartanyan, Garutt, and Sher, 1993; Lister, 1993; Long, Sher and Vartanyan, 1994). So apparently the woolly mammoth managed to survive past the end of the Ice Age on an isolated island. It is possible that the carbon-14 dates are wrong, or that the Ice Age ended around 4,000 years ago.

Many of the other animals of the mammoth steppe became extinct or disappeared from whole continents at the same time as the woolly mammoth. In North America alone, 135 species in 33 genera of large mammals disappeared (Ward, 1997, p. 141; Monastersky, 1999, p. 360). Twenty-two genera of birds went extinct from North America at the end of the Ice Age (Grayson, 1977). Other continents were hit hard with extinctions during and soon after the Ice Age, including South America and Australia. In all, 167 genera of large mammals greater than 100 pounds (45 kg) disappeared from entire continents (Martin and Steadman, 1999, p. 17). Why?

Scientists do not know why the extinctions occurred, and the question has tortured their minds for more than *200 years!* Mass extinctions at the end of the Ice Age, when the climate and environment was improving, remains an enigma to this day. Ward (1997, p. 120) writes:

> This great extinction — truly a mass extinction — represents one of paleontology's most fundamental mysteries.

CHAPTER FOUR

A MAMMOTH NUMBER OF MAMMOTH HYPOTHESES

One can imagine that with so many woolly mammoth mysteries, there would be numerous ideas or hypotheses dreamed up over the years. This is indeed the case. Efforts to understand the mysteries associated with the woolly mammoth have led to an abundance of hypotheses — all with mammoth problems. The hypotheses range from native beliefs to astral catastrophes.

ANCIENT AND NATIVE BELIEFS

During the Middle Ages, the local population thought the woolly mammoth remains were prehistoric giants (Kurtén, 1986, p. 50). Before the days when geology developed, a famous Russian intellectual insisted the beasts were elephants that died during a vast military campaign led by Chinghiz Kan (Howorth, 1880, p. 550). Then there is the entertaining idea that the bones were from elephants that had run away from Hannibal's army as the army crossed the Swiss Alps (Tolmachoff, 1929, p. viii).

Many natives of Siberia were superstitious and feared the mammoth bones and carcasses, believing that if they viewed a carcass, they would fall ill or die (Howorth, 1887, p. 83). The natives thought the gigantic beasts once lived underground and tunneled forward and backward (Howorth, 1887, p. 73–74). To explain the remains they found along riverbanks they concluded that when the beast came near the surface to smell the air or see the light it immediately would die. In about 1600, the

Chinese emperor K'ang-his (Kangxi) wrote a book on animals in which he supported the Siberian belief that the carcasses were the remains of five-ton rodents who lived beneath the earth's surface (Kiger, 2000). The "freshness" of some meat from the carcasses encouraged their belief that the beasts were still living underground, and that they soon died upon viewing the light (Dillow, 1981, p. 323).

THOUGHTS FROM EARLY GEOLOGISTS

I believe there is a lot of merit to the ideas of the early geologists. Most of them seemed to provide a straightforward interpretation of the evidence without biases that have crept into modern interpretations, such as the principle of uniformitarianism.

Knowledge of the existence of woolly mammoth fossils filtered into Europe in the 1600s (Howorth, 1887, p. 48). Trade in mammoth ivory began in the 1700s. Agassiz, Cuvier, Buckland, and most geologists of the time believed the fossils pointed to a once *warmer climate* in Siberia (Grayson, 1984a, p. 11–16). Cuvier thought the woolly mammoth became extinct because of abrupt climatic deterioration and were buried by local flooding or other events (Grayson, 1984a, p. 9; Berger, 1991, p. 116). Following Cuvier with his periodic catastrophic inundations and extinctions, many scientists took the Noachian flood as the last of many catastrophes that wiped out the mammoths.

Charles Lyell at first believed the mammoths lived in southern Siberia and were floated down the rivers to northern Siberia before burial (Howorth, 1887, p. 60). This idea did not last too long, mostly because the bones showed no indication of having been moved (Tolmachoff, 1929, p. ix), and many bones are far from rivers (Howorth, 1880, p. 551). Lyell, the father of the uniformitarian doctrine, ended up grudgingly conceding that the climate must have been a little warmer, but tried to fit the mammoth and the frozen carcasses into his belief of gradual extinctions and faunal replacement (Grayson, 1984a, p. 16). Lyell's explanation is preferred by most scientists today (Hopkins et al., 1982).

Sir Henry Howorth (1887) was probably the first to attempt a grand synthesis for the demise of the woolly mammoths in Siberia. He first gathered a massive amount of information on the woolly mammoths, especially in Siberia. He then concluded that a giant flood, likely a shallow Noachian flood that affected only the surface of the earth, swept across all lands of the world, killing the Siberian mammoths. He offered support from the flood traditions of many cultures from around the world. He considered uniformitarianism — "the present is the key to the past" — wholly inadequate to explain the mammoth mysteries. Today, Howorth would be considered a neo-catastrophist, similar to those scientists who believe the dinosaurs died out from a meteorite impact.

Upon rereading Howorth, I was impressed with the substantial amount of data that he had gathered from earlier observations by explorers and travelers. In listing the known Siberian carcasses, Tolmachoff (1929) extensively referred to the Howorth collection of data. Howorth's descriptions of the mammoth distributions and the characteristics of the other fauna, as well as the buried flora, that accompanied the mammoths in Eurasia and North America seem amazingly up to date.

ASTRAL CATASTROPHES AND CATASTROPHIC CRUSTAL SHIFTS

The anomaly of the woolly mammoth carcasses in Siberia has inspired such angst among scientifically minded individuals that several hypotheses of global catastrophism have been invented. I suppose Howorth would be considered the first catastrophist, but the ideas discussed in this section are more modern beliefs. None of these individuals is a Christian, as far as I know.

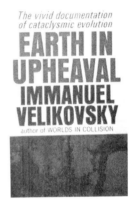

Immanuel Velikovsky wrote two influential and popular books on astronomical or astral catastrophes called *Worlds in Collision* (1950) and *Earth in Upheaval* (1955). His books sold in the millions. Few remember Velikovsky or his ideas and the considerable consternation he fomented among orthodox scientists. Charles Ginenthal (1997) provides an updated, modern defense of Velikovsky's hypothesis.

According to Velikovsky, astral catastrophes caused great upheavals over the earth. The demise of the woolly mammoths in Siberia played a *lead* role in his books. He weaves the mysteries of the mammoth, the Ice Age, and many other puzzles from the earth sciences into a catastrophic adventure featuring Venus and Mars moving through the solar system and skimming close by the earth. Then somehow, and despite astronomical odds, these two planets were captured in stable orbits around the sun. He envisioned the astral catastrophes taking place about 3,500 years ago. He believed many of the miracles of the Old Testament, but suggested an astronomical explanation. Velikovsky perceptively points out the multiple problems inherent in explaining the past. Like Howorth, Velikovsky considered the geological doctrine of uniformitarianism inadequate to solve the many mysteries of the past. He cannot help but add an element of exaggeration, as in the following reference to the "muck" of Alaska:

> *Under what conditions did this great slaughter take place, in which millions upon millions of animals were torn limb from limb and mingled with uprooted trees?* (Velikovsky, 1955, p. 13).

Others have also noted the twisted and torn trees with disarticulated mammals in the muck of Alaska (Hibben, 1943, p. 256). The Alaskan muck, with its mixture of plant and animal remains, is really no mystery substance, as some have suggested. It has a more mundane explanation, which will be discussed later in the book.

Velikovsky and Ginenthal suggest that a sudden shift of the axis of the earth to vertical took place as Mars or Venus passed close to the earth. This caused the Ice Age to end. The warmer Siberian climate attracted migrations of mammoths. Later, about 3,500 years ago, they contend the axis shifted back to the present 23½ degrees, bringing a rapid cooling, and freezing the mammoths in their tracks by a quick freeze. Some died before they could swallow the food in their mouth and before their last meal decayed in their stomachs. With this pole shift, Velikovsky and Ginenthal account for the demise of the mammoths, the cause of the Ice Age, and many other riddles of the recent past.

Velikovsky's and Ginenthal's hypothesis has many problems, but one is fatal. A pole shift to a more vertical axis would *result in an ice age*, not a sudden warming. This may seem strange to many people, because a perpetual spring or fall sounds ideal. However, not many realize an Arctic spring and fall is *not* warm. The song, "North to Alaska," does not have a verse about springtime in Alaska being 40 below zero Fahrenheit (-40ºC) for nothing. With the earth's axis vertical, an endless spring or autumn would cause the snow and ice to build up. The snow and ice would reflect more sunlight back into space, adding to the cooling. The cooling and ice age would slowly spread into the mid latitudes. Even worse for their theory, the snow and ice would *accumulate* in the lowlands of Siberia and Alaska. These areas we know were never glaciated. These lowlands are the land of the mammoths that inspired Velikovsky's hypothesis in the first place. The astral catastrophe theory in practice would cause the *reverse* of what they hoped to explain.

Other popular intellectuals and writers have accepted and embellished on Velikovsky's ideas. Ivan Sanderson (1960) published a short piece in the *Saturday Evening Post* suggesting a rapid shift of the earth's crust over the mantle, instead of a shift of the poles. He thinks this caused worldwide volcanism and cooling and a quick freeze of the woolly mammoths.

Charles Hapgood (1958, 1970) also expounded on Velikovsky's ideas and agreed with Sanderson that the earth's crust shifted. He proposed that Siberia moved north and North America south to freeze the mammoths and end the Ice Age. He thought the violent atmospheric disturbances and volcanic cooling, caused by the last displacement of the earth's crust, specifically killed the Siberian mammoths. His first book was even endorsed in the foreword by Albert Einstein, who seemed to recognize that many climatic mysteries of the past were not being explained well, or even addressed, by mainstream geologists.

I have two problems with Hapgood and several others that postulate such catastrophes — they are not careful with their data and are quick to jump to conclusions. A good example of this occurred when Hapgood (1958, p. 234–235) stated that Baron Toll, a Siberian explorer, reported a 90-foot (27 m) high fruit tree on the

New Siberian Islands. The tree was said to be perfectly preserved in permafrost with its roots intact, and seeds, green leaves, and ripe fruit still clinging to its branches. However, Hapgood does not reference Toll at all, but uses a secondhand report from Bassett Digby (1926, p. 151), who reported that Toll discovered a 90-foot alder tree on Bol'shoi Lyakhov Island, one of the New Siberian Islands, among the Ice Age animals. The alder (*Alnus fructicosa*) was intact with roots and seeds. Hapgood obviously embellished the facts.

THE QUICK FREEZE

In many of the above hypotheses, the mammoths are quick-frozen. This hypothesis is suggested to account for the half-digested state of the stomach contents of several mammoths, the undecayed meat on a few mammoths, and the undecayed nature of many of the bones and tusks. The quick freeze idea actually is an old one, originating from the early 19th century. It probably began with Baron Cuvier and apparently was popular in his time (Grayson, 1984a). It is a reasonable suggestion, given the observations. The quick-freeze hypothesis was given a boost by Birds Eye Frozen Foods Company in 1960. Based on heat conduction through beef, they calculated that a sudden plunge to a temperature below −150°F (−100°C) was necessary to account for the state of preservation of the stomach contents of the Beresovka mammoth (Sanderson, 1960). Proponents of the quick-freeze idea have great difficulty finding a viable mechanism to account for such a catastrophic cooling. More will be said about this intriguing hypothesis later.

MAINSTREAM SCIENTIFIC HYPOTHESES

Mainstream scientists do not seem to have honestly faced the raw data. They seem to be mentally constrained by their uniformitarian straightjacket, which undergirds their interpretation and conclusions.

William Farrand (1961, 1962) typifies many scientists' position on the woolly mammoth's life and extinction in Siberia. He believes that the climate played little or no role in the demise of the Siberian mammoths because the animals were well adapted to cold. He concludes there is much evidence that ancient Siberia had a similar climate to today, although he admits there is some puzzling data indicative of a little warmer climate. He does not believe there are millions of mammoths entombed in the permafrost and thinks the animals that did live there could have subsisted on the vegetation that grows in Siberia today. Farrand (1962, p. 450) leans strongly toward the uniformitarian view that the woolly mammoth data *". . . can be adequately explained by the everyday processes which we can observe around us."*

It is questionable whether the woolly mammoth could have adapted to Siberia's present frigid temperatures or the even colder climate of the Ice Age. The bog vegetation that dominates Siberia's summers would provide woefully inadequate nutrition for the "well dressed giants." Worse, the Siberian summers would melt the permafrost enough to cause the mammoths to mire. Not to be forgotten, it is well substantiated that there were millions of mammoths in Siberia. In conclusion, uniformitarianism does not answer some very essential problems with the existence of millions of apparently well-fed mammoths living in Siberia and becoming extinct within a short time.

CHAPTER FIVE

THE EXTINCTION WARS

The worst problem uniformitarian scientists encounter with the extinction of the Siberian woolly mammoths is that they disappeared not just in Siberia but everywhere at about the same time. Another major difficulty they face is that many other animals also went extinct at the same time, near the end of the Ice Age. On North America, 70 percent of mammals weighing over 100 pounds (40 kg) disappeared (Martin and Klein, 1984; Stone, 2001, p. 94–143; Agenbroad and Nelson, 2002, p. 87–99). This represents about 100 species of large animals that included mammoths, mastodons, saber-toothed cats, giant ground sloths, giant beavers, giant peccaries, dire wolves, short-faced bears, and many others. The American mastodon is a type of elephant that lived mainly in the eastern half of the United States during the Ice Age. It differs from the woolly mammoth in being shorter and more heavyset, and having less hair and less curvature of the tusks (G. Haynes, 1991). About three-fourths of mammal species went extinct on Eurasia (Stone, 2001, p. 102). Mass extinctions also occurred in the Southern Hemisphere. Australia lost 90 percent of its large animals including the giant kangaroos and wombats (Agenbroad and Nelson, 2002, p. 88). Strangely, these mass extinctions occurred at a time when the climate was supposed to be warmer with more glaciated land becoming exposed upon melting. Their paradigm or major belief system leaves them with a climate that does not explain how the animals found enough food to thrive or how they survived the inhospitable Ice Age climate. (Possible explanations for disharmonious associations are presented in appendix 2.)

There are two main hypotheses in vogue today to account for these extinctions at the end of the Ice Age: (1) either they died because of the climate change, the overchill hypothesis, or (2) man killed most of the large animals in a great slaughter, the overkill hypothesis (Martin and Klein, 1984; Stone, 2001, p. 94–143; Agenbroad and Nelson, 2002, p. 87–99). The two sides in this conflict are at such odds that it is almost a war between them — a war of ideas.

A third hypothesis has recently entered the dispute, namely that people sparked the extinctions by introducing epidemic diseases, the overill hypothesis (Monastersky, 1999). The disease vectors could have been introduced to the wild animals by the organisms that normally accompany man, such as dogs, cats, rats, fleas, etc. However, there is little evidence to support this new hypothesis (Agenbroad, 1998, p. 23; Martin and Steadman, 1999, p. 18). Howorth (1887, p. 179) examined the possibility of disease long ago and concluded that it was extremely unlikely. This was because disease could not affect that many animals over such a wide area. Furthermore, evidence for disease should be seen in the remains, but the animals appear to have been healthy when they died.

Extinction by Climate Change?

Many geologists favor massive extinctions from the climate changes that occurred at the end of the Ice Age. The timing is certainly suggestive. Unfortunately, there are several objections to climate change alone being the culprit. The most common and serious argument is that the animals survived all the many supposed previous glaciations and interglacials with few extinctions (Stuart, 1991, p. 457). Since there are now thought to be about 30 separate ice ages (Ehlers, 1996, p. 5), why would there be such a mass extinction only after the last? Daniel Fisher (1996, p. 315) summarizes this argument:

> *Climatic hypotheses for late Pleistocene extinction face the challenge of explaining why this [last] deglaciation event had consequences for the fauna that were so much more drastic than earlier [ice age] events.*

Climate enthusiasts counter that the climate change from the Ice Age to the present climate was unique and much harsher than the previous interglacials (Graham and Lundelius, 1984; Guthrie, 1984, p. 290). But, this is unlikely. Stuart (1991, p. 546) points out that there should be little, if any, difference between the present interglacial and previous ones.

Another objection is that as the ice sheets were disappearing and the climate was warming, more land became available for grazing animals (Agenbroad, 1998, p. 23). Instead of the overchill hypothesis, it should be the underchill hypothesis (Agenbroad and Nelson, 2002, p. 97). The animals also could have migrated to a more suitable habitat as the climate changed (Stuart, 1991, p. 457). So, the likelihood of climate change causing their demise is still questionable.

Then there is the high probability that if the mammoths died out by climate change, their condition would show evidence of starvation or other climate-induced trauma. Comments of most workers indicate that the mammoths were apparently healthy when they died. According to Jeffrey Saunders, the Columbian mammoth on the Great Plains of the United States shows no evidence of long-term stress at the end of the Ice Age (Saunders, 1992, p. 140).

If climate change caused the extinctions, one would expect evidence of more deaths in the north, closer to the ice sheets, than the southern part of the United States. However, 60 percent of the deaths occurred in the south. This is considered a firm refutation of the climate idea by some (Monastersky, 1999, p. 360)

Table 5.1 summarizes the evidence against the climate change hypothesis. These are formidable objections.

EXTINCTION BY MAN?

The alternative hypothesis is that man is responsible for the Ice Age extinctions, since man seems to be the only added variable to the last ice age compared to the previous 29 ice ages that uniformitarian scientists believe occurred. The overkill hypothesis as it is called is rather old, going back to the time of Howorth in the late 1800s (1887, p. 170). But Paul Martin and colleagues (Martin and Klein, 1984; Steadman and Mead, 1995; MacPhee, 1999) have revived it. Because of the objections to the climate change hypothesis, and noting that the time of extinction coincided with the time of man entering the New World, Martin believes man rapidly exterminated the animals in a great slaughter. According to Stewart, the fact that most of the animals that became extinct were large and were not replaced by other animals suggests that man was the culprit (Stuart, 1991). One of Martin's overkill models is the "Blitzkrieg model," named after the ferocious German advances early in World War II.

Table 5.1
Summary of the Evidence against the Climatic Hypothesis
for the Extinction of the Woolly Mammoths and
Other Large Mammals at the End of the Ice Age

1) Animals survived many previous ice ages and interglacials.

2) The present interglacial was not harsher than previous interglacials.

3) The climate warmed while ice sheets melted.

4) More land was exposed as ice sheets melted.

5) Skeletons and carcasses were apparently healthy when they died.

6) Most deaths of animals were well south of the ice sheet boundary in the United States.

Of course, overkill advocates are quick to mention all the animals and birds that man has sent to oblivion during recorded history. They remind us that within 600 years of man's arrival in New Zealand, about 1000 A.D., many bird species, including the giant moa, were exterminated (Stuart, 1991, p. 458). Scientists, who favor the overkill hypothesis, point out that some mammoth remains in the New World have Clovis spear points associated with the skeleton. The Clovis people are supposed to be the first humans entering the New World from Alaska about 11,000 years ago. There are little less than two dozen associations between mammoths and Clovis spear points (Fisher, 1996, p. 300).

However, there are problems with the overkill hypothesis. The question can legitimately be asked: how can man kill so many animals within a few hundred years, especially when some of these animals ranged all over the Northern Hemisphere and were quite adaptable to various habitats? People were likely sparse at the time. The hunters had only spears, not a very efficient method to destroy millions of animals. These people depended upon hunting for food. They likely would not wantonly have killed off massive amounts of animals, like the buffaloes killed by rifles on the Great Plains of North America in the 1800s. Hunting for sport and wasting the meat would be very unlikely. To hunters and gatherers, the tusks and meat would be very useful, yet most of the mammoth tusks remain untouched (Howorth, 1887, p. 171). Hunters would surely have absconded with the tusks, so that few skeletons of mammoths would possess tusks. Stone (2001b, p. 116) describes the problem with overkill this way: "Considering the sheer number of species that went extinct, that argument runs thin — even if Clovis men were hunting from morning until night."

Advocates of overkill counter that the animals, in North America at least, were not afraid of man and had not developed defenses against them (Monastersky, 1999), since the animals preceded man to North America. So, goes the theory, the animals were essentially "tame," and it was like killing cattle. However, many think that it would not take long for the animals to adapt to aggressive people

In answer to the objection that many genera of birds also went extinct in North America (Grayson, 1977), Steadman and Martin (1984) respond that most of them were large carrion feeders and depended on a supply of large mammals.

In reference to recent extinctions of island birds and animals, such as on New Zealand, overkill critics point out that these species cannot migrate off the island and are especially vulnerable to hunting pressure (Stuart, 1991, p. 459). Furthermore, most of the modern-day mass extinctions or mass killings occurred with *rifles*, which early hunters with spears, of course, did not possess.

As far as the mammoth/spear point associations in the New World, critics of overkill further point out that there are relatively few of these sites in all of North America (Stuart, 1991, p. 458). And even the mammoth/spear point associations do not mean that man hunted the mammoth, but the associations could just as well mean that man killed some sick or dying mammoths (Haynes, 1999).

Furthermore, there are few, if any, signs of associations between man and the remainder of the extinct animals (Fisher, 1996, p. 300). This is why Martin advocated his Blitzkrieg model, which happened *so fast as not to leave much evidence.* One problem with Martin's *ad hoc* subsidiary hypotheses is that there are many moa kill sites in New Zealand from the historical extinctions (Haynes, 1999, p. 230). This is overkill with much evidence lying around.

Grayson (1984b) rightly challenges Martin's view and maintains that because of such subsidiary explanations, overkill is untestable. The migrating Clovis hunters are assumed to be rather backward people using simple weapons, like spears. Some of these animals are dangerous and when wounded would be ferocious. How many would dare to spear a woolly rhinoceros? Furthermore, the hide of the mammoth is quite tough and would be very hard for a spear to penetrate. Based on the dissection of an elephant which died in a zoo, Laub (1992, p. 101) comments:

> *Our own experiences with the elephant carcass left us skeptical about the wisdom of seeking to bring down a mammoth or mastodon primarily with spear thrusts. A thick coat of fur during at least part of the year, added to the thick skin known to have been present in mammoths (preserved in frozen carcasses) and presumed in mastodons, would probably have diminished the force of a striking spear.*

Stone (2001b, p. 112) corroborates in describing an experiment with simulated Clovis weaponry and a dead zoo elephant. The Clovis points mostly failed to penetrate the rubbery skin.

Another argument against the overkill hypothesis is that in Africa man and animals are said to have coexisted for a million years or so with very few extinctions. Digby (1926, p. 67), long ago, had a good answer to this objection: Africa teems with food year around, and man had no need to wipe out animals. However, Digby's argument can be turned around to question the overkill hypothesis in North America, since game was likely plentiful at the time.

Another problem for the overkill hypothesis is that some of the animals that disappeared were unlikely to have figured in the human diet (Stuart, 1991, p. 459). Then, there is the objection that many animals that should have been hunted to extinction, such as the bison, elk, moose, and reindeer, have survived to this day.

Although overkill enthusiasts lift up the North American extinction record as support, the correspondence of the meager archaeological record and mass extinctions in northern Eurasia and Australia seems contradictory (Stuart, 1991, p. 459, 547–548; Agenbroad, 1998, p. 23). The extinctions in Eurasia and Australia are believed to stretch out over a period of about 40,000 years. This record is contrary to both the overkill and climatic hypotheses (Stuart, 1991, p. 546).

A number of the extinct mammals were carnivores, like the saber-tooth tiger. Why would these carnivorous animals also go extinct? Overkill enthusiasts counter that it is because the herbivores died out. This argument does not hold water because some large herbivores, such as the bison, elk, deer, reindeer, etc, remain to this day (Pielou, 1991, p. 266).

Some scientists question the presumed date of the North American extinctions as concurrent with man entering the New World about 11,000 years ago. Most of these dates are based on carbon-14 dating. Krishtalka (1984, p. 226) points out how the "dating" is likely a *selection* process:

> *Their selective acceptance of only the "good" dates — those that fit the model (for example dates for human beings in North America no older than 12,000 yr B.P., and those for mammoths no younger than 10,000 yr B.P.) — may play fast and loose with the evidence that doesn't fit.*

Grayson reinforces this possible juggling of carbon-14 dates to arrive at preconceived conclusions:

> *The timing of Ice Age extinctions is really very poorly understood. . . . Radiocarbon chronologies are bad in North America and worse in Europe* (Bower, 1987, p. 285).

Table 5.2 summarizes the evidence against the overkill hypothesis.

Can Both Be Correct?

Many scientists advocate that both climate and man caused the late Ice Age extinctions (Stuart, 1991, p. 548–549). They agree that neither hypothesis by itself seems likely. For instance, Ward (1997, p. 162) states:

> *However, no one seems to have considered the possibility that, at least as they were defined through the late 1980s, both hypotheses might be wrong.*

After testing the Blitzkrieg model, Beck (1996) found that both main models appear to be wrong. As a result of tests and the many arguments against either hypothesis alone, many scientists have settled on believing that a combination of climate change and overkill explains the extinctions. Gary Haynes (1991, p. 264–317) examined the problems with both hypotheses, but leans mostly toward climate change with man killing off already dying animals. I believe his stance on this issue has merit.

Some consider the combination of both hypotheses to be a weak approach because the combination is almost untestable (Martin and Steadman, 1999, p. 18). But Burney (1999, p. 162) cautions that the more complex solution should not be rejected just because it is complex.

Table 5.2
Summary of the Evidences against the Overkill Hypothesis
for the Extinction of the Woolly Mammoths and
Other Large Mammals at the End of the Ice Age

1) The population of people was sparse while animals were widespread over the Northern Hemisphere.

2) Hunters only had spears and knives.

3) Mammoth hide and hair was difficult to penetrate with a spear.

4) Hunters normally don't wantonly kill animals they use for food.

5) Most mammoth tusks were left with the skeletons.

6) Overkill was unlikely with island extinctions by man because the animals could not flee far.

7) There are relatively few mammoth-spear point associations.

8) Spear points associated with mammoths could be the result of man killing weak or dying animals.

9) There were few associations between man and other extinct animals.

10) There were many moa kill sites on New Zealand, while there were few mammoth kill sites.

11) Africans have not killed off many animals over thousands of years.

12) Many of the extinct animals would not have been part of man's diet.

13) Many animals that should have been hunted to extinction survive today.

14) Dating associations between man and extinctions are questionable.

THE DEBATE RAGES ON

Back in 1926 when Digby wrote his book on the mammoths, the extinction of the woolly mammoths had already caused much consternation among scientists for one hundred years:

> *Many scientists, including the great palaeontologists of this and other countries, have wrinkled their brows for a century over the problem of flesh-and-blood mammoths* (Digby, 1926, p. 51).

One would expect that after 75 more years the problem would have been solved, not only for woolly mammoths, but also for the other animals that went extinct.

Summarizing the results of a conference on extinctions, Grayson (1984b, p. 807) writes in frustration:

> *We have accumulated facts on the nature of ancient floras and faunas, on past climates, on human prehistory, and on the chronology of it all. These are precisely the kinds of facts that scientists have assumed all along are needed to provide an adequate explanation of late Pleistocene extinctions.*
>
> *Nonetheless, from an historical perspective one of the most interesting lessons to be learned from this volume is that we are apparently no closer to that adequate explanation, or at least to agreement as to what that adequate explanation is. . . . The accumulation of facts, it would seem, has been of surprisingly little help in resolving one of the major problems that confronts the student of mammalian history. There is a question that can hardly be avoided, one that is nearly as interesting as the causes of the extinctions themselves: why has the huge increase in our knowledge of the past failed to move the issue detectably closer to a resolution? Why has so much time made so little difference?"*

In a more recent conference on mass extinctions, Alroy (1999, p. 105) throws up his hands:

> *After many decades of debate, the North American end-Pleistocene megafaunal mass extinction remains a lightning rod of controversy. The extraordinarily divergent opinions expressed in this volume show that no resolution is in sight.*

Despite the enormous expense and accumulation of data, scientists are stymied. The extinction wars continue. Could the problem be in their basic assumptions regarding the past?

CHAPTER SIX

THE MULTIPLICATION OF ICE AGE THEORIES

Researchers have generated a lot of theories to explain the mysteries surrounding the mammoths, but questions about the cause of the Ice Age have also spawned a multitude of ideas. Ice Age theories can be divided into two general groups. One group is extraterrestrial — something happened in our solar system or the Milky Way galaxy or even on the sun to start an Ice Age. The second group of theories is terrestrial. They propose that something in Earth's complex climate changed to start an Ice Age.

EXTRATERRESTRIAL THEORIES

Not until the mid 1800s did the scientific world finally accept that an Ice Age actually occurred. At that time, the cause of the Ice Age was first ascribed to a loss of light from the sun. The temperature of the earth is controlled by the amount of sunlight that reaches the earth. Differences in sunlight cause the cold polar and warm tropical regions. These differences in temperature power the earth's wind system and storm movements. The theory goes that if the power of the sun could somehow be reduced, temperatures in the higher latitudes would drop and lead to an Ice Age.

However, no one knows whether the amount of sunlight changed in the past. No one was around to observe such a change, and observations are necessary for an idea to be verified as a scientific theory. It is true that the intensity of the sun does change a little, depending upon the number of sunspots, but the change is very small. As far as anyone knows, the sun has maintained a nearly constant intensity throughout Earth's history. In meteorological jargon the assumed reliability of the solar output is called the *solar constant.*

Even if there were less sunlight in the past, it would not necessarily lead to an Ice Age. Colder temperatures are less able to hold water vapor. Therefore, the amount of rain or snow would be *reduced, not increased.*

Other scientists have proposed that the solar system moved through a dust cloud to cause an Ice Age. They suggest that perhaps this dust cloud was a dirty arm of the Milky Way galaxy. The dust between the sun and earth would block out some of the sun's rays and lead to a build-up of ice. Unfortunately, this theory also suffers from a lack of evidence and also does not provide for the copious amount of snow needed to produce an Ice Age.

TERRESTRIAL THEORIES

Many scientists today are concerned about the build up of carbon dioxide in the atmosphere since more carbon dioxide brings a greenhouse effect. Increased carbon dioxide in the atmosphere absorbs more infrared radiation from the earth, heating the lower atmosphere. Conversely, if there were less carbon dioxide in the past, the climate would become cooler. Scientists believe there was about 30 percent less carbon dioxide during the Ice Age than there was at the start of the industrial revolution. This is based on measurements of carbon dioxide trapped in small air bubbles in the Greenland and Antarctica ice sheets.

Other greenhouse gases, such as methane, have increased substantially more than carbon dioxide, but they have a weaker effect on greenhouse warming. It is convenient to consider these other greenhouse gases in terms of carbon dioxide, so scientists have transposed these other greenhouse gases into *carbon dioxide equivalents.* The net effect of these other greenhouse gases is similar to increasing carbon dioxide another 30 percent. Thus, "greenhouse" gases have increased 60 percent since the industrial revolution. However, this has produced at most only a 1°F (0.6°C) global temperature rise. It is likely that part of this warming was not caused by the increase in greenhouse gases but due to other causes (Michaels and Balling, 2000), but let us assume it was. Reducing carbon dioxide by 30 percent during an Ice Age would probably produce a less than one-degree drop in temperature — definitely not enough to start an Ice Age.

Mountain building can be used to explain the cold climate of an area. It is possible mountain building could have initiated an ice sheet. It is well known that as a person ascends a mountain, the temperature cools. It is also well known that mountains receive much more rain and snow than the adjacent valleys. So, as the theory goes, if the land were higher, the temperatures would be colder and the snowfall greater.

However, although the mountainous regions of North America, Europe, and Asia today are high, they have very few glaciers, and they do not have an ice sheet covering them. Another problem is that the ice sheet in North America developed over the *low* areas of northeast Canada. Another glitch is the altitude of the land in the United States from North Dakota to Maine is not very high. So postulating that mountain building in the past caused an Ice Age does not help at all. Besides, the high mountains are still with us, and there are no ice sheets covering northern North America, Europe, and Asia.

Another ingenious Ice Age theory is that if the sea ice melted over the Arctic Ocean, the increased evaporation would provide the needed high latitude moisture. Due to the snow and ice build-up, the climate would then cool and the Arctic Ocean would refreeze and reverse the build-up of ice. The cycle would continuously repeat itself. This theory provides an explanation for the many ice ages that scientists claim took place in the past 2.5 million years of geological time (Donn and Ewing, 1968).

The theory has merit in that it focuses on the necessary moisture that most theories neglect. It is likely, however, that the added moisture would be insufficient to begin an Ice Age. It is true that increased evaporation from an iceless Arctic Ocean would provide more snow in northern Canada and Eurasia. However, the heat transmitted to the atmosphere from the water during the winter would most likely keep the continents too warm during the summer for snow and ice to build up. The theory fails to account for the tremendous summer cooling required for an Ice Age. Moreover, no one mentions how the Arctic Ocean ice could have melted, or whether there is any evidence of it having happened in the recent past. In the standard view, the ice on the Arctic Ocean has not melted for at least the past supposed million years of geological time.

Other theories involve increasing volcanic dust, trapped in the upper atmosphere, blocking some of the sunshine and, therefore, causing cooler temperatures and an Ice Age (figure 6.1). This theory also has merit because volcanic dust and gases do bring cooler temperatures. The problem is that each supposed ice age lasts 100,000 years. Volcanic dust and gases, on the other hand, fall out of the stratosphere in one to several years. An inordinate amount of volcanism would be required to sustain cold summer temperatures throughout such a long ice age.

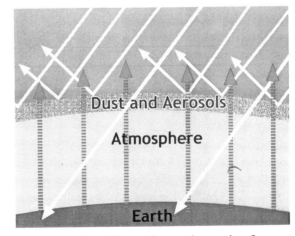

Figure 6.1. Volcanic dust and aerosols reflect sunlight back to space, cooling the land.

One desperate theory has the West Antarctic ice sheet slipping from its undersea moorings and out into the deep ocean. As it floats around in the southern ocean, more sunlight reflects back into space and cools the earth. However, displacing the West Antarctic ice sheet from its current location could hardly change by much the amount of sunlight already reflected back to space. Moreover, if the snow and ice did somehow increase in the Southern Hemisphere by this mechanism, it would have little impact in the Northern Hemisphere. The two hemispheres generally act independently of each other with little exchange of heat or moisture between them.

A theory that gives up on most other theories is that an ice age is simply caused by chance fluctuations in the climate. Since small climate changes occur on short time scales, it is supposed that large climate changes occur over long periods of time. This assertion is backed up by sophisticated mathematics. The plausibility of this theory, however, is open to serious question. According to what is generally believed about the ice ages, ten ice ages waxed and waned regularly every 100,000 years. This defies the rules of chance. Since the theory cannot be tested, it does not qualify as a scientific theory.

SUMMARY

Scientists abhor a theoretical vacuum. It has been difficult finding even a somewhat plausible theory to explain even one ice age. Adding to the difficulty, geologists became convinced early on that there were many ice ages. So, a mechanism that could produce more than one would be favored. One particular theory out of the many has recently become popular since the 1970s. It is called the astronomical or Milankovitch theory of the Ice Age. It is not new; meteorologists had previously rejected it more than once (see boxed section).

When a phenomenon cannot be explained by existing data, the theories multiply. In 1968, in a volume on the causes of climate change, Erik Eriksson counted over 60 theories on the cause of the Ice Age. Although many have merit, each has fatal flaws. After a lifetime of studying the Ice Age, J.K. Charlesworth (1957, p. 1532) commented on the status of all these theories, including the astronomical theory:

> *Pleistocene [Ice Age] phenomena have produced an absolute riot of theories ranging "from the remotely possible to the mutually contradictory and the palpably inadequate."*

That is not saying much for Ice Age theories; Charlesworth is essentially saying that all these theories are mammoth failures. Twenty-two years later, in 1979, Brian John, reminiscing on Charlesworth's words, relates that the situation has not improved. In fact, he says that it is worse: *"Things have become even more confused since then . . ."* (John, 1979, p. 57).

THE ASTRONOMICAL THEORY OF THE ICE AGES

Many people believe the earth travels around the sun like clockwork — never changing. However, it has been discovered that the earth's orbit around the sun does change a little. Its path transforms from a circle to a slightly flattened circle, called an ellipse, and back again to a circle. It would take 100,000 years or so for each cycle.

Evolutionary scientists have extrapolated the eccentricity millions of years back in the past (see figure 6.2). The difference of the earth's orbit from a circle to an ellipse is called the eccentricity. An eccentricity of zero is a circle.

The earth's orbit itself revolves around the sun. This is especially noticeable when the orbit is an ellipse. Such a cycle is hard to visualize. Think of it as an elliptical path around the sun, and that the path slowly rotates around the sun. The orbital path would make one rotation about every 22,000 years and is called the precession of the equinoxes. In the current orbit of the earth, the sun is closest in January and farthest in July (figure 6.3). In about 11,000 years, the sun will be closer to the earth in July and farthest in January.

Many have been taught that the 23.5-degree tilt of the earth's axis with respect to the earth's orbital plane about the sun never changes and causes the

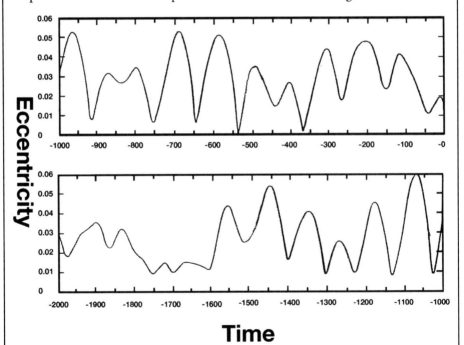

Figure 6.2 The variation in the earth's eccentricity for an assumed past two million years. Units are in thousands of years (Vernekar, 1972).

(Monograph is from the American Meteorological Society)

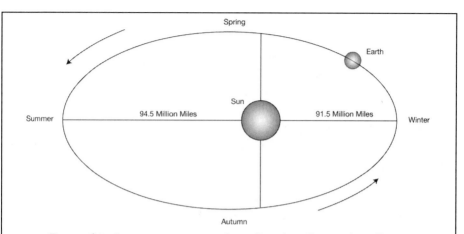

Figure 6.3. Present eccentricity of Earth's orbit (flattened to illustrate the phenomenon). Seasons are in reference to the Northern Hemisphere.

seasons. It is true that this tilt causes the seasons. However, the tilt also changes a little with time. It wobbles back and forth from 22.1 degrees to 24.5 degrees and back to 22.1 degrees. A full cycle would take 40,000 years, assuming there were no other forces.

The slight gravitational pull of the moon and planets on the earth cause all these cyclical changes of the earth's orbit. The variations are small with correspondingly slight changes in the amount of sunlight around the globe (figure 6.3). The change in solar radiation caused by all three orbital variables is shown in figure 6.4. Scientists postulate that a decrease in the sunlight at higher latitudes in summer, caused by changes in the earth's orbital geometry, would cause an ice age. Alternatively, an increase in sunlight in the summer would cause an ice sheet to melt. Since the above changes in sunlight are cyclical processes, it would favor multiple ice ages repeating in a regular fashion — an attractive concept.

James Croll first proposed the astronomical theory in the late 1800s. It helped persuade scientists to believe in many ice ages as opposed to just one. According to the theory in the late 1880s, the last ice age ended about 70,000 years ago. Scientific evidence was marshaled to "prove" that this termination time was true. But, the astronomical theory was not well developed until the 1920s and 1930s, when Milutin Milankovitch, a Serbian meteorologist, worked out many of the details with more precision. According to the revised *Milankovitch theory,* as the astronomical theory is often called, the Ice Age peaked about 18,000 years ago. Data, once again, were tweaked to "prove" this time for Ice Age maximum. Soon after Milankovitch refined the theory, it came under a withering barrage of criticism, mostly from meteorologists. It was quickly discarded in the 1950s and 1960s.

It is somewhat common in the history of science for a discarded theory to make a comeback (Charlesworth, 1957, p. viii). This has proven true with the

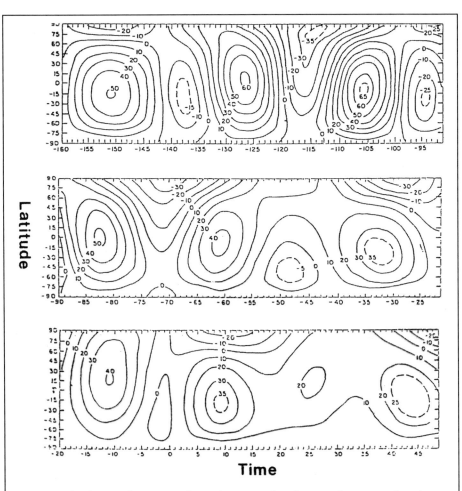

Figure 6.4. The net change in solar radiation in langleys per day received at the top of the atmosphere of the Northern Hemisphere caloric summer for an assumed time interval of 160,000 years in the past to 50,000 years in the future. Minus latitude is for the Southern Hemisphere. Units are in thousands of years. (Vernekar, 1972)

(Monograph is from the American Meteorological Society)

Milankovitch theory. New technology applied to deep ocean-floor sediments and the persistence of several prominent scientists has revived the theory. Based on properties of the ocean-bottom sediments, oceanographers concluded there have been over 30 distinct ice ages that have repeated regularly, each completely melting during what is called an interglacial period. Some even consider the mystery of the Ice Age as solved (Imbrie and Imbrie, 1979).

Despite the enthusiasm of most scientists toward the astronomical theory, it has a number of serious, most likely fatal, flaws. The changes in summer sunshine at high latitudes postulated by the theory are too small to generate an ice age.

Heating at higher latitudes depends only partially on the amount of sunshine. Northward transport of heat by the atmosphere and ocean currents are also important, but mostly neglected by proponents of this theory. Heat transport would lessen the cooling effect caused by reduced sunshine. Between heat transport and the already small effect of reduced sunshine, the cooling would be negligible.

Meteorologists have known about this weakness in the theory for a long time. It contributed to its earlier demise. Famous astronomer Fred Hoyle (1981, p. 77) expressed his sentiments for the Milankovitch theory by saying:

> *If I were to assert that a glacial condition could be induced in a room liberally supplied during winter with charged night-storage heaters simply by taking an ice cube into the room, the proposition would be no more unlikely than the Milankovitch theory.*

The "night-storage heaters" are the other processes that supply heat to higher latitudes, while the ice cube represents the slight cooling due to the astronomical theory.

Data from oceanic sediments supposedly show that the 100,000-year eccentricity cycle is the most important cycle for repeating ice ages. This particular cycle, however, is the smallest of the three orbital variations by far. It causes almost no change in the summer sunshine at higher latitudes. Scientists are greatly perplexed and have been shopping around for a secondary mechanism to boost their theory.

Another serious problem is that the ice age cycles supposedly occur at the same times in both the Southern and the Northern Hemispheres. But the decreased sunlight caused by the precession of the equinoxes generally alternates between hemispheres, as shown in figure 6.4. When the Northern Hemisphere has a slightly lower intensity of sunlight during the summer, the Southern Hemisphere has an increased intensity of summer sunlight. Since the two hemispheres are generally separated climatologically, why the supposed ice ages and interglacials would cycle in phase has never been answered.

With so many scientific objections to the astronomical theory, one may ask why it is so popular. I believe it is because the apparent statistical matches from deep-sea cores have swayed most scientists. There are many problems, however, in relating properties of deep-sea cores to the astronomical theory. Accurate dates are needed, but the dating methods are not all that accurate. Unfortunately, the numbers that make up the statistics seem to have a high degree of interpretation mixed into them. One never knows how much is interpretation and how much is fact. Another reason for the popularity of the theory is that such a dramatic event as the Ice Age of the recent past demands an explanation and any explanation is better than none — even if it is the weak astronomical theory.

CHAPTER SEVEN

THE GENESIS FLOOD
CAUSED THE ICE AGE

In order to understand the mysteries of the woolly mammoth, we need to first understand the Ice Age. This is because the woolly mammoth is a denizen of the Ice Age (see appendix 4). I will first delve into a biblical theory for the development of one Ice Age. We will then be prepared to answer the questions surrounding the woolly mammoth.

Scientists have collected mounds of evidence proving that ice once covered most of Canada and parts of the northern and central United States. Evidence is also found in northern Europe, northwest Asia, many of the large mountain ranges of Eurasia, and high mountainous areas of the Southern Hemisphere and tropics. But the truth is, scientists still do not know the cause of the Ice Age as succinctly stated by David Alt (2001, p. 180): *"Although theories abound, no one really knows what causes ice ages."* Uniformitarianism has not been able to explain the Ice Age, or events related to the Ice Age. Ice sheets are not developing and melting today so we have no way to actually observe how they developed in the past. The woolly mammoths are extinct, so we cannot witness whether they could survive in Siberia. Large lakes are not filling the deserts of the earth. Animal and plant distributions were different during the Ice Age, unlike any pattern observed today. And, we have not observed the kind of mass extinctions that occurred at the end of the Ice Age.

It is doubtful that evolutionists will find a present process that can explain the origin of the Ice Age or the mass extinctions of large mammals. It is very likely the difficulty in knowing the cause of the Ice Age does not lie in the data that has been gathered for over two centuries but in the assumptions. It is my conviction, and that of many others, that the *assumption of uniformitarianism needs to be rejected.* I believe it is this assumption and the antagonism of mainstream scientists toward catastrophism that has blinded their minds toward a solution of the Ice Age, as well as for the woolly mammoths. Guthrie (1984, p. 292), speaking in regard to the common disharmonious associations and subsequent extinctions associated with the Ice Age, discovered early in his career:

> *Looking at the extinction problem through the eyes of a young paleontologist in the early 1960s, I encountered my first important lesson — that the present can be used to understand the past only with sensitive discretion. In fact, much of the past may have no modern analogue.*

Larry Marshall (1984, p. 791–792) sums up a book on Ice Age extinctions by saying:

> *Many chapter authors argue that the old axiom — the present is the key to the past — no longer stands. Guthrie (chap. 13) speaks of the standards tied*

Figure 7.1. Time frame for the Ice Age in relationship to the Flood.
(Illustration by Daniel Lewis of AIG.)

to normalcy of present as being erroneous when looking at the Pleistocene. The present can no longer be regarded as the norm.

They conclude that uniformitarianism cannot be applied to the recent past — the time of the Ice Age and the woolly mammoth. It is this doctrine of uniformitarianism that has retarded understanding of these many mysteries. Catastrophism offers a more logical and less flawed solution to the dual mysteries.

I believe that we need to revisit the rejected biblical world view, one that takes the straightforward account in Genesis 1–11 as early earth history. This account and many other traditions describe a global Flood. The global Flood, believed by most scientists in the 1700s and early 1800s was really never proved wrong. Scientists in the mid to late 1800s simply decided they wanted to assume uniformitarianism instead. One of the results of a global Flood would be the perturbation of the climate before it reached the equilibrium we observe today (figure 7.1). It is within this transitional climate that the mysteries of the Ice Age and woolly mammoth find a reasonable solution.

THE FIRST REQUIREMENT — COOLER SUMMERS

From the description of the Genesis flood in the Bible, we have been able to glean enough information to form an idea about what the world was like during and immediately after the catastrophe. Genesis chapters 7 and 8 record:

> *In the six hundredth year of Noah's life, in the second month, on the seventeenth day of the second month, on that day all the fountains of the great deep burst open, and the floodgates of the sky were opened. And the rain fell upon the earth for forty days and forty nights. . . . And the waters prevailed and increased greatly upon the earth . . . so that all the high mountains everywhere under the heavens were covered. . . . And the water prevailed upon the earth one hundred and fifty days. . . . and the water receded steadily from the earth. . . . And in the second month, on the twenty-seventh day of the month, the earth was dry* (NASB).

Scripture indicates that much of the water for the Flood came from the "fountains of the great deep." The deep or great deep refers to the ocean (Batten, 2004, p. 154). The bursting open of the fountains of the great deep implies the ocean rose up and covered the land or that oceanic or subterranean sources of water burst forth onto the land (Fouts and Wise, 1998; Batten, 2004, p. 169–170).

Monumental geological and hydrological activity occurred early in the Flood. Gigantic earthquakes could have caused large cracks or rifts in the earth's crust, explosively releasing subterranean water and triggering volcanic activity. By inference, the mountains before the Flood were fairly low, and even if the mountains were above 10,000 feet (3,000 m) the strong currents of a worldwide Flood would have

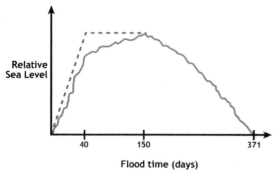

Figure 7.2. This graph shows the relative rise in sea level in 150 days followed by a gradual fall in 221 days. The reason the curve is not smooth is because several variables would cause the sea level to oscillate up and down during the general rise and fall. The dashed line represents an alternative interpretation in which the Flood peaks in 40 days.

eroded the mountains that did exist. Since the fountains of the great deep are mentioned before the rains, it is likely that they caused most of the rainfall. Rainfall was the second contributor to the flood waters.

According to the biblical record, the floodwaters increased and covered the earth by the 150th day, the fastest rise likely occurring in the first 40 days followed by a slow rise or "prevailing" for the next 110 days (figure 7.2). (Some creationists believe that the Flood peaked in 40 days, which is the alternative dashed line in figure 7.2.) The Flood waters then receded from the future continents for the next 221 days when the ocean basins subsided and the mountains rose as recorded in Psalm 104:6–9 (NASB; Oard, 2001a, b).

Interbedded within the sedimentary rocks is evidence of incredible volcanic activity that has no parallel today. Vast, unusually thick layers of volcanic flows and ash interlayer sedimentary rocks and fit the worldwide Flood paradigm very well. It appears that at the end of the Flood the world was covered by huge volumes of volcanic ash and gas that had spewed into the atmosphere (Oard, 1990, p. 23–38). The abundant ash and gas trapped in the stratosphere would act as an "anti-greenhouse" (see figure 6.1 on page 63). Instead of warming the earth, it would reflect sunlight back into space and cool it. At the same time, infrared radiation would continue to escape the earth.

Scientists recognize that volcanic dust and gas can substantially cool the earth. Most people in the United States remember the eruption of Mount St. Helens in Washington State in May of 1980. I watched as a dark "dry fog" spread from Oregon into central Montana where I lived. The darkness lasted for two days. Although I saw it as a major event, this eruption was actually small compared to many during the past two hundred years. The largest include Agung on the island of Bali in 1963; Krakatoa, Indonesia, in 1883; Tambora, Indonesia, in 1815; and Laki, Iceland, in 1783. Large modern eruptions usually cool a region or hemisphere a degree or two Fahrenheit (about 1°C). The cooling normally lasts one to three years as the ash and gases slowly fall out of the stratosphere.

Tambora was the largest eruption and is credited with causing the "year without a summer" in 1816. An unprecedented series of cold spells chilled the northeastern United States and adjoining Canadian provinces. Heavy snow fell in June, and frost caused crop failures in July and August. Even Europe felt the chill that summer.

David Keys (1999) makes a case that a massive volcanic eruption in Indonesia caused the darkness, cooling, crop failures, and social upheaval that was recorded in 535 A.D.

The extensive volcanism that would result from a worldwide Flood would have a much greater impact on the climate than in historical times. Volcanic ash and gases from the Flood would probably take at least three years to fall out. Three years would be enough time to start an Ice Age. The eruptions would need to continue for many years after the Flood to sustain it (Oard, 1990, p. 67–70). Geologists recognize that there was extensive volcanic activity during the Ice Age. Ice Age researcher Charlesworth (1957, p. 601) writes:

> *. . . signs of Pleistocene [Ice Age] vulcanicity and earth-movements are visible in all parts of the world.*

In the western United States alone there were more than 68 different ash falls, mostly coinciding with the Ice Age. Some of the volcanic eruptions were very extensive.

In the South Pacific, an exceptionally large ash layer from an eruption in New Zealand was discovered. It spread a thick layer of ash over four million square miles (10 million sq. km) and would have darkened the entire earth for several months. This eruption would have caused a tremendous cooling of the continents.

The Ice Age eruptions were much larger than what we have experienced during the past 200 years. So evidence indicates that after the Flood, volcanic eruptions would have been able to replenish the stratospheric dust and gasses and sustain the cooling. Since the eruptions were more or less random as the earth gradually settled down after the global Flood, volcanism would show peaks and lulls within a pattern of gradual decline (figure 7.3).

The effect of severe volcanic eruptions has been compared to the aftermath of a nuclear war. Computer models of a nuclear war show dust and soot causing a "nuclear winter." During a "nuclear winter," continental summer temperatures can drop below freezing in a matter of days. Toon and others (1982, p. 197) speculate with regard to nuclear winter:

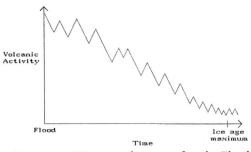

Figure 7.3. Waning volcanism after the Flood.

Sub-freezing temperatures for six months over the entire globe could possibly lead to extensive snowfield buildup over large areas of the continents. Such snowfields would greatly increase the albedo [reflectivity] of the earth and could sustain themselves indefinitely.

The large eruption in New Zealand is an analogy for the worst nuclear winter models that block out nearly all sunlight all over the world for several months. So, nuclear winter models provide insight into how continental areas can cool enough from atmospheric dust and gases for an ice age to develop.

If volcanic activity is such a good cooling mechanism, why haven't uniformitarian scientists incorporated it into their Ice Age models? They realize that volcanic ash and gases cool the planet but can't invoke volcanism because they believe each ice age lasted 100,000 years. There has not been enough volcanism to be significant over such a period of time. Paul Damon (1968, p. 109) writes:

. . . volcanic explosions would need to be an order of magnitude [ten times] more numerous than during the past 160 years to result in continental glaciation equivalent to the Wisconsin glacial episode.

The Wisconsin glacial episode is the last glaciation, according to the uniformitarian multiple glaciation system. One researcher, however, has attempted to incorporate volcanism to start an ice age. Bray (1976) postulates that a short period of enhanced volcanism may initiate the needed summer snow cover. Bray (1976, p. 414) states:

I suggest here that such a [snow] survival could have resulted from one or several closely spaced massive volcanic ash eruptions.

Then he relies on a snow cover to take over and continue the summer cooling for an ice age. Unfortunately, there could not be enough volcanism to sustain such an "ice age" for more than a few years without constant eruptions. The snow would quickly melt when the sunshine increased.

The creationist's time scale is telescoped, putting all these tremendous volcanic eruptions into a relatively short period after the Flood. *It is the short time frame that makes the difference.* The atmospheric consequences of frequent eruptions would allow an ice age to develop and be sustained.

THE SECOND REQUIREMENT — HEAVY SNOW

Extensive summer cooling of the land is the first requirement needed for an ice age to develop. High snowfall is the second. Cooling alone cannot generate more precipitation, since cold air holds less moisture, not more. This is the major reason why uniformitarian Ice Age theories fail.

*Figure 7.4. Steam fog from a pond caused by colder
atmospheric temperatures and warm water.*

In the Ice Age model after the Flood, the abundant moisture needed for an ice age would be produced by evaporation from a warm ocean at mid and high latitudes. Why would the oceans be warm? First, it is likely the pre-Flood ocean was warmer than now. Secondly, if the water from the "fountains of the great deep" came from within earth's crust, much hot water would be added to the pre-Flood ocean. The earth's crust warms about 10°F per 1,000 feet (2°C per 100 m) depth. If the water for the fountains came from 3,000 feet (900 m), it would be quite warm. If it came from 10,000 or more feet (3,000 m), the water would have been hot. Third, intense tectonic activity during the Flood and lava flows would add more heat. Earthquakes and rapid ocean currents during the Flood would mix this warm water with the pre-Flood ocean. As a result, the ocean immediately following the Flood would have been warm from pole to pole and from top to bottom. Because of this, the Arctic and Antarctic Oceans would have had no sea ice and, as strange as it may seem in today's climate, may have been warm enough for a pleasant swim.

The importance of warm surface water temperatures is that the warmer the water the greater the evaporation (figure 7.4). For example, if all other variables remain constant, water evaporates three times faster at an ocean temperature of 86°F (30°C) than at 50°F (10°C), and seven times faster than at 32°F (0°C). So a universally warm ocean would generate a high amount of evaporation.

Would all this heat from a warm ocean keep the high and mid latitudes too warm for the Ice Age? In some areas it would — until the ocean cooled enough by evaporation and contact with colder air. The warm ocean at mid and high latitudes is a key to unraveling the mysteries of the woolly mammoths that will be developed in chapter 14. Although the oceans would be warm, the continents would be cool due to the volcanic ash and dust in the stratosphere. The heat released by the warm ocean and its mixing with the air over the land would result in milder winter temperatures compared to today. The main effect of the volcanic ash and gasses would be to cause the land to cool during the summer.

In summary, the Flood and its aftershocks provide the volcanic dust and gases that bring the summer cooling indispensable for the Ice Age. Water from the "fountains of the great deep" and mixing during the Flood provides a warm ocean. In the mid and high latitudes the warm ocean would cause copious evaporation and produce massive amounts of snow. The two ingredients required for an Ice Age, cool temperatures and tons of snow, were dramatically fulfilled immediately after the Genesis Flood. This unique climate would persist for hundreds of years after the Flood as the intensity of the two mechanisms slowly decreased.

CHAPTER EIGHT

THE SNOWBLITZ

The Genesis flood uniquely and providentially provides the two ingredients necessary for an ice age. From this point on we can use basic meteorology to estimate the storm patterns and where the ice sheets would develop. Because of the dynamic combination of cool summers in mid and high latitude continents adjacent to warm oceans, some areas would quickly develop an ice sheet. Other areas had to wait until the ocean cooled enough because warm onshore flow would keep some lands too warm. Surprisingly, some areas that at first sight appear ideal for glaciation would not be glaciated at all, such as the lowlands of Alaska and Siberia.

"Snowblitz" is a word used to describe how a large area becomes covered quickly with snow and ice. This contrasts with the idea that an ice sheet started in the high mountains of the higher latitudes and slowly crept southward at a glacial pace. The post-Flood Ice Age model reveals that the Ice Age developed *over large areas all at once*, immediately after Noah's flood (Oard, 1990, p. 38–65).

RAPID ACCUMULATION OF SNOW AND ICE

Most of the snow that fell during the Ice Age would have been associated with storms rather than as continuous snowfall. Understanding the location of the storm tracks is essential to predicting where the snow and ice first built up. In today's climate, storms take a variety of paths, but because of the earth's topography and general temperature patterns, storms favor certain areas. Presently, they develop most frequently around Iceland in the North Atlantic Ocean and in the

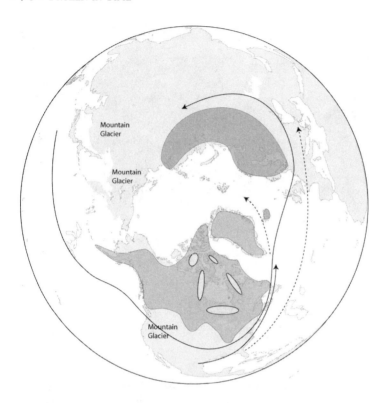

Figure 8.1. Distribution of snow and ice and storm tracks at maximum glaciation. Circular areas within the North American ice sheet represent postulated ice domes. Little sea ice has formed as yet.

Mountain Glacier

Mountain Glacier

Mountain Glacier

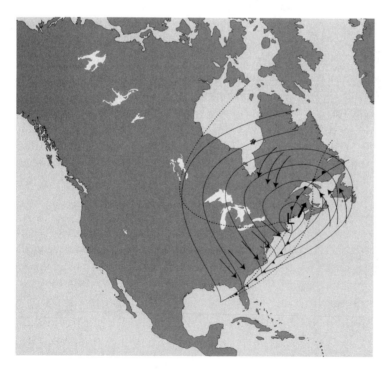

Figure 8.2. A northeaster storm that should be typical during the Ice Age, showing the areas of precipitation within the dotted line. Arrow north of low center (L) is the direction of movement. Multiple arrows are wind directions.

Aleutian Islands in the North Pacific. These are called the Iceland and Aleutian lows, respectively.

During the Ice Age, storms also tended to favor certain paths. Because of strong temperature contrasts between land and sea, storms in the Northern Hemisphere would develop more frequently just south of the growing ice sheets and along the east coasts of Asia and North America (figure 8.1) (Oard, 1990, p. 46–55). It is important to remember that these storm tracks would be averages with a fair amount of chaotic storm tracks.

In the Northern Hemisphere most of the precipitation from snowstorms falls on the north and northwest side of the storm (see figure 8.2). This is the coldest part of the storm. With a main storm track just south of the developing ice sheets, the ice sheets would continue to grow, especially along the periphery. The first several years after the Flood, snow would have covered a large area of the continental interiors of the mid and high latitudes. The Ice Age would start as a snowblitz with snow blanketing large areas of Canada and the northern United States right away, and accumulating in many mountainous areas. The ice would not need to develop in northern Canada and move slowly into the northern United States.

As long as the volcanic ash and gases remained thick in the stratosphere, and the mid and high latitude ocean surface remained warm, the snow would continue to fall and would rapidly build up. There likely would be only minor summer melting early in the Ice Age, mainly along the edge of the ice sheets.

A number of minor climatic processes would either reinforce or dampen the cooling caused by the volcanic ash and dust in the stratosphere. One of these is snow-cover cooling. Once a snow cover is established, the temperature cools about another 10°F (6°C) because of snow's greater reflectivity to sunlight. This reinforces the cooling already caused by volcanic ash and gases.

To keep the snow quickly and continuously accumulating, the sea surface temperatures must remain warm at mid and high latitudes. But, as rapid evaporation occurs from the ocean and cool continental air blows over the ocean, the ocean surface will cool. This creates a damping effect on evaporation. This is countered for a time by chilled surface water sinking and being replaced by warmer water from below. Additionally, an enhanced ocean circulation will continually feed warm water from further south into the higher latitudes (figure 8.3). So, the ocean surface temperatures will remain relatively warm for a long time at mid and high latitudes, despite the cooling effects, ensuring the high water vapor demanded for productive storms.

The Ice Age still had seasons due to the changing angle of the sun but would have cooler summers and milder winters. The seasonal contrast over continental areas would be much less than we see today, maybe on the order of 15°F (8°C).

The potential for rapid glaciation can be demonstrated by considering a famous type of storm from the east coast of North America — the northeaster (figure 8.2). These storms commonly dump a foot or more (25 cm or more) of snow. The storm

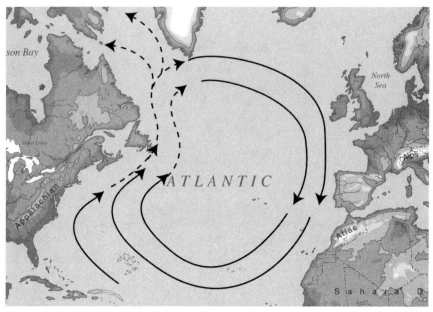

Figure 8.3. Postulated surface ocean circulation in the North Atlantic during the Ice Age. The solid line represents vertically rising ocean water, while the dashed line represents sinking water.

of the century, on March 12–15, 1993, dropped up to 56 inches (140 cm) of snow in the eastern United States (Oard, 1997b, p. 56–57). Figure 8.4 shows a cross section through the northern part of a northeaster with warm moist air

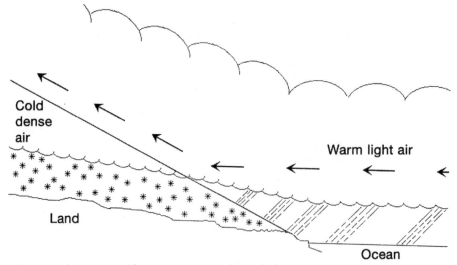

Figure 8.4. An atmospheric cross section through the northern part of a northeaster. The straight slanted line is the boundary between cold and warm air.

from the Atlantic Ocean rising up over a surface inversion with cold, dense air on land. In fact, I expect that an inversion occurred over most areas where the ice sheets developed with warm moist air overriding the cold air. Northeasters during the Ice Age would be more frequent and much stronger than what we experience today. They would generally produce in the neighborhood of three times the snowfall over twice the area, mostly because of the stronger temperature difference between the developing ice sheet and the warm ocean.

To show the potential of northeasters for a snowblitz, assume one northeaster every week for a year moved parallel to the East Coast, dropping 20 inches (50 cm) of snow in New England and southeast Canada. This is about twice the average for these types of storms, but it is a rather conservative figure considering the amount of water vapor available during the Ice Age. The ratio of snow to water is commonly 10 inches of snow to 1 inch of water. After the snow is converted to ice, this 20 inches of snow would become about 2 inches (5 cm) of ice. In the first year of the Ice Age, assuming no summer melting, 104 inches (264 cm) of ice would collect. If this rate continued for 200 years, the ice would be 1,733 feet (530 m) deep, more than enough for a developing Ice Age.

Assume that other storm tracks passed through southeast Canada and New England. In addition to the northeaster, there would be a main storm track that stretched parallel to the southern boundary of the ice sheet (see figure 8.1). This would have an overland path and would not contain as much water vapor as a northeaster that picks up its supply from the warm ocean off the east coast. In 200 years, the continental storm path could add another 500 feet (150 m) of ice. So, there is potential for as much as 2,200 feet (670 m) of ice to be deposited from these two main storm tracks in just a 200-year period.

THE EARLY ICE SHEETS

A number of factors would contribute to the timing and spread of glaciation early in the Ice Age. The ice sheets would accumulate rapidly in the areas closest to the main storm tracks and the moisture source of the warm ocean. Glaciation would be delayed in areas that were too close to the warm ocean. The warm ocean heats the air above it and as this onshore flow of air spreads inland, it would keep the adjacent land relatively warm. This is why Seattle, Washington, rarely falls below freezing and rarely sees snow.

Figure 8.5 shows the estimated areas of early ice build-up. Southeast Canada and New England would lie in a very favorable area for rapid accumulation of snow and ice. That is probably why Labrador was one of the ice domes of the Laurentide ice sheet of central and eastern Canada (see figure 9.3 on page 92). The southern interior of Canada and the northern Midwest of the United States, being farther from the moisture source would have had a relatively thin ice sheet at this time.

For a time, the lowlands of Scandinavia and British Columbia would be too warm for ice because of strong onshore airflow of relatively warm air. The mountains, however, would quickly develop thick ice caps that would tend to gradually

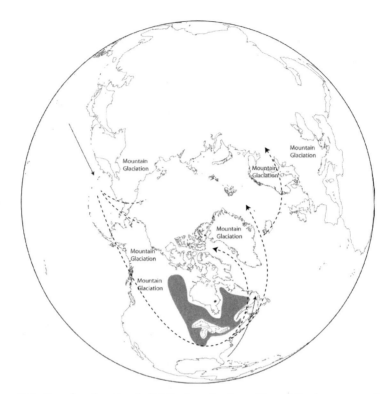

Figure 8.5. Postulated major (solid line) and minor (dotted line) storm tracks and snow cover in the Northern Hemisphere at the beginning of the post-Flood Ice Age.
(Redrawn from Ruddiman and McIntyre, 1979.)

descend into the valleys. Because of the warm Baltic Sea and North Atlantic Ocean, snow and ice build-up on continental Europe would be delayed. The British Isles, surrounded by warm water, would not be glaciated at all at the beginning. Greenland at this time would also be surrounded by warm water and would probably have snow and ice mostly in the mountains.

There would be an interesting distribution of snow and ice over the northern areas of the ice sheets, those lands bordering the Arctic Ocean. Remember that right after the Flood the Arctic Ocean would have no sea ice as the water temperature would be quite warm. During the first several years of the Ice Age, this warm water would often be subject to cool air masses overriding it. This would cause strong evaporation. At the same time, the air would be heated up by contact with the warm ocean and the release of latent heat from the water vapor when it condensed. The warm air would keep the areas bordering the Arctic Ocean ice free at the beginning of the Ice Age. But the heavy moisture in the area would greatly boost snow and ice accumulation farther inland from the Arctic Ocean, a bit like the Donn and Ewing Ice Age theory (see chapter 6). This explains why the Keewatin portion of the Laurentide ice sheet, northwest of Hudson Bay, was an ice dome during the Ice Age (see figure 9.3 on page 92).

In contrast, the uniformitarian Ice Age model has great difficulty accounting for this ice dome. Donn and Ewing (1968, p. 102–103) state the problem:

> *It is difficult to imagine a source of moisture for the maintenance of the prominent northwestward extension [to the Keewatin district] of the Canadian ice sheet in view of the pronounced barrier effect of the large Laurentide ice sheet to the south.*

Today, the Keewatin area is one of the driest places in North America. During the Ice Age that uniformitarian scientists envision, Keewatin would be too far north to receive much precipitation. Uniformitarian scientists cannot postulate moisture from the Arctic Ocean because in their scenario this ocean would be covered with sea ice, but the ice-free warm Arctic Ocean in the post-Flood Ice Age model can account for the Keewatin ice dome.

The distribution of warm water immediately after the Flood has other interesting consequences. It is likely that the Great Lakes and Hudson Bay were large, warm bodies of water and would retard ice build-up over and close to them. Strong evaporation from these bodies of water would help build the snow and ice around them, but at some distance from their shores.

The area just east of the Rocky Mountains in North America would be unglaciated at this time because of warm air from the Pacific Ocean overriding the mountains and descending as mild chinook winds. This is called the ice-free corridor. The warm Arctic and North Pacific Oceans would also have kept most of Siberia and Alaska unglaciated at this time. It was warm enough in the lowlands of Siberia and Alaska and the ice-free corridor to allow all the animal migrations into the Americas during the early and middle part of the Ice Age. By now you are getting an idea as to why the woolly mammoths would be able to live in Siberia and Alaska during the Ice Age and why the lowlands would remain unglaciated.

The Southern Hemisphere, with its huge warm ocean extending to the coast of Antarctica, would have a rather simple storm pattern. Since the warm water would abut the coast of East Antarctic, the main tracks would circle around this cold continent. This large land area would glaciate rapidly, especially when one considers all the warm water from the vast Southern Hemisphere oceans. West Antarctica would be more complicated. A significant portion of West Antarctica would still be a series of islands with warm water between. It is likely that early in the Ice Age, only the mountains of West Antarctica had ice caps (figure 8.6).

It is possible that a few of the higher mountain areas of the Southern Hemisphere and the tropics had ice caps early in the Ice Age, but these probably would be small until later.

THE WET DESERTS

One major mystery of the Ice Age listed in chapter 3 is the evidence of large lakes, rivers, and the fossils of aquatic animals in current deserts and semi-arid areas.

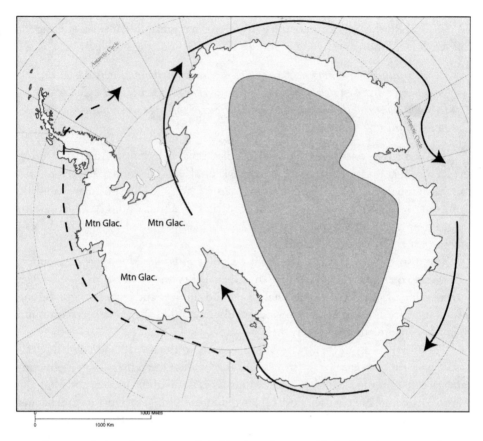

Figure 8.6. Postulated major (solid line) and minor (dashed line) storm tracks and snow cover (dark area) over Antarctica at the beginning of a post-Flood Ice Age. "Mtn Glac." means mountain glaciation.

The Genesis flood and the Ice Age caused by the Genesis flood can easily account for the evidence of "wet deserts."

Other than the main storm tracks shown in Figure 8.1, it is challenging to predict the atmospheric circulation during the Ice Age. It is this circulation that also determines the precipitation on the planet. This is because warm ocean water and atmospheric evaporation strongly influences the atmospheric circulation. The effect of so much moisture injected directly into the air above the ocean and the release of latent heat spread around the Northern Hemisphere is difficult to compute. Having the continents cold with a small seasonal contrast adds to the difficulty because it is so different from today. No computer simulations of the atmosphere have been performed with anything close to these conditions. Larry Vardiman (Vardiman, 2001) from the Institute for Creation Research has done some work with a simple climate model using a warm ocean and discovered many unique possibilities. These are

Figure 8.7. Shorelines carved into a terminal moraine when Mono Lake was much higher during the Ice Age.

suggestive of atmospheric patterns significantly different than today. Storm tracks, heavy precipitation belts, monsoons, and other climatic features would be unique to this Ice Age era. Perhaps in the future a sophisticated ocean-atmospheric climate simulation of the Ice Age can be executed.

One thing that can be stated is that such a unique Ice Age climate would cause much more precipitation all over the earth, simply because of the greater evaporation from a warm ocean. Furthermore, this precipitation would be distributed differently than it is today. This climate has the potential to cause copious precipitation in currently arid and semi-arid areas, such as the southwest United States. Of course, all the water in the lakes in the southwestern United States did not need to come from heavy Ice Age precipitation. As the floodwaters drained off the continents, while the land rose at the end of the Flood, water would be trapped in basins that had no outlet. The precipitation during the post-Flood Ice Age simply maintained the lakes left over from the Flood. Evidence for the maintenance of these lakes is shown by beaches that have been carved into terminal moraines near Mono Lake, California, and at the edge of valleys along the Wasatch Range of central Utah (figures 8.7 and 8.8).

Figure 8.8. Shoreline of Lake Bonneville on moraine at the mouth of Little Cottonwood Creek and Bells Canyons, Wasatch Mountains, Utah.

The Sahara Desert is another good example of a "well-watered desert." It had a fairly wet climate for several hundred years. This provided a healthy, flourishing environment for the people and animals that inhabited the area.

At the end of the Ice Age, mainly during deglaciation, a great desiccation occurred, producing the deserts and semi-arid areas we observe today. It is important to note: a post-Flood Ice Age has the potential to explain wet deserts, while the uniformitarian model with cold Ice Ages has great difficulty.

CHAPTER NINE

THE PEAK OF THE ICE AGE

After the Flood drained off the land, the world's ocean and land temperatures were constantly changing as they strove toward the relative equilibrium we experience today. It took centuries of climate change for this to work itself out. The warm ocean gradually cooled while the glaciers grew and spread. The Ice Age wound down as the amount of volcanic ash and dust in the stratosphere slowly decreased and the earth's climates became more stable. Finally, there came a time when the two main mechanisms of the Ice Age, volcanic material in the stratosphere and the warm ocean, diminished so much that they could no longer sustain a net build-up of ice over the globe. This was the peak of the Ice Age or glacial maximum.

GLACIAL MAXIMUM

As glacial maximum approached, the ocean water and atmosphere at mid and high latitudes cooled enough for many areas close to the ocean to glaciate (see maps on pages 35 and 36). The change in water and land temperatures allowed the ice sheets to expand out onto the continental shelves off eastern Canada and New England. Ice spread from the mountains of British Columbia and Washington State into the surrounding lowlands. East of the Rocky Mountains, ice descended onto the high plains and coalesced with the Laurentide Ice Sheet blocking the ice-free corridor.

Ice caps starting in the mountains of Greenland and Scandinavia swept down onto the lowlands. The Baltic Sea was covered with ice by then, so ice blanketed much of northern continental Europe and northwest Asia. About midway through the Ice Age the British Isles developed mountain ice caps. They would have filled in the valleys and covered the Irish Sea by the end of the Ice Age. However, it is doubtful there was a connection between the small ice sheet on the British Isles and the Scandinavian ice sheet across the North Sea.

By glacial maximum the East Antarctica ice sheet in the Southern Hemisphere had become enormous. In West Antarctica, ice descended out of the mountains and filled up the surrounding depressions that were below sea level to form one large West Antarctica ice sheet. The West Antarctica ice sheet merged in places with the East Antarctica ice sheet. The mountains of South America, New Zealand, and Tasmania, were covered by ice caps. A small portion of the mountains in southeast Australia was capped by ice.

In the tropics, glaciers descended to fairly low altitudes as they crept down the high mountains. Mount Kilamanjaro and Mount Kenya in Africa retain an ice cap to this day, but during the peak of the Ice Age, the ice had descended 3,000 feet (900 m) lower than today. A 3,000-foot lower snow level was about the same for other high mountains of the tropics. Uniformitarian scientists have been puzzled by tropical mountain glaciation. Few theories, including the popular astronomical theory, predict tropical mountain glaciation during the Ice Age. The Ice Age model, based on the climatic aftermath of the Genesis flood, predicts that all glaciation would be simultaneous from the Northern Hemisphere, through the tropics, and into the Southern Hemisphere.

DOES GLACIATION TAKE A LONG TIME?

Uniformitarian scientists claim that it takes about 100,000 years for an Ice Age cycle. In the Flood model, it would be rapid — some would consider it catastrophic. The volcanic effluents in the stratosphere and a warm ocean are a powerful Ice Age breeding mechanism.

Estimating the length of the Ice Age depends mainly upon how long it would take for a warm ocean after the Flood to cool. Once the ocean cooled below some threshold temperature, there would not be enough evaporation to sustain net ice sheet growth. With less snow and less volcanic pollution, the summer sun would be more effective in melting the ice sheets during the summer. To calculate the rate a warm ocean would cool, I made estimates of the average temperature of the ocean at the end of the Flood and the threshold temperature of the ocean at glacial maximum. Then I used heat balance equations for the ocean and the atmosphere to reach glacial maximum and came up with an estimate of the time it would take for an Ice Age. Since there is speculation involved in the estimates of the terms of the equations, I used minimum and maximum estimates for the variables involved and then chose midrange values to come up with a ballpark number. The details have been worked out in the book: *An Ice Age Caused by the Genesis Flood* (Oard, 1990, p. 93–98, 199–210).

I started with a warm average ocean temperature of 86°F (30°C) right after the Flood. This temperature was chosen because all the heat inputs during the Flood would have been tremendous, but marine organisms still survived. The water must

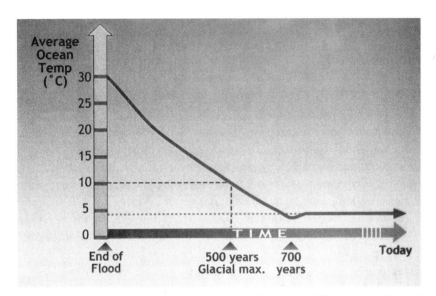

Figure 9.1. Graph of the average temperature of the ocean following the Flood. The average ocean temperature cooled below today's average as the Ice Age glaciers melted because the atmospheric temperature at higher latitudes was much below the present.

have been quite warm, but not too hot for life. Since the average ocean temperature today is about 39°F (4°C) and there are no ice sheets, except on Antarctica and Greenland, the threshold temperature when glacial maximum was reached would be warmer than today. I estimated an average ocean temperature of 50°F (10°C) when the Ice Age peaked. This represents an oceanic cooling of 36°F (20°C). Plugging in maximum and minimum estimates of the variables into the ocean cooling equation, I calculated a minimum cooling time of 174 years and a maximum time of 1,765 years. Using values in the mid range of the variables, I ended up with about 500 years to reach glacial maximum. Figure 9.1 shows a graph of the change in ocean temperature with time since the Flood in relationship to Ice Age events. Regardless of whether minimum or maximum values are used in the equation, the ice sheets develop in a very short time compared to the uniformitarian estimate of around 100,000 years.

I also discovered that the rate of glaciation was controlled by the amount of volcanic dust and gases in the stratosphere at any one moment. The more the volcanic effluents, the faster the evaporation and the greater the ice built up and spread. The less the volcanic debris, the slower the ice built up. It is conceivable that glaciers retreated a little during volcanic lulls, only to surge during times of greater volcanism. Variable amounts of volcanism would have resulted in active ice sheets.

ICE SHEET THICKNESS

It may seem impossible to calculate the thickness of the ice sheets at the peak of the Ice Age, but there is a method that can be used to provide a ballpark average.

It can be done by estimating the amount of available moisture, the percentage of the precipitation that falls on the ice sheets, and the length of time to reach glacial maximum. This also has been developed in more detail elsewhere (Oard, 1990, p. 98–100, 211–215). I will only give the reader the highlights.

There are two main sources of moisture: (1) evaporation from the warm ocean at mid and high latitudes, and (2) atmospheric moisture transport from low latitudes. As it turns out, the first variable is the main source of moisture. Based on maximum and minimum values for the proportion of the moisture to fall on the ice sheet, I obtained for the Northern Hemisphere a minimum depth of 1,700 feet (500 m) and a maximum depth of 2,970 feet (900 m). Using variables for the mid range, I estimated an average depth of 2,300 feet (700 m). The average yearly precipitation over the ice sheets would have been 55 inches/year (1.4 m/yr). This rate is three times the current average precipitation over land north of 40°N (Peixoto and Oort, 1992, p. 168). This is a conservative increase from today considering the huge amount of evaporation at mid and high latitudes from a warm ocean.

Since nearly all of the ice in the Southern Hemisphere ended up on Antarctica, I made a similar calculation for the average ice depth on Antarctica. Interestingly, the best estimate came out to be about 3,900 feet (1,200 m). The yearly average precipitation in water equivalents would have been 95 inches/year (2.4 m/yr). Antarctica had a thicker ice sheet because of a greater ocean-to-land distribution. In other words, the Southern Hemisphere oceans were able to supply more water vapor to storms circling Antarctica.

The above estimates for ice depth are averages. It is expected that some areas of the ice sheet would be thicker and other areas thinner. The depth depends upon how close the area was to a main storm track and the amount of moisture the storm carried. The latter factor is usually related to how close the storm was to the moisture source — the warm ocean.

The above estimates also assume no summer melting. This is probably a good assumption for most of the ice sheet, but along the periphery, some summer melting would be expected. The periphery is a 400-mile (640-km) wide strip along the edge of the ice sheets. Summer melting would tend to decrease the ice depth along the edge. However, I never took into account a third moisture source, and that is the moisture picked up over wet non-glaciated land in the mid and high latitudes. With possibly three times more precipitation than today over non-glaciated lands with large lakes occupying currently desert and semi-arid areas, significant evaporation would have occurred from land. Some of this evaporation from this third source of moisture would have been added as snow to the ice sheet. This should mostly compensate for summer melting. Therefore, neither variable was considered in the ice depth calculations. I assumed that summer melting and extra snow supplied from evaporation originating from non-glaciated lands would cancel each other out.

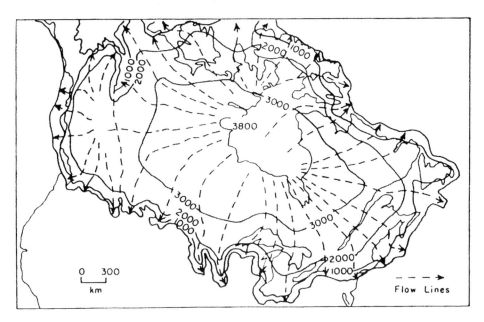

Figure 9.2. This illustration shows the view of Denton and Hughes of the Laurentide ice sheet of eastern and central Canada and the Cordilleran ice sheet over British Columbia.

Uniformitarian Ice Thickness Estimates Exaggerated

Uniformitarian scientists have claimed that the ice piled up to over 10,000 feet (3,000 m) thick over eastern Canada during the Ice Age with an average more like 5,000 feet (1,500 m) (figure 9.2). The Scandinavian and Cordilleran ice sheets were similarly thought to have been thick. These ice depths are much thicker than the depths calculated for the post-Flood model. Which estimate comes closest to the actual depths? First, I will examine the basis for uniformitarian estimates and then provide data that indicates that the ice sheets were thinner (Oard, 1990, p. 100–107).

Uniformitarian geologists mostly have assumed that the melted ice sheets from the Ice Age were of *similar* thickness to those on Greenland and Antarctica. This is part of their "present processes occurring over millions of years" mindset. They have reasoned that, given enough time, these past ice sheets should have built up to the size of the present ones. Arthur Bloom (1971, p. 367), in referring to the past Laurentide ice sheet, states:

> *Unfortunately, few facts about its thickness are known. . . . In the absence of direct measurements about the Laurentide ice sheet, we must turn to analogy and theory.*

The only analogy or examples we have today are the Greenland and Antarctica ice sheets. As for theory, uniformitarian scientists assume the ice developed in the far north of North America and flowed uphill to the southern periphery after many thousands of years. In this case, the ice at the center, in Canada, would have to be very thick since glaciers on fairly level terrain flow from a region of thicker ice to areas of thinner ice. In other words, the downward slope at the top of the ice sheet determines the glacial motion over generally level terrain. So, based on both analogy and theory, the uniformitarian estimate of the ice thickness is quite large, but it is totally speculative.

Geologists have also used estimates of sea level lowering to infer ice sheet thickness. However, it is difficult to determine how low the sea fell during the peak of

Figure 9.3. The new multidomed model of the Laurentide ice sheet with two main centers over Labrador and Keewatin. Arrows are postulated flow paths out from these domes. There are several other smaller domes postulated, one of which is shown as the Foxe/Baffin Ice Dome.

the Ice Age because the evidence is underwater. It is interesting that geologists have often estimated the drop in sea level *based on their postulated ice sheet thickness*. This is circular reasoning, since both lower sea level and ice thickness are *both* unknown. When it comes right down to it, geologists are really guessing ice sheet thickness. Ericson and Wollin (1967, p. 136) admit: *"The estimates vary because one can only guess how thick ice sheets were."*

There is some recent evidence, however, that the past ice sheet thicknesses were significantly lower than uniformitarian scientists expected. Instead of one big Laurentide ice sheet with a center over Hudson Bay, most geologists now conclude that there were at least two main ice domes, one east of Hudson Bay in Labrador and one west and northwest of Hudson Bay, the Keewatin dome (figure 9.3). This is based mainly on the direction of striated bedrock and the dispersion of glacial debris. There probably were other ice domes, for instance the Foxe/Baffin Dome in figure 9.3. Another dome possibility built up just north of the Great Lakes. Regardless, two or more domes instead of one dome imply a thinner ice sheet.

Furthermore, the periphery of the Laurentide ice sheet in the north central United States is now known to have been much thinner than earlier thought. The original estimates of thicker ice were based on the thick periphery of the Antarctica ice sheet. The evidence for a thinner periphery comes from observations that the tops of mountains in north central Montana, the western Cypress Hills of southeast Alberta, and the Wood Mountain Plateau in southwest Saskatchewan were all found to be above the ice (Klassen, 1994). Ice thickness in southern Alberta and Saskatchewan was rather variable, but was around 1,000 feet (300 meters) deep. The ice surface slope in southern Alberta to its southern terminus was nearly flat (Mathews, 1974). This thickness is about 1/5 the thickness postulated by using the edge of the Antarctica ice sheet as an analogy. With such a flat slope and a general uphill topography from southern Canada into Montana, mainstream scientists are left with a quandary: how did the ice sheet spread into north central Montana moving uphill? According to the way glaciers move, it should have been impossible. The most likely explanation is that the snow and ice had to form generally in place, as predicted in the post-Flood Ice Age model.

Further evidence for a thin ice sheet comes from the northern Midwest United States. It is now known that ice lobes along the margin in this area surged southward. These surges left behind lateral moraines. The gentle slope of these lateral features indicates that the ice sheet must have been notably thin (Clayton et al., 1985; Beget, 1986). The driftless area in southwest Wisconsin suggests thin ice lobes missed this area entirely. If the periphery ice were not thin, the driftless area would have been buried by ice.

Not only was the southwest and south-central periphery of the Laurentide ice sheet thin, but recent evidence indicates the northwest margin in the eastern Yukon Territory was also thin (Beget, 1987). The southeast margin in New England was relatively thick. There is little information from other areas of the periphery of the Laurentide ice sheet.

Occhietti (1983, p. 13) sums up the significance of the new observational data:

> *These results change the concept of the Laurentide ice sheet radically. They imply, notably, a much smaller ice volume, and complex margins.*

Chapter Ten

Catastrophic Melting

According to the creation-Flood Ice Age model, glacial maximum was reached when the ocean temperature cooled to an average of 50°F (10°C). At this ocean temperature, the net melting of the glaciers would be slow. Precipitation would still be substantial, but would decrease with time. As the oceans continued to cool, the amount of water evaporating into the atmosphere would continue to decrease proportionate to the ocean's surface temperature. Accelerated melting would mark the end of the Ice Age.

Warmer Summers, Colder Winters

As the Ice Age waned, volcanism gradually decreased as the earth became used to the new configuration of land and water caused by the Flood. Less gas and ash spewed into the stratosphere, and more sunlight warmed the summers. Summers, of course, would not be as warm as they are today in the mid and high latitudes because the nearby ice sheets and increased sea ice would keep the land somewhat cool.

A decrease in volcanic activity would also affect the tropics. Temperatures there would warm quite quickly and would soon approximate today's climate. Due to the slower melting of the ice sheets at higher latitudes, the tropical to polar temperature difference would be greater than it is today. This difference in atmospheric temperature is very important for understanding the demise of the woolly mammoth and other animals. This is because such a temperature difference would cause strong, windy, dry storms.

At the same time as the decreased volcanism, the ocean water would continue cooling and sea ice would gradually develop in the polar latitudes. These two factors would result in a drying atmosphere in this phase of the Ice Age. Sea ice would form quickly because meltwater from melting ice sheets would flow out over the ocean water at mid and high latitudes. Fresh water has a tendency to float on the denser salt water, making it easier to form ice. Sea ice, especially with fresh snow on top, would reinforce the winter cooling trend by reflecting sunlight back into space. It would also stop the heat of the warmer water from entering the atmosphere. Thus, sea ice would increase the cooling of the atmosphere, which would further increase ocean cooling, sort of like a chain reaction.

The net effect of this climatic change would be that winters would become quite cold and the summers mild as the ice sheets melted. Winters would be significantly colder than today, and summers warmer, but not as warm as today. The atmosphere would also become drier and drier. The climate over mid- and high-latitude continents would become more continental with colder winters and warmer summers. During the earlier phase when the ice was building up, the climate was equitable, having little seasonal contrast, but during deglaciation, snowfall on the ice sheets would be light and would easily melt by the time summer arrived. The winter cooling and drying would continue until the ice sheets melted. Figure 10.1 shows the generally expected temperature trend through the Ice Age to the present for the mid- and high-latitude continents of the Northern Hemisphere.

Such colder winters and summers than today at the end of the Ice Age would also affect the ocean temperatures. It is likely that for a while the average ocean temperature cooled below its present average of 39°F (4°C) (see figure 9.1 on page 89).

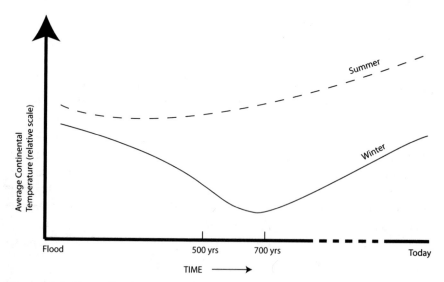

Figure 10.1. Generalized winter and summer temperature changes through the Ice Age to the present for the mid- and high-latitude continents of the Northern Hemisphere.

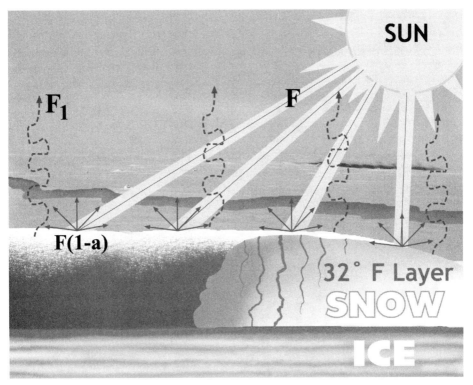

Figure 10.2 The energy balance over a snow cover in which the solar radiation, the major melting variable, is represented by F, while the solar radiation absorbed at the top of the ice sheet is represented by F(1-a), where "a" is the albedo or reflectivity of the surface. Infrared radiational cooling (F_1) is represented by the squiggly dashed lines. The melt water either flows as a stream on top of the ice or sinks vertically through the 32-degree layer.
(Drawn by Dan Lietha of AIG.)

How Fast Would the Ice Sheets Melt?

The summer melting rate for snow and ice can be estimated by using a heat balance equation of the snow or ice cover (Oard, 1990, p. 114–119; 217–223; Peixoto and Oort, 1992). It would work similar to the heat balance equations for the atmosphere and ocean. The heating and cooling terms are added up with the difference being the melting rate (figure 10.2). This equation is easy to apply and is often used to estimate snowmelt today. The only difficulty with applying the equation to the melting of an ice sheet is in trying to estimate the summer temperatures of the atmosphere near and over the ice sheet. Here is where I made several reasonable assumptions. First, I assumed the atmosphere above the ice sheet was about 18°F (10°C) cooler than it is today. This seems reasonable from climate simulations that are done without volcanic material in the stratosphere. For the calculation, I used temperature and sunshine data from central Michigan. Michigan was chosen because it would

Figure 10.3a–c.

be typical within the periphery of the Laurentide ice sheet. I assumed winters during deglaciation would be so dry and cold that little new snow would accumulate, and the snow that did accumulate would easily melt by May 1. I also assumed melting stopped on September 30, much earlier than today. These seem like reasonable and conservative estimates of the melting time and the date of May 1 even allows for the top of the ice sheet to be "primed," warmed to 32°F (0°C), so that all the meltwater for the five warm months would flow out of the ice sheet and not be refrozen within it.

As with the previous equations, I used minimum and maximum values for the terms in the equation. One of the most important variables in the snowmelt equation is the reflectivity of the snow, which varies from about 80 percent of the sunlight for fresh, cold snow to 40 percent or lower for wet snow. A reflectivity of 40 percent is reached after several weeks of melting. If ice is exposed at the surface, the reflectivity is further reduced to between 20 and 40 percent. In the low-altitude glaciers of Norway, the reflectivity in the melt zone has been observed to fall as low as 28 percent. So, a reflectivity for the periphery of the ice sheet of 40 percent was assumed to be a maximum value during summer melting.

Reflectivity can be lowered even more if dust from dry storms is added to the ice surface. The end of the Ice Age would bring huge dust storms, especially just south of the ice sheets. These storms would develop from the large temperature differences between polar latitudes and the subtropics. So, the ice sheet surface along the periphery most likely accumulated a large quantity of dust. After the melt season, the dust would concentrate on the snow or ice surface. Figure 10.3a–c shows three snapshots of a pile of snow after a snowstorm. As the snow melted, the debris within the snow became more and more concentrated on the surface. As a result of more concentrated debris, more sunlight was absorbed by the snow and less reflected. The reflectivity of a permanent snow cover in Japan was observed to drop as low as 15 percent in late summer due to dust from air pollution. So a 15 percent reflectivity, representing a dusty snow or ice surface, was used as the minimum reflectivity.

Plugging the minimum and maximum estimates for reflectivity and the other variables into the snow melt equation, I obtained minimum and maximum estimates of melting. I averaged the two extreme melt rates for a best estimate and ended up with a melting rate of about 30 feet per year (10 m/yr).

According to this estimate, if central Michigan had an average ice depth of 2,300 feet (700 m), the ice would melt in only 75 years! Farther north, the amount of sunlight is, of course, less and the snow surface was probably less dusty. So, the ice would melt more slowly in the interior ice sheets. If the ice were of average thickness in the interior, it would take in the neighborhood of 200 years for this ice to disappear. It is expected that the melting rates for other ice sheets and mountain ice caps would correspond to those of the Laurentide ice sheet, so the total time for deglaciation would be in the neighborhood of 200 years. This is surprisingly fast — the melting would be catastrophic!

This melt time requires much less time than the uniformitarian estimates. The Flood model rate of 30 feet/year (10 m/yr) at the periphery compares very closely to modern measurements in the cool, commonly cloudy melting zones of glaciers in Alaska, Iceland, and Norway. Sugden and John (1976, p. 39) state that glacial melting can be rapid as indicated by:

> . . . many mountaineers whose tents in the ablation [melting] areas of glaciers may rest precariously on pedestals of ice after only a few days.

The present-day glaciers do not disappear at this melt rate because they are nourished by a huge amount of mountain snow in the winter that continually flows into the melting zone.

The question immediately comes up as to why uniformitarian scientists believe that ice sheets took many thousands of years to melt? The reason, like many aspects of Ice Age research, is because of their dating methods and theories, especially the astronomical theory of the Ice Age, which vastly stretches out every physical process. Mainstream scientists rarely use equations for snow and ice melt; they depend instead on their assumption of a long time-period.

All indications are that a melting rate of 30 feet/year (10 m/yr) of ice is reasonable along the periphery. Such a melting rate in a cool Ice Age climate has ominous consequences for theories and models that depend upon the uniformitarian assumption or present processes. At such a melting rate, ice sheets could *not even get started* within a uniformitarian climate even if a mechanism for cold enough temperatures could be found. An Ice Age simulation by Rind, Peteet, and Kukla

(1989) started by placing 30 feet (about 10 m) of ice everywhere the ice sheet covered. Then they ran their Ice Age climate model fully expecting the ice to grow with the higher reflectivity that the snow and ice would provide in the model. Instead of growing, the 30 feet of ice melted everywhere in 5 years! The main reason is because summer sunshine is very powerful at mid and high latitudes. This experiment makes one wonder how an ice sheet could develop within the uniformitarian climate. We touched on this difficulty in chapter 3.

Putting it all together, I conclude that it took about 500 years for the Ice Age to reach its maximum and 200 years to melt. This is a total of 700 years from start to finish — a time much different than uniformitarian theories. Given the unique conditions that existed after a worldwide Flood, I have also concluded that there was only one Ice Age. It was indeed a rapid, even a catastrophic, Ice Age. It could easily have occurred between the time of the Genesis flood and the time historical records first were written in northern Europe.

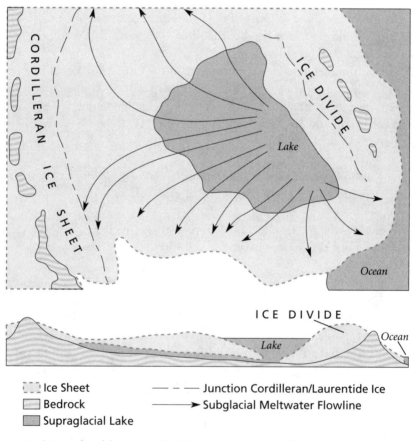

Figure 10.4. Postulated location of a lake in the vicinity of Hudson Bay and subglacial flow paths from this lake. The bottom diagram is a northeast-southwest cross section.

(Redrawn from Shaw, 1996, p. 226, by Mark Wolfe.)

Catastrophic Flooding

Is there evidence for catastrophic melting at the end of the Ice Age? Scientists have found an increasing amount of evidence of catastrophic flooding during deglaciation. One example is the Lake Missoula flood, which was rejected for over 40 years because it seemed too "biblical" (see the boxed section later in this chapter). It was finally accepted in the 1960s since the evidence for it is overwhelming (Oard, 2004a).

With the acceptance of the Lake Missoula flood, geologists have found strong evidence for catastrophic Ice Age floods in other areas of the Northern Hemisphere (Oard, 2004a, p. 59–67). A flood on par with the Lake Missoula flood was discovered coming out of the Altay Mountains of south-central Siberia (Baker, Benito, and Rudoy, 1993; Carling, 1996). A glacier during the Ice Age had enclosed a large lake just over 1,600 feet (485 m) deep. The ice dam failed and water about 1,500 feet (450 m) deep flowed down the Chuja River Valley and eventually into the Ob River of western Siberia. Another Ice Age flood was the Bonneville flood that occurred when ancient Lake Bonneville, the largest Ice Age lake in the southwest United States, dropped about 300 feet (about 100 m) in several weeks, initiating catastrophic flooding down the Snake River of Idaho.

One of the more interesting, but speculative, Ice Age flood or floods are the subglacial (under the ice) catastrophic bursts postulated by John Shaw and other collaborators (Sharpe and Shaw, 1989; Shaw and Gilbert, 1990; Shoemaker, 1992a,b; Gilbert and Shaw, 1994; Sjogren and Rains, 1995; Shaw, 1988, 1996; Shaw et al., 1996; Brennand, Shaw and Sharpe, 1996; Kor and Cowell, 1998; Munro-Stasiuk, 1999; Beaney and Shaw, 2000). Shaw, in his most radical suggestion, postulates a large lake in the vicinity of Hudson Bay that discharged about 50 times more water than glacial Lake Missoula (figure 10.4). One major pathway for the subglacial flood started in the northwest territories of Canada and passed southwest through northern Saskatchewan, ran almost the length of Alberta, and ended in northern Montana (Rains et al., 1993). A second major pathway is believed to have started around southern Hudson Bay or Labrador and flowed south into southern Ontario, the eastern Great Lakes, and New York. This later subglacial flood is believed to have carved the Finger Lakes of New York.

Of course, Shaw's hypothesis has generated considerable controversy, especially the suggestion of a huge lake in the vicinity of Hudson Bay. After reviewing most of the evidence, I have concluded that his case is strong. If he is correct or partially correct, the current uniformitarian Ice Age paradigm needs to be almost totally rewritten to allow for a gigantic lake near Hudson Bay. He suggests the lake had to exist near the peak of the Ice Age because flooding generally occurred when the ice boundary was close to its maximum extension. Such a large lake and catastrophic flooding when there was supposed to be a huge ice sheet over Canada is uniformitarian Ice Age heresy — at least currently. Mounting evidence is convincing many mainstream scientists that the Ice Age was very different from uniformitarian expectations.

Catastrophic Deglaciation Flooding by Glacial Lake Missoula

Geologist J. Harlen Bretz, while examining the geology of eastern Washington in the 1920s, discovered a most unusual phenomenon. He discovered huge, deep canyons etched into hard lava. This caused him to surmise that only a flood of heretofore unheard of proportions could have formed them. The Grand Coulee had been gouged 900 feet (275 m) deep and 50 miles (80 km) long. The flood carved out the canyon where Palouse Falls is located in southeast Washington when water overtopped a lava ridge forming a canyon six miles (10 km) long and 500 feet (150 m) deep.

At first, Bretz did not understand where all this water could have originated. At the same time, J.T. Pardee postulated that a large lake existed in western Montana that was dammed by a lobe of the Cordilleran ice sheet in northern Idaho. Bretz finally made the connection and dubbed it the Lake Missoula or Spokane flood. Figure 10.5 shows glacial Lake Missoula in western Montana and the path of the Lake Missoula flood through the Pacific Northwest.

Geologists of that era were not prepared to hear of such a catastrophe. It seemed too much like the biblical flood against which they had a strong bias, so Bretz's idea was severely challenged. For 40 years the geological establishment criticized his idea and made up other theories that, today, seem farfetched. Finally, in the 1960s, with the advent of aerial photography and better geological work, Bretz's "outrageous hypothesis" was verified.

At the peak of the Ice Age, thick ice filled the Lake Pend Oreille River Valley in northern Idaho blocking the Clark Fork River. Meltwater from the ice flooded the valleys of western Montana, gradually filling them until they could hold no more. It had risen to about 4,200 feet (1,280 m) above sea level, based on abundant shorelines observed in the valleys of western Montana, most notably the hills east and northeast of Missoula (figure 10.6). The water depth was 2,000 feet (600 m) at the ice dam. The lake contained 540 cubic miles (2,200 cubic km) of water, half the volume of present day Lake Michigan.

Glacial Lake Missoula burst through its ice dam, probably in a matter of hours, and roared over 60 mph (30 m/sec) in places through eastern Washington into the Columbia Gorge and emptied into the Pacific Ocean. It was 450 feet (135 m) deep when it rushed over Spokane, Washington. It eroded 50 cubic miles (200 cubic km) of hard lava and silt from eastern Washington. Scoured-out lava over eastern Washington resembles a large braided stream from satellite pictures, although the stream had to have been 100 miles (60 km) wide!

Much of the basalt rock has been rolled into huge gravel bars that are commonplace over the very dry scablands of eastern Washington. They look like normal gravel bars found in rivers, but on a stupendous scale. One near

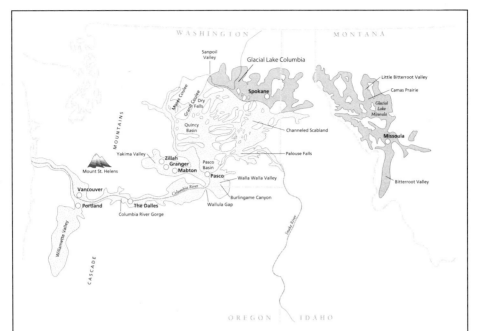

Figure 10.5. Map of the Pacific Northwest, showing the path of the Lake Missoula flood (dotted pattern) and glacial Lakes Columbia and Missoula (dark pattern). The Channeled Scabland is the part of the flood path in eastern Washington. (Drawn by Mark Wolfe.)

Figure 10.6. Shorelines of glacial Lake Missoula along the edge of the Little Bitterroot Valley, 75 miles (120 km) northwest of Missoula, Montana.

Figure 10.7. A gravel bar along the Snake River, Washington, from the Lake Missoula flood.

the Columbia River south of Vantage, Washington, is 20 miles (32 km) long and about 100 feet (30 m) high. Another bar is 300 feet (90 m) high and fills up portions of the Snake River Valley (figure 10.7). The rushing water scoured the lava so badly that it formed the lava badlands near Moses Lake, Washington.

As the floodwater came to the narrow constriction through the Horse Heaven Hills, called Wallula Gap, it backed up and formed a lake 800 feet (245 m) deep. From there, the waters rushed up the surrounding valleys, including the Walla Walla and Yakima River Valleys. The rushing water formed a series of repeating beds of sand and silt called rhythmites. Bretz noticed these unusual deposits lying on top of lava flows and included them in his evidence for the Lake Missoula flood. The best outcrop is found in Burlingame Canyon in the Walla Walla Valley (figure 10.8). The canyon was cut in about one week by water diverted from an irrigation canal, exposing the series of rhythmites. Thirty-nine of these sand and silt couplets have been counted and have inspired several theories on how they formed during the Lake Missoula flood.

As the muddy water churned down the Columbia River Gorge, the flood enlarged the gorge between The Dalles and Portland, Oregon. Leaving the gorge, it spread out in the wide lowlands of the Willamette Valley, depositing a layer of silt rhythmites about 50 feet (15 m) thick and laying a huge gravel bar in the Portland area that is 400 feet (120 m) deep and covers 200 square miles (500 square km). The water continued racing toward the Pacific Ocean where it carved a small canyon in the continental slope. It took about a week for Lake Missoula to empty.

Strewn all along the flood path are large erratic boulders that could have only been floated in by icebergs. Most of the boulders are granite from outcrops in northern Idaho and northern Washington. One found in the central Willamette Valley attests to the power of icebergs to transport boulders during the Lake Missoula flood. Originally it weighed 160 tons (145,000 kg), before tourists broke off pieces for souvenirs. Today the rock is only 90 tons (82,000 kg). A rock of this size and composition could not have been rolled into place by water. It is composed of argillite, a slightly metamorphosed shale that is too delicate to take the rigors of water transport. Its nearest possible source is in extreme northeastern Washington. Argillite is also abundant in northern Idaho and western Montana. The boulder had to have been transported at least 500 miles (800 km). Ice rafting during the Lake Missoula flood is the only reasonable explanation.

Geologists today overwhelmingly accept the Lake Missoula flood. Before, they had trouble believing there was a flood of these proportions; later many debated how many such floods took place during the Ice Age. In the 1980s,

Figure 10.8. Burlingame Canyon, south of Lowden, Walla Walla Valley, Washington. Note the layered rhythmites on the sides of the canyon.

opinion swayed from one or a few floods to anywhere between 40 and 100. The rhythmite layers found in Burlingame Canyon have played a key role in this controversy. A recent analysis of most of the data has revealed that there probably was just one Lake Missoula flood, similar to what Bretz originally believed (Shaw et al., 1999; Oard, 2000a, 2004a).

CHAPTER ELEVEN

ONLY ONE ICE AGE

We often hear glacial geologists speak of numerous ice ages, as if it is certain. They hypothesize up to 30 different ones, each separated by interglacials, during the past 2.5 million years (Kennett, 1982, p. 747). An interglacial is the period between ice ages when all of the glaciers melted, except for Antarctica and Greenland. Each ice age is believed to have occurred at regular intervals of 100,000 years during approximately the past million years. The ice sheets are said to build up in 90,000 years and melt in the subsequent 10,000-year interglacial. Before a million years ago, ice ages cycled about every 40,000 years, they believe. Furthermore, uniformitarian scientists also postulate more ancient ice ages as far back as 2 to 2.5 billion years ago (see boxed section later in this chapter). Figure 11.1 shows a plot of these ice ages in the evolutionary/uniformitarian time scale.

WHY MULTIPLE ICE AGES?

In the mid 1800s, when scientists began to realize that ice sheets had overrun large tracts of land in the mid and high latitudes, they at first thought there had been only one ice age. As they began to look at glacial debris in more detail they concluded that ice ages may be more complicated than they had originally thought. At the periphery of the ice sheets they found glacial debris layers separated by sand and gravel. This, they thought, was proof of multiple glaciations.

The idea of multiple glaciations caught on. It quickly became the new ice age paradigm — a supermodel in which to fit subsequent research data. After all,

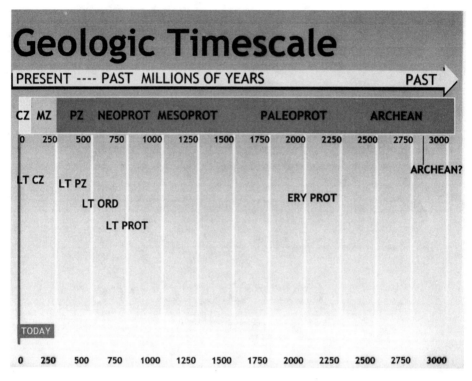

Geologic Timescale

| PRESENT ---- PAST MILLIONS OF YEARS | | | | | | | | | | | PAST |

CZ	MZ	PZ	NEOPROT	MESOPROT		PALEOPROT		ARCHEAN	

| 0 | 250 | 500 | 750 | 1000 | 1250 | 1500 | 1750 | 2000 | 2250 | 2500 | 2750 | 3000 |

ARCHEAN?

LT CZ   LT PZ

LT ORD   ERY PROT

LT PROT

TODAY

| 0 | 250 | 500 | 750 | 1000 | 1250 | 1500 | 1750 | 2000 | 2250 | 2500 | 2750 | 3000 |

Figure 11.1 Schematic of the five main ice age periods in uniformitarian earth history. The Archean "ice age" is still speculative. The ice age labeled LT CZ (late Cenozoic) represents the post-Flood Ice Age that uniformitarian geologists call the Pleistocene or Quaternary. The other four labeled "ice ages" or "ancient ice ages" are considered to be caused by giant landslides during the Genesis flood and not real ice ages.

according to the uniformitarian principle, if there was one ice age, why not many? Multiple ice ages, to many scientists, was a more satisfying idea because the idea conformed to their assumption of uniformitarianism and helped fill its need for time. A number of scientists, however, still thought the evidence was equivocal and that one ice age could cause multiple till layers. They attributed the layers to an ice sheet edge advancing and retreating. But their view eventually lost favor.

That generation of scientists died and a new one took its place, one that was conditioned to think in terms of multiple glaciations. The new breed of geologists went on to consider how many ice ages there were. Scientists settled on about four ice ages in the early 1900s, due to the work of Albrecht Penck and Eduard Bruckner, who convinced the world that four river terraces north of the Alps showed meltwater deposits from four different ice caps. So, the four-ice-age hypothesis was born and caught hold. Scientists who believed in an early version of the astronomical theory of the ice age saw more than four ice ages in the river terraces, since their theory demands many more than four. However, the astronomical theory was considered

Table 11.1. The Classical Glacial-Interglacial Sequence of the North-Central United States	
Glacial	Interglacial
Wisconsinan	Holocene or recent
Illinoian	Sangamon
Kansan	Yarmouth
Nebraskan	Aftonian

too feeble to cause ice ages, so the belief in four ice ages prevailed and was *accepted doctrine* for about 60 years.

From the Alps research, glacial geologists working in other areas also saw only four ice ages (Bowen, 1978, p. 10–19). Four ice ages became conventional wisdom along the edge of the former ice sheet in the Midwest of North America and in northern Europe and Asia. Table 11.1 shows the glacial and interglacial classification from the Midwest that was in vogue for about 60 years. There is an interesting progression that occasionally occurs in science, especially historical sciences, that wrong concepts get "proved" over and over again. This is called the bandwagon effect or reinforcement syndrome. During the time when the four-ice-age theory dominated thinking, all relevant data was fitted into this theory. There appeared to be no contradictions.

It was all fiction, developed on preconceived ideas of how glaciers are expected to behave. In the 1970s, ideas changed and now scientists are postulating 30 regularly repeating ice ages! Nevertheless, as with all ruling theories, all of the data has been, once again, massaged into the new ruling theory. Few scientists dare risk their careers and grant money to point out the theory's glaring contradictions.

History indicates that the number of glaciations has never been on a solid footing. It has changed according to the popular ideas of the time.

ONE RECENT ICE AGE?

It may come as a surprise to many people, but there is strong evidence there was only one fairly recent ice age (Oard, 1990, p. 135–166).

In an earlier chapter, I showed just how meteorologically difficult it is for any ice age to develop using present processes. For snow to survive a summer in the northern United States, summer temperatures would have to drop to an average of about 20°F (-7°C), 50°F (28°C) below normal, and the snow needs to be regularly replenished. According to uniformitarianism, this abnormal climate has to persist for thousands of years. If one ice age is difficult to produce, how much more difficult would it be to form 2, 4, 15, or 30 ice ages in succession?

When we examine the glacial debris called till, we learn that it was deposited predominantly from the *last Ice Age* even within the uniformitarian paradigm. Moreover, most of this till is from the *last advance* of the *last* ice age (Sugden and John, 1976, p. 133). Sugden and John (1976, p. 138) state in reference to ice ages other than the last:

> *We shall not, therefore, consider these [previous] glaciations in any detail — a task which would in any case be difficult because of the scarcity of supporting evidence.*

The glacial deposits themselves point to only one ice age.

When you compare the till to the bedrock below, you usually discover that the debris is the same as the bedrock material and, therefore, was not transported very far. Feininger (1971, p. C79) writes:

> *Earlier in this report, the nearness of most glacial boulders to their source was cited as evidence that glacial transport is generally short. Even stronger evidence to support this view can be read from the tills themselves. Where the direction of movement carried a continental ice sheet from one terrain to another of markedly different rock type, the tills derived from each terrain are predominantly restricted to the area of their corresponding source rock.*

A short distance of transport would be expected in one ice age, but in multiple ice ages, the debris should be bulldozed farther and farther from its source. Since most glacial till is from local bedrock, one ice age is a more straightforward deduction.

A few areas within the periphery of the ice sheet in North America were never glaciated at all. These are called driftless areas and have been mentioned in a previous chapter. Evidence the driftless area in southwest Wisconsin was never glaciated is the spires of sandstone that would have been planed off (figures 11.2 and 11.3). How can a thick ice sheet over a 100,000-year period in the uniformitarian paradigm

Figure 11.2. Sandstone spires in southwest Wisconsin indicating the area has never been glaciated, otherwise the ice sheets would have planed the area.

Figure 11.3. Close-up of a sandstone spire shown in figure 11.2.

have missed these areas? Even more puzzling is how 30 or more ice ages could have missed these driftless areas. A thin ice sheet that formed and melted rapidly has a much greater chance of leaving a few areas unglaciated at the margin than many long ones.

With the many presumed glaciations of Canada, Canada's bedrock should be heavily eroded. However, the terrain, in truth, shows little erosion (Eyles, 1983, p. 4). The bedrock under the local cover of sedimentary rocks is of the same topographical roughness as that found on the exposed crystalline bedrock (figure 11.4).

The characteristics of ice age animals points to a single ice age. During the approximately two to three million years that uniformitarian scientists allot to multiple glaciations, the animals remained much the same (Bowen, 1978, p. 38). There is very little fossil information available to differentiate between various glacials and interglacials. Their explanation is that very little evolution took place because the many ice ages apparently did not stress the animals to change. Then for some mysterious reason, dozens of large mammals and birds went extinct after the "last" ice age. This appears doubtful within their evolutionary paradigm. One ice age with characteristic plants and animals is a more reasonable deduction.

If there were multiple interglacials, animals such as reindeer and woolly mammoths would successfully recolonize previously glaciated territory. Their bones should be abundant in these areas, but they are

Figure 11.4. Schematic showing that the same topographic roughness of the granite in southeast Canada continues under the sedimentary rocks to the south.

rare and are found mainly at the periphery of ice sheets and in non-glaciated areas.

Lastly, if the uniformitarian version of multiple ice ages were true, at least 1 of the 30 ice ages should have glaciated the lowlands of Siberia, Alaska, and the Yukon. Could it be there really were no interglacials?

The broad-scale evidence for only one ice age is summarized in table 11.2. When it comes right down to it, the uniformitarian scientists actually *assume* there were multiple ice ages. Young and others (1994, p. 683) admit:

Glacial reconstructions commonly assume a multiple-glaciation hypothesis in all areas that contain a till cover.

It all adds up to a strong case for one recent Ice Age.

How Can One Ice Age Explain the Evidence for Multiple Ice Ages?

Although scientists have been operating under preconceived concepts for interpreting glacial data, they do have some physical evidence that supports the multiple glaciation hypothesis. This mainly consists of presumed interglacial deposits between layers of till and the old appearance of some glacial debris, especially in the north central United States.

The foremost evidence for multiple glaciation comes from the periphery, where till layers are sometimes separated by layers of sand, gravel, clay, or even organic material. However, the sand and gravel are glacial melt debris. It is easy to sandwich this debris between layers of till, even within the interior of a single ice sheet (Eyles, Dearman, and Douglas, 1983, p. 222). The edge of an ice sheet or glacier is now known to oscillate many times over short periods. Glaciers advance, retreat, readvance, and even surge. A surge is a sudden increase in glacial flow that goes from normal to perhaps one hundred times faster over a period of a few months and sometimes for as long as three years. During a surge, a glacier has often moved many miles. Scientists now recognize that surges were common at the edge of the ice sheets. Even scientists who are committed to the present processes paradigm are coming to the conclusion that one ice sheet can cause multiple till layers with non-glacial deposits or melt debris between them. Derbyshire (1979, p. 77) writes:

TABLE 11.2. SUMMARY OF EVIDENCE SUPPORTING ONLY ONE ICE AGE

1) One ice age meteorologically difficult
2) Most till local
3) Most till predominately from the "last"
4) Most North American loess from the "last"
5) Interior till thin and coarse-grained
6) Bedrock slightly eroded in interior areas
7) Inadequate thickness of periphery till
8) Driftless areas within periphery
9) Little change in flora and fauna
10) Fossils rare in glaciated regions
11) Most extinctions after the "last"

Long-standing problems of interpretation of complexly interbedded tills of the Pleistocene glaciations have been resolved as a result of the realization that

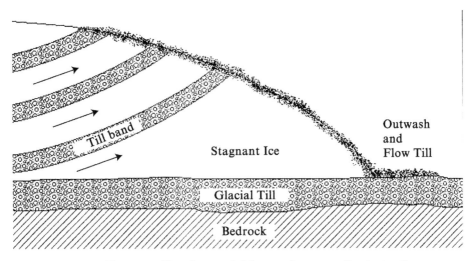

Figure 11.5. Shearing of basal ice and debris at the snout of a glacier. Retreats and advances of the glacier cause a complex mixture of till, flowtill, and outwash deposits after the ice melts that have been mistaken for multiple glaciation.

not all tills are of subglacial origin, and that a formation of several tills inter-bedded with meltwater stream deposits may be the product of a single advance and retreat of the glacier.

Derbyshire (1979, p. 78) even shows how shearing layers of debris-rich till over a stationary lower layer of ice would result in stacked debris bands that look, upon melting, like multiple till sheets (figure 11.5). Most of this shearing takes place at the ice sheet margin and can be repeated many times. Other authors confirm Derbyshire's conclusion.

It is interesting that the first claim for multiple ice ages was later shown to be a likely minor oscillation at the edge of *one* glacier (Imbrie and Imbrie, 1979, p. 56). Based on new concepts of glacial dynamics, geologists have concluded that only one ice age affected much of Alberta, Canada (Oard, 1995c). Beaney and Shaw (2000, p. 51) recently summarized the evidence for western Alberta:

> *The suite of landforms was interpreted as evidence for multiple advance and retreat cycles of the Laurentide ice sheet. These interpretations are brought under question with the conclusion that there was only a single glaciation, the Late Wisconsinan, of the western part of the Alberta Plains. . . .*

Organic remains, commonly associated with interglacials within the multiple glaciation paradigm, are rare in glaciated areas, as Charlesworth (1957, p. 1025) states:

. . . glacial deposits are virtually unfossiliferous; interglacial accumulations, if fossiliferous, occur in isolated and discontinuous patches. . . .

Eyles (1983, p. 9–16) finds that organic material associated with till can be incorporated by glacial readvances. So, a dynamic ice sheet that oscillates at its margin would be expected to pick up organic remains, especially plant material, now and then. If an ice sheet advances far enough, it could cover forests and animal bones that would be located just south of the sheet, especially if the Ice Age had mild, wet winters and the animals and plants lived close to the edge.

In the Midwest, sticky clay layers, called gumbo are found either between till sheets or on top of glacial debris. This has been interpreted as a soil that took much time to develop during an interglacial period. However, many of these "soils" are controversial. Some soil scientists believe this clay can form in areas of poor drainage, which means that the clay can form quickly in a wet climate. It is even possible that some of the clay layers could form at the bottom of a lake adjacent to the ice sheet. Soils usually have an organic layer at the top, but the Midwest clay layers nearly always are missing the top organic layer (Birkeland, 1984, p. 33). In conclusion, the idea that these clay layers represent interglacial times between ice ages is a stretch.

The old, weathered appearance of some glacial deposits could be explained by several processes within a post-Flood ice age. One possibility is that much heavier precipitation in an equable climate could cause faster weathering. Another, more likely, possibility is acid rain. One of the primary volcanic gases during the Ice Age was SO_2. When combined with water, SO_2 will form sulfuric acid. The resulting acid rain would tend to cause very rapid weathering and an old appearance in a short time.

In summary, one dynamic ice age during the unique post-Flood climate can account for many, if not all, of the features of the glacial deposits that appear to support multiple glaciations. Other interpretations, like clay soils, may simply be a misinterpretation.

IS THE NEXT ICE AGE DUE SOON?

A global superstorm is coming soon, say Art Bell and Whitley Strieber (2000) in their provocative new book, *The Coming Global Superstorm*. They give dire warnings of a storm so devastating that it will quickly usher in another ice age.

The entire American Midwest would be under a sheet of ice, one that would extend across Siberia and northern Europe as well. . . .

The ice keeps coming back, and we aren't sure why. But something acts as the trigger, and we know that this event is a sudden one. . . . the victims — some of them frozen so quickly that their dinners are still in the mouths — will not be found again for thousands of years. Like the mammoths who preceded them in the last storm, their remains will suggest to the future that something strange and terrible happened. . . . For the past 3 million years, earth has been in an agonizing cycle of alternating Ice Ages and brief warming periods." (Bell and Strieber, 2000, p. 13, 103, 139, 160).

Notice that the quick freeze of the woolly mammoths in Siberia is used as an analogy of what will happen to man in a future ice age. Daniel Grossman in the July 22, 2003, *New York Times* warns us:

> *If the past is any indication, the earth is at the end of another such warm period, poised to descend into a new Ice Age.*

Their evidence for such a frightening scenario consists of the popular idea that ice ages have repeatedly occurred over 90 percent of the past 2.5 million years and that each intervening warm spell lasted only 10,000 years. According to uniformitarianism, the last ice age ended about 10,000 years ago, so the next one is about due. To further support their theory, they contend that solar radiation absorbed in the higher latitudes has fallen to the level of the peak of the last ice age. This is thought to be due to the earth's orbital geometry in accordance to the currently popular astronomical theory of the ice ages.

Large fluctuations in oxygen isotope ratios in Greenland ice cores are also thought to signal rapid climatic changes. Oxygen comes in three isotopes with different numbers of neutrons in the atoms. When there is more oxygen-16 than oxygen-18 in the ice, the climate is assumed to have been colder. For the past 30 years, glacial geologists have drilled ice cores on the Greenland ice sheet. In the early 1990s, they were surprised to discover rapid changes in oxygen isotope ratios, which suggested to them there were rapid changes in climate, possibly up to 36°F (20°C) within a few decades (Hammer et al., 1997, p. 26, 315)! There is much evidence that ice cores from the Greenland and Antarctic ice sheets support the creation-Flood Ice Age model and not the uniformitarian model (Oard, 2004b).

This is an example of how uniformitarian beliefs can get us into a lot of trouble. As we already know, ice ages are not easy to develop. Although the summer radiation at higher latitudes is similar to what it was at the peak of the Ice Age, the world is nowhere close to producing another ice age. Secondly, there was only one trigger known to be strong enough to produce an ice age — the Genesis flood. God has promised not to send another

Figure 11.6

Flood on the earth. The rainbow's association with rain and thunderstorms is a frequent reminder of His promise from Genesis 9:11–17 (figure 11.6). If there will never be another global Flood, then there obviously will never be another ice age.

Were There Ancient Ice Ages?

Geologists believe ice ages existed not only in the recent past but also in the ancient past. Figure 11.1 shows the times of supposed ice ages within geological time. Ancient ice ages go back 2 to 2.5 billion years ago in the standard geological time scale. Creationists, on the other hand, would consider that most of the sedimentary layers on the earth were laid down by the Flood. Because of the acceptance of multiple ice ages, those opposed to creation question how ice ages can occur with only one flood. Anti-creationist Arthur Strahler (1987, p. 263) points out what he thinks is a major contradiction to the biblical time scale in this way:

The Carboniferous tillites cannot be accepted by creationists as being of glacial origin for the obvious reason that the tillite formations are both overlain and underlain by fossiliferous strata, which are deposits of the Flood. During that great inundation, which lasted the better part of one year, there could have been no land ice formed by accumulation of snow.

Tillite is the consolidated equivalent of glacial till. I believe Strahler is correct in that there could have been no land ice or glaciation during the Flood. Then how do we explain the rocks that are used as evidence for ancient ice ages?

The rocks representing these assumed ice ages look like hardened glacial till (figure 11.7). Furthermore, they exhibit other features that are thought by many to only be caused by ice. They show striated rock surfaces, striated rocks within the till, and stones in finely layered sediments. Figure 11.8 shows a picture of striated and polished bedrock below "tillite" from the most famous ancient glaciation, the late Paleozoic or Carboniferous/Permian "ice age" from southern Africa. The stones in finely layered sediments are suggestive of lakes adjacent to a glacier in which debris-rich icebergs break off and float out over the lake. As the iceberg melts, stones in the ice are dropped into the fine mud on the lake bottom.

Figure 11.7. Hardened glacial till. Note the stones of various sizes embedded in a finer-grained matrix.

Figure 11.8. Striated bedrock below "tillite" from the supposed late Paleozoic glaciation in southern Africa.
(Photo by Gordon Davison)

Supposed ancient ice ages are not unlike other challenges from geologists to the Genesis flood and the creation's short time scale. Further analysis of the data is called for, and it provides a different explanation for these rocks (Oard, 1997a). The rocks in question have a number of peculiar properties suggesting that they likely are not ice age related. First, the vast majority of these "tillites" are *marine* deposits. Second, they hardly show the dimensions of glacial debris, being geographically small and commonly thick, unlike glacial deposits that are the opposite. Third, the stones in the "tillite" are generally small and random, while glacial deposits from the recent Ice Age commonly contain masses of boulders. Fourth, there are a number of geological features for the presence of ice that should exist in these "tillites" but are absent. Fifth, paleomagnetism indicates that most of the numerous "ice age" deposits older than 500 million years in their geological time scale occurred *near the equator*. This data has spawned the serious consideration that the earth was totally glaciated for several long stretches of time from about 3 billion years to 500 million years ago (Kirschvink et al., 2000). Lastly, the so-called glacial debris is intimately associated with warmth indicators such as carbonates and dolomites.

So, we observe a number of glacial-like features in the "tillite" rocks and a number of features hostile to ice ages. Are there other geological processes that

Figure 11.9. Landslide debris that scratched the bedrock. Some of the stones in the debris are scratched.

can account for the data used to postulate ancient ice ages? Yes, there are other processes that can account for the data we observe, namely underwater landslides of various sorts. Landslides can striate bedrock as they slide over it and at the same time scratch up the stones in the landslide material. Figure 11.9 is a photo of a landslide that scratched the bedrock below and the stones in the debris. Schermerhorn (1974, p. 681–682) takes other geologists to task for not considering other mechanisms for striated stones:

> *To repeat the most important point, great caution is urged in the use of striated stones as glacial pointers. It is a point that has been stressed time and again by many stratigraphers, without apparently leaving much impression.*

It seems that geologists have developed too strong a bias toward ancient ice ages to seriously consider other mechanisms for the observed rocks.

The very dynamic Genesis flood produced rapid sedimentation and landslides of unstable sediments. These landslides could duplicate the large scale of some of these "tillites." Landslides would be caused by tectonic motion and huge earthquakes that occurred during the Flood. It is known that the larger the landslides, the farther they travel. Hence, monstrous Flood landslides are bound to cause some unconsolidated sediments to slide long distances and come to rest on nearly level strata, as is observed in these supposed ancient ice age deposits.

Landslides in the Genesis flood can also result in striated bedrock, striated rocks in the debris, and other supposed glacial features. The Flood is probably the only possible mechanism that can explain one unique feature of a "tillite" in the Sahara Desert. A grooved substratum has been observed in the Sahara Desert that covers many hundreds of square miles. However, in the Sahara Desert these grooves *mostly all* point north! Ice sheets have never been observed to produce such consistent directional indicators over such a wide area. Large underwater landslides during the Flood would be expected to continue moving in the same direction once the motion was initiated, and thus groove and striate the bedrock in the same direction over many hundreds of square miles.

So these so-called ancient ice ages can be explained as gigantic underwater landslides during the Genesis flood (Oard, 1997a).

CHAPTER TWELVE

DO ICE CORES SHOW MANY TENS OF THOUSANDS OF YEARS?

In the sequence of events in the creation-Flood Ice Age model, at the end of deglaciation, the Ice Age was effectively over. Yet some ice sheets continued to grow. The Greenland and Antarctica ice sheets are remnants left over from the post-Flood Ice Age (figures 12.1 and 12.2). They were protected from melting by their location in the polar latitudes and by the high altitude of the ice deposited during the Ice Age. The altitude of the ice is an important factor since the atmosphere cools at an average of 3.6°F per 1,000 feet (6°C per 1,000 m).

It is interesting to note that the Greenland and Antarctica ice sheets may never have grown to their present size, if it were not for the initial thickness of ice at the end of the Ice Age. Some scientists believe that if the ice somehow disappeared, it probably would not return in the present climate. This is especially the case for Greenland.

Many ice cores have been drilled deep into both the Antarctica and Greenland ice sheets since the 1960s (see figures 12.1 and 12.2). It is observed today that these ice sheets incorporate dust, acids, pollution, etc. that cycle with the seasons. Near the top of the ice sheets, annual layers can be distinguished by measuring the many variables related to the seasons. From the top of the Greenland ice sheet, glaciologists further

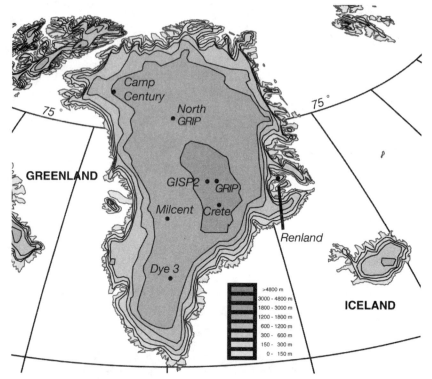

Figure 12.1. Map of Greenland showing ice thickness above sea level with major ice core locations. (Redrawn by Ron Hight.)

claim that they can count the annual layers downward, like counting the rings in a tree to determine its age. They arrive at 110,000 years for the top 90 percent of the ice sheet (Meese et al., 1997). Is their claim justified?

ARE THERE 110,000 ANNUAL LAYERS IN THE GREENLAND ICE SHEET?

The claimed 110,000 annual layers in the GISP2 ice core to near the bottom of the Greenland ice sheet is not a straightforward deduction. The annual layers, indeed, show up well near the top of the ice sheet. However, the situation becomes much more complicated deeper down in the ice sheet. Essentially, the uniformitarian scientists must make assumptions for the bottom and middle portion of the ice sheet in order to determine the annual layers.

The main assumption is that the earth is very old — billions of years old. They *assume* that the Greenland and Antarctica ice sheets have existed for many millions of years. Furthermore, they believe these ice sheets have more or less maintained their present height in a state of *equilibrium* during all this time. They think the amount of snow and ice added each year is approximately balanced by the ice that is lost by melting and calving of icebergs into the ocean. Because of their assumptions, uniformitarian scientists believe that the annual layers thin drastically as they

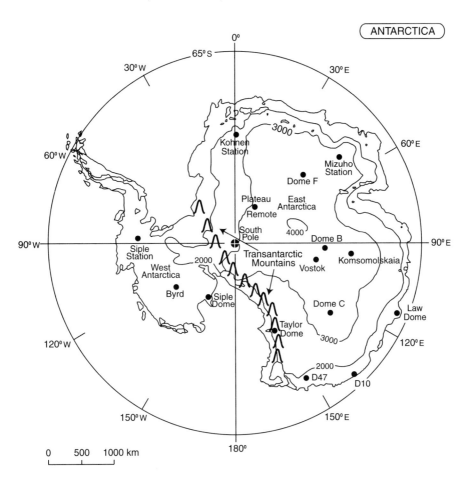

*Figure 12.2. Map of Antarctica showing ice thickness above
sea level with major ice core locations.*
(Redrawn by Ron Hight)

are covered by more snow and ice (figure 12.3). The upshot of their assumptions is that the *amount* of annual layer compression believed to have occurred depends upon *how old one believes the ice to be*. For an ice sheet in equilibrium for millions of years, the annual layers would, theoretically, thin rapidly and become almost paper thin near the bottom of the ice.

On the other hand, if the ice built up rapidly, as in the creationist model during the Ice Age, the annual layers would be very thick at the bottom and thin upward to the present average annual layer thickness. There would be some compression of ice during this short time, of course, but far less than the uniformitarian model suggests (Vardiman, 1993). Figure 12.4 shows these contrasting views of the annual layer thickness with depth.

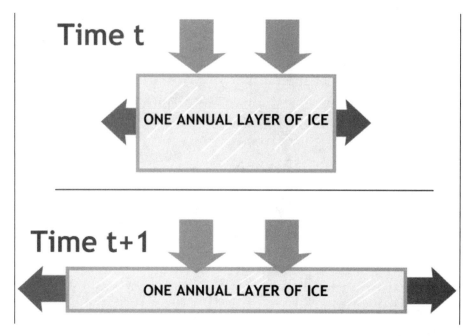

Figure 12.3. Annual layers of ice are compressed vertically and stretched horizontally due to pressure from accumulating snow and ice above.

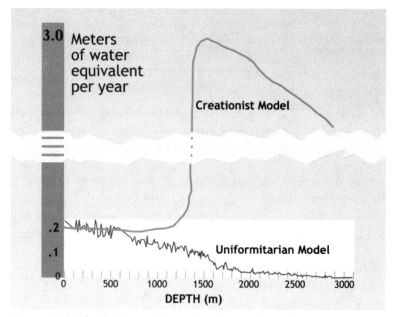

Figure 12.4. The thickness of annual ice layers down the GRIP ice core on central Greenland, calculated according to the uniformitarian (De Angelis et al., 1997, p. 26, 683) and creationist (Oard, 2001c) models.

The assumed thickness of the annual layers is important because it constrains the *expected* annual thickness in the measurements. The measurements can deviate a little from the assumed annual layer thickness but not by much. For instance, in the oxygen isotope method, uniformitarian scientists normally need eight measurements per annual cycle to pick up the "annual" signature. As an example, halfway down the GRIP Greenland ice core at about one mile (1,600 m) deep, uniformitarian scientists believe the annual layer thickness is 4 inches (10 cm) (De Angelis et al., 1997, p. 26683). The measurements for oxygen isotopes would then be spaced every 1/2 inch (1 cm) apart.

Since the creationist model postulates an annual layer thickness significantly thicker, say 12 inches (30 cm) as an example, the uniformitarians have taken more measurements than needed and are, therefore, measuring multiple cycles of oxygen isotopes within one year. This is how the number of annual layers becomes greatly exaggerated (Oard, 2001c, 2003, 2004b).

As already stated, the uniformitarian and creationist estimated annual thickness is much the same at the top of the Greenland ice sheet. The difference between the two models becomes more and more significant deeper in the ice core. Because of extreme annual layer thinning at the bottom of the core in the uniformitarian model compared to the creationist model, the uniformitarian scientists may be counting 100 layers that they think are annual. These layers in the creationist model may represent only one year. So, the uniformitarian scientists in actuality would be counting storm layers or other cycles of weather that can often duplicate the annual cycle (Oard, 2004b). For instance, a storm has a warm and cold sector with different measurements of the variables, producing a cycle in the variables. These storm oscillations may be on the order of several days. Even the uniformitarian scientists recognize that storms and other phenomenon, like moving snow dunes, may result in the counting of an annual cycle, as Alley and others (1997, p. 26378) state:

> *Fundamentally, in counting any annual marker, we must ask whether it is absolutely unequivocal, or whether nonannual events could mimic or obscure a year. For the visible strata (and, we believe, for any other annual indicator at accumulation rates representative of central Greenland), it is almost certain that variability exists at the subseasonal or storm level, at the annual level, and for various longer periodicities (2-year, sunspot, etc.). We certainly must entertain the possibility of misidentifying the deposit of a large storm or a snow dune as an entire year or missing a weak indication of a summer and thus picking a 2-year interval as 1 year.*

Have They Measured 700,000 Years in the Antarctic Ice Sheet?

The method of counting annual layers only works with the high accumulation Greenland ice sheet. However, the deep Antarctic ice sheet cores have been dated to over 300,000 years showing multiple ice age cycles. The new deep Dome C ice core from the top of the Antarctic ice sheet is claimed to have drilled seven ice age cycles for a total of about 700,000 years near the bottom. Are these ages objective?

Except for coastal ice cores that show only one ice age cycle, the Antarctica ice sheet is dated by *assuming* that the astronomical theory of the ice age is correct (Oard, 2004b). In fact, this assumption also undergirds the annual layer dating of the Greenland ice sheet (Oard, 2004b). This is how they obtain three or more ice age cycles, with each cycle being 100,000 years long. They simply count the assumed number of ice age cycles and multiple by 100,000 years, the assumed period for the astronomical theory. These dates are not objective; they simply are based on the assumption of the astronomical theory and old age, which was discussed in chapter 6. It is easy to reinterpret the data from the ice sheet within the creationist's framework, as we will see in the next section.

GREENLAND AND ANTARCTICA ICE SHEETS — REMNANTS OF THE POST-FLOOD ICE AGE

At the peak of the Ice Age, the average thickness of the ice sheets in the Northern Hemisphere was estimated to be 2,300 feet (700 m), while on Antarctica it was 3,900 feet (1,200 m). The ocean water was still relatively warm at an average of 50°F (10°C). It still needed to cool another 11°F (6°C) to reach the current average of 39°F (4°C). The relatively warm water adjacent to Greenland and Antarctica during deglaciation would have continued to cause significantly greater ocean evaporation resulting in relatively high precipitation to fall on the Greenland and Antarctic ice sheets.

If the rate of ice growth after the peak of the Ice Age continued, 30 percent more ice would be added to Greenland and Antarctica as the ocean cooled to its present temperature in the 200 years of deglaciation. At the end of this period, the average ice depth on Greenland would be about 3,000 feet (900 m) and Antarctica around 5,000 feet (1,525 m). The average depth of the Greenland ice sheet today is 5,250 feet (1,600 m) with a maximum depth of 11,045 feet (3,367 m) (Bamber, Layberry, and Gogineni, 2001). The current average thickness for the Antarctic ice sheet is 6,230 feet (1,900 m) with a maximum of around 13,775 feet (4,200 m) (Bamber and Huybrechts, 1996; Vaughan et al., 1999; Huybrechts et al., 2000).

The average precipitation in water equivalent on the Greenland ice sheet is 12 in/yr (30 cm/yr) with more than 60 in/yr (150 cm/yr) on the southeast corner and below 8 in/yr (20 cm/yr) for a substantial part of the high northern half of the ice sheet (Thomas and PARCA Investigators, 2001, p. 33,692; Bales et al., 2001). The average precipitation for Antarctica is 7 in/yr (19 cm/yr), which varies from relatively high values near the coast to around 2 in/yr (5 cm/yr) for the majority of the high East Antarctica ice sheet (Huybrechts et al., 2000, p. 56). It is interesting that the precipitation is so low over the high altitudes of the Antarctic ice sheet that the region is considered a *polar desert*.

The precipitation of the southeast Greenland ice sheet is surprisingly high. During World War II, six P-38 Lightning fighters and two B-17 Flying Fortress aircraft were forced to ditch on the southeast Greenland ice sheet, 18 miles (29 km) from the ocean. A team went back to recover them in the late 1980s and discovered that the planes were buried under 260 feet (80 m) of ice and snow that had accumulated since 1942 (Bloomberg, 1989)! These planes did not end up buried in the ice and snow because they absorbed solar radiation and sank into the ice sheet. They are at this depth because of the high precipitation that covered them. Such high precipitation is not typical for the remainder of the ice sheet, but gives us a hint of the possibilities when the ice sheet was much lower and the climate much different in the Ice Age.

Based on strict biblical chronology and assuming no gaps in the ancestral lists, the Ice Age ended about four thousand years ago. Since then, many hundreds of feet of ice would be added to the Greenland and Antarctica ice sheets. Of course, ice would also be lost during this time. This loss would mainly be from surface melting, which is only significant on the Greenland ice sheet, and iceberg calving. In spite of melting and calving, these two ice sheets very likely continued to build to their present altitudes in the 4,000 years since the end of the Ice Age.

The model presented in this book can account for the current prominence of the Greenland and Antarctica ice sheets during a short Ice Age of about 700 years and the present climate for another 4,000 years (Vardiman, 1993). Figure 12.5 shows a timeline for the buildup of the ice sheets from the end of the Flood to the present.

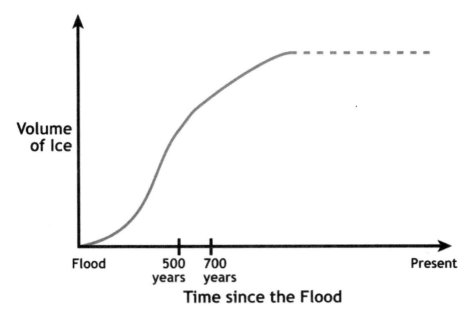

Figure 12.5. Time-line for the build-up of the Greenland and Antarctica ice sheets from the time of the Flood to the present.

Wild Ice Core Interpretations During the Ice Age

The uniformitarian interpretation of the "annual layers" within the bottom half or Ice Age portion of the ice cores drilled near the top of the Greenland ice sheet has resulted in some wild ideas (Oard, 2002). Some of the variables in the lower sections of the cores show dramatic and rapid changes (figure 12.6). Based on their uniformitarian assumption, mainstream scientists are now forced to come to strange conclusions. They see these oscillations within the Ice Age as representing temperature changes on Greenland possibly up to 36°F (20°C) in periods as short as a few decades (Hammer et al., 1997)!

Such oscillations continue down into the very bottom of the cores, thought to represent the previous interglacial period. Some scientists think these oscillations are radical temperature changes during an interglacial. Since we live in a supposed interglacial, such radical changes are considered possible in today's climate. Since these core changes probably represent the climate around the North Atlantic Ocean, climate researchers fear that the present climate could undergo a similar change in the future, induced possibly by global warming (Oard, 2004c). Currently, they are desperately searching for some sort of mechanism that would cause such catastrophic climate change to explain these oscillations in the very bottom of the ice cores. They are considering a few possibilities, such as a halting of the ocean currents in the North Atlantic Ocean. However, other scientists believe the very bottom of the Greenland ice sheet was disturbed by ice sheet flow, and the oscillations, therefore, are climatically meaningless.

In the creationist model, on the other hand, such rapid oscillations, whether in the Ice Age portion or the lower supposed interglacial portion, could simply be the *signature of annual layers or decadal temperature changes caused by variable amounts of volcanic dust and aerosols in the stratosphere*. This is because the creationist annual layer is so much thicker in this part of the ice core. Therefore, we do not have to fear the possibility of a catastrophic climate change in the near future.

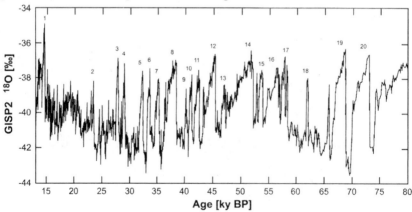

Figure 12.6. Plot of oxygen isotope fluctuation, considered proportional to temperature, during the Ice Age in the GISP2 ice core (from M. Schultz, 2002).

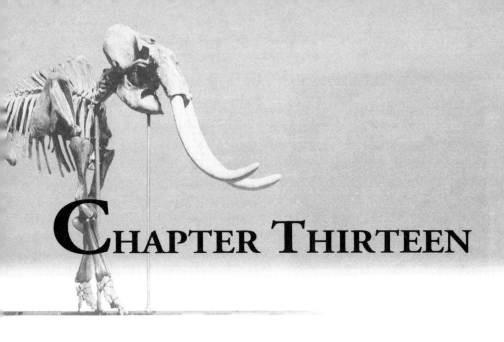

CHAPTER THIRTEEN

WHERE WAS MAN
DURING THE ICE AGE?

When we think of Ice Age man, we usually think of a brutish, ape-like, cave-man that hunted woolly mammoths and woolly rhinos. According to evolutionary theory, the Ice Age is the time when man evolved through a series of missing links. (See boxed section later in this chapter for a discussion on supposed missing links.)

Biblical history records events during or soon after the Ice Age. This epoch includes the Book of Job and the life and times of the Jewish patriarchs. The Bible's focus is on events that took place in the Middle East after the Flood. So, we should not expect to read about an Ice Age in the Bible.

Based on Genesis 10 and 11, we can deduce that for the first 100 years after the Flood, man lived exclusively in the Middle East. After leaving the ark, Noah and his three sons and their wives and their offspring settled and remained in the Tigris-Euphrates River area until the Tower of Babel incident. When Noah and his family left the ark, God commanded them to multiply and fill the earth once again (Gen. 9:7). They chose to not spread out from there in disobedience to God. Within a fairly short time, rebellion against God began. It reached a crisis point when the people of Babel built a tower to reach into "heaven." The rebellion very likely involved astrology. God judged them by giving them a confusion of language that resulted in their dispersal over the earth (figure 13.1). This happened about

Figure 13.1. The confusion of languages at the Tower of Babel.

100 to 300 years after the Flood. By then the Ice Age was well underway.

DISPERSION SOUTH

Many people decided to head southwest and southeast from the warm Tigris-Euphrates Valley (figure 13.2). Those heading southwest settled around the Dead Sea, Palestine, Egypt, the Sahara Desert and the remainder of Africa. At that time, the summer climate of the entire area was still cooler and wetter than our present climate. This accounts for the thriving post-Flood civilizations found in areas that are now inhospitable. A few hundred years after the Flood and well into the Ice Age, the Sahara was teeming with life, as witnessed by the remains of aquatic animals and the extensive rock art discovered in the Sahara Desert.

Other groups headed southeast into India, Southeast Asia, New Guinea, Australia, and eventually to New Zealand and the islands of the western Pacific. The Australian Aborigines would be included in this early group.

DISPERSION NORTHWEST

Those that headed northwest had to be hearty (Oard and Oard, 1993). They were migrating toward the Scandinavian ice sheet in northern Europe and northwestern Asia. They probably had no idea that an ice sheet existed when they first headed north, but soon they saw ice caps in the mountains. The volcanic ash and aerosols in the stratosphere made their days a little dark and cold, but game was

Figure 13.2. Dispersion from the Tower of Babel.
(Drawn by Daniel Lewis of AIG.)

plentiful. It was unlikely they could grow crops because the summers were too cool and the growing season too short, but they probably gathered berries and roots along the way. Large game was a possible factor for them moving farther and farther north. Eventually a few entered the land of the woolly mammoths. Caves were the most practical places to live. Your classic European "caveman" then became a reality, but he was neither brutish nor ape-like. They are known as Neanderthal and Cro-Magnon man and were probably of average or greater intelligence, surviving in a harsh environment, and were not missing links.

Neanderthal (or Neandertal) man was once considered a link between apes and humans, but this was because of evolutionary bias. He did have some unusual facial features, but his brain was *a little larger* than modern man, whose brain averages almost three times the size of an ape brain. That should have spoken volumes to the early evolutionists who are always anxious to find a missing link. Over one hundred skeletons of Neanderthal man have been found in the caves of Europe, western Asia, and northern Africa. Their skeletons from the neck down are almost identical to modern man. Neanderthal Man had brow ridges, lacked a chin, and the back of his head extended backwards. These skull features could be either unique genetic features, a result of inbreeding, or been caused by disease. Some of their features could have been caused by diseases like rickets and arthritis that some of them were known to possess. Rickets is caused by a lack of vitamin D, which would be a common result of living in caves during the cloudy, bleak days of the Ice Age.

Cro-Magnon man, who looked as modern as you and I, seemed to follow the Neanderthals into Europe sometime later. They also lived in caves. They, along with the Neanderthals, used stone tools, probably because any metal tools they possessed upon leaving Babel had worn out. They also left their artwork on cave walls throughout the region. The Cro-Magnon people most likely interacted with Neanderthal man. Life would have been challenging for both groups in those days, but the abundant game kept them alive. For an account of what life was probably like living in a cave close to the ice sheet as seen through the eyes of a 12-year-old boy, read *Life in the Great Ice Age* (Oard and Oard, 1993).

The Cro-Magnon and Neanderthals very likely intermarried and are included within the Europeans and Asians of today. We find skeletons from the Ice Age period that show a mixture of features from both groups of people.

Large game would have become scarce during the extinctions at the end the Ice Age, but since summers were becoming warmer, man was able to start planting and harvesting again. He built tribal dwellings, then villages, and then cities. Civilization and agriculture developed rapidly. Life in the great Ice Age was only a blip in the life of man in Europe and western Asia. Evolutionary archeologists and anthropologists have thought that the development of agriculture was slow in Europe, but this is very likely due to their evolutionary bias in which man evolved from the apes over millions of years. Some archeologists now are recognizing that agriculture could have developed in Europe rapidly:

> *The realization that recent hunter-gatherers can turn to herding and crop cultivation if they perceive this to be advantageous has major implications for studies of agricultural origins in Europe* (Dennell, 1992, p. 91).

ORIGIN OF THE NATIVE AMERICANS

Other families left the Tigris-Euphrates Valley heading east and northeast (figure 13.2). They, too, would have been a hardy people, since the continental interior of Asia was relatively cold with ice caps developing in the higher mountains. Those spreading due east were the ancient Oriental tribes who settled in eastern Asia.

Some of the tribes would have moved northeast into Siberia. Winters were cold in this region, but not nearly as cold as they are today. Game was overwhelmingly abundant. This is where the woolly mammoths lived by the millions. There are quite a number of signs that early man inhabited Siberia, especially southern Siberia. Just recently, archeologists discovered that man lived during the Ice Age along the Yana River in north central Siberia (Pitulko et al., 2004; Stone, 2004). This time would be, according to evolutionary theory, during the "paleolithic" (old stone age) and "neolithic" (new stone age) periods. These classifications from the 1800s are now seen as simplifications:

> We saw earlier how the nineteenth-century scheme for European prehistory divides it into a sequence of ages based on the material used for cutting tools — first stone, then bronze, then iron. Archaeologists today realize that while these can be useful divisions, they don't necessarily correspond to major changes in the way prehistoric people lived or prehistoric communities functioned (Scarre, 1998, p. 13).

As the tribes continued on their journeys, some remained in Siberia while others with more wanderlust continued moving on. It is even possible that as they approached the mild Pacific or Arctic Ocean, the climate was warmer than interior Asia. This might have motivated them to continue migrating east.

Soon some of the nomads reached the Bering Strait between Siberia and Alaska. Because it was either shallow or dry, they crossed into the New World and became the first Native Americans to reach Alaska. The lowlands of Alaska had mild winters and cool summers at this time. As always, some people would settle down and others would continue migrating. From Alaska, they continued on into the Yukon Territory of northwest Canada and southeast along the east slopes of the Rocky Mountains and down the ice-free corridor (figure 13.3).

It would have taken most of the Ice Age for there to be enough snow and ice piled up on the land to expose the shallow Bering Strait and shelf for man to walk over to Alaska. This is assuming the current depth of the Bering Strait. There would have been only a narrow window of opportunity to walk by foot into Alaska. Such a time would have occurred near the end of the Ice Age when conditions became colder. Because many animals had already preceded man into North America, I lean toward the option that the Bering Strait was shallower early in the Ice Age and became exposed earlier. Then man and beast would have migrated into North America early in the Ice Age.

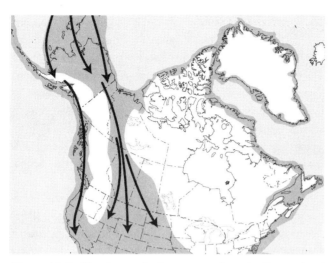

Figure 13.3. The dispersal of man rounding the Bering land bridge and into North America through an ice-free corridor. An alternate coastal route is also shown.

Most Native Americans traveled by land, but it is possible others migrated down the Pacific Coast. They could have built boats, crossed the Bering Strait, and floated along the coasts of Alaska and western British Columbia into Washington state and from there south and east. The waters of the Pacific Ocean would still be warm and the glaciers still would occupy the mountains of British Columbia this early in the Ice Age.

Archeologists have uncovered a large ancient garbage dump mostly of fish bones on Heceta Island near Ketchikan, Alaska. A report in *Science News* (Bower, 1988) states:

> *The animal remains show that these people were experienced in offshore fishing and made extensive use of water transportation. . . . [There was] a relatively mild coastal climate and access to abundant marine food sources would have greatly benefited maritime immigrants, compared with hunters crossing a bitterly cold [ice-free] corridor between massive sheets of ice.*

This statement is within a uniformitarian Ice Age context. Within the post-Flood Ice Age model, the ice-free corridor along the east slopes of the Rocky Mountains would not be nearly as cold in the winter due to downslope chinook winds.

The corridor probably would still be open since it was still early or midway in the Ice Age when the first migrations occurred. Animals had used the corridor earlier, since they started their spread about a few hundred years before man. The corridor closed late in the Ice Age as ice sheets from British Columbia and central Canada merged, but there is evidence that the first people probably made it through before closure and not after. One piece of evidence for this lies with the Taber child, found in southern Alberta below 60 feet of glacial till and post-glacial debris (Stalker, 1977). A number of archaeologists have disputed the pre-glacial implication of the Taber child (Martin and Steadman, 1999, p. 39), but its location indicates that it is pre-glacial.

The first Native Americans, called various names by archeologists, such as Clovis or Folsom man, would have had no difficulty spreading south into southern North America, Central America, and eventually into South America. The journey from the Tigris-Euphrates Rivers to the southern tip of South America did not need to be a grueling journey, as some have envisioned (Fagen, 1987), nor did it need to take a long time. If the tribes were nomadic hunters and they averaged two miles a day for only four of the warmest months, they would move at the rate of 250 miles (400 km) a year. The distance to the southern tip of South America is about 15,000 miles (24,000 km). At the rate of 250 miles (400 km) each summer, the people could have made the journey in only 60 years.

Sixty years is a crude back-of-the-envelope calculation to estimate the *minimum* time it would take to reach South America. The actual migration would likely have been more complicated and slower. Migration could have happened in spurts. Some tribes could have settled for a while in a location before moving on. We know some tribes did settle along the route, such as the Eskimos. Why would the more wandering tribes keep moving? There are many possible reasons, already alluded to before. Some could have simply possessed wanderlust and traveled for the same reason people climb a mountain — because it is there. Others could have been forced to move due to human conflicts of various sorts. It could have been the younger generation spreading outward into more promising territory away from their more settled elders. The tribes could have thought hunting would be better farther along, just like the saying "the grass is greener on the other side of the mountain." Regardless, it need not take much time for people, as well as animals, to populate North and South America.

WAS THERE A PURPOSE TO THE ICE AGE?

Some may wonder whether there was a God-ordained purpose for the Ice Age. In other words, did God cause the Ice Age that would have some benefit for man? Or was the Ice Age simply a climatic consequence of the Genesis flood?

We know the Flood had a purpose. It was to destroy the wickedness of man and start over because ". . . the Lord saw that the wickedness of man was great on the earth, and that every intent of the thoughts of his heart was only evil continually" (Gen. 6:5; NASB). That was an extremely bleak situation, and God was forced to take drastic action. The confusion of languages at the Tower of Babel also had a purpose. It was a judgment from God with the goal of causing man to finally fill the earth after the Flood. I also believe that God could see where such an ungodly, idolatrous union of people would lead down the road, and it was not good. Any number of evil results could have happened. Many other biblical events can be understood as "coming from God" to fulfill His purpose. What about the Ice Age?

It is difficult to conclude one way or other whether the Ice Age had a purpose for man. The Ice Age is not mentioned in the Bible; it is a climatic deduction from the biblical event of the Flood. One could think that if such a great event as the Ice Age had a purpose, God would have mentioned it. However, the Bible was practically all written after the ice melted. The Book of Job is probably the only book written during the Ice Age. Job does mention snow and ice, but he could have observed such features during winter. There are also events not mentioned in the Bible that have a purpose for man. Furthermore, the Ice Age occurred in the far north or in the mountains, far from contact with most people. Therefore, the Ice Age would produce little harm for mankind.

There are two purposes I would like to suggest. Ice Sheets and glaciers grind up the rock to silt size. This silt is called rock flour. While the Ice Age was ending, this rock flour would have been blown all over the world by the strong, dry storms during deglaciation. There is even much dust in the Ice Age portion of the Greenland and Antarctica ice sheets. We will visit this topic more when I get back to the woolly mammoth. The interesting aspect of this wind-blown silt is that it is a very rich soil. A number of places in the world where the wind-blown silt is especially thick are super agricultural areas. These areas include the Midwest of the United States, the Ukraine, and large areas of China.

Another possible purpose for the Ice Age could have been to aid the repopulating of the earth, as described in this chapter. Mild winters and cool summers, the characteristic of the early and mid Ice Age, would have helped people to migrate across the Sahara Desert, which was much cooler and wetter, and into central and southern Africa. Such a climate would have aided man and beasts to migrate into Siberia and pass into North America. On the other hand, mild winters and cooler summers with more precipitation would have made the Tigris-Euphrates area a much more ideal location to live than today. Maybe this is the reason people settled there and did not want to leave.

ARE THERE MISSING LINKS BETWEEN MAN AND APES?

If man ascended from the apes or an ape-like creature over several million years, a multitude of fossil links should be found. This transition was theorized to have occurred during the time of the Ice Age — possibly even caused by the Ice Age as some scientists postulate. Why people evolved, but not animals, at this time is an obvious contradiction to evolutionary theory. Paleoanthropologists, as missing link hunters are called, have combed the world for over 100 years expending huge amounts of time and money in their search for the missing links. Indeed, they have found a few candidates, but the number is rather small, and the interpretation of the fossil scraps is open to debate. Every paleoanthropologist seems to have his own interpretation as to how the bones should be arranged.

As a result of their enthusiasm and intense competition to find the missing link, paleoanthropologists have run into a great deal of trouble. Neaderthal man, early on, was seized as the missing link, but experts later realized that their own bias created this link. Neaderthal man is just a variety of man.

Exaggerated missing link claims have even been made on the basis of one tooth. The "Nebraska man" found in Nebraska in 1922 ended up being a pig's tooth.

Fraud was easy to foist on these desperate fossil-man hunters. The so-called Piltdown man, despite obvious clues, fooled all of the leading palaeontologists in the early and mid 20th century. This "missing link" ended up being the jaw of an ape connected to the braincase of a man.

The most recent candidates for missing link status have lasted a little longer, but amidst controversy. *Ramapithicus*, based on scraps of teeth and jaws, was thought to be the first missing link between man and apes. However, more material has been found. It ended up being an extinct ape. The original analysis of its missing link status was once again found to be loaded with bias.

Australopithicus is the next in line. It can be coined, "Mr. Missing Link." There are now a variety of such creatures in this group, including Lucy, found by Donald Johanson in Ethiopia (Johanson and Edey, 1981; Johanson and Shreeve, 1989). It is even claimed Lucy walked upright like humans. Most of the scraps labeled *Homo habilis* would also fall into the category of *Australopithicus*. Paleoanthropologists emphasize their "human-like" characteristics and usually downplay their ape-like features. Based on a computer analysis of many parts of the available skeletons of *Australopithicus*, Charles Oxnard (1975) categorized it as a unique ape, not in the line between apes and man. Of course, one would expect unique features with an extinct animal because that is part of the definition of being extinct.

Australopithicus is overwhelmingly apish. It has the brain size of an ape, its skull looks like an ape, and it is questionable that it walked upright, according to Sir Solly Zuckerman (1970, p. 61–94), one of the leading evolutionary experts on this fossil during the middle of the 20th century. Just recently, an analysis of the elbow area of Lucy and one other *Australopithicus* fossil revealed the bones of a knuckle walker, comparable to some living apes (Richmond and Strait, 2000; Stokstad, 2000; Collard and Aiello, 2000). Unfortunately, in their desire to keep the missing link status of *Australopithicus*, paleoanthropologists have relegated this new evidence as a *throwback from a previous ancestor*, claiming that the knuckle-walking ability was not used.

Sir Solly Zuckerman (1970, p. 64,94), waxing philosophical about this entire enterprise of attempting to find the missing link, laments:

> *As I have already implied, students of fossil primates have not been distinguished for caution when working within the logical constraints of their subject. The record is so astonishing that it is legitimate to ask whether*

much science is yet to be found in this field at all. . . . So much glamour still attaches to the theme of the missing-link, and to man's relationship with the animal world, that it may always be difficult to exorcise from the comparative study of Primates, living and fossil, the kind of myths which the unaided eye is able to conjure out of a well of wishful thinking.

The last candidate for missing link status is *Homo erectus*. This designation includes a fair variety of fossils, some of which are questionable. Early members of the category include the equivocal Java man and Peking man. Since this time, many fossils of *Homo erectus* have been unearthed. As it turns out, *Homo erectus* is only a little different than Neanderthal man. The main difference is that *Homo erectus* generally had a smaller stature and brain size, but still within the normal range of man. And just like Neanderthal man, modern people and mixed types lived in the same region at the same time. There is only one conclusion that can be drawn and that is *Homo erectus* was a breed of man, as documented extensively in Marvin Lubenow's book *Bones of Contention* (Lubenow, 2004).

CHAPTER FOURTEEN

MAMMOTHS THRIVE EARLY IN THE POST-FLOOD ICE AGE

We have developed the post-Flood Ice Age model based on the climatic aftermath of the Genesis flood. Now we are in a position to delve into the mysteries of the woolly mammoth.

The questions surrounding the life and death of woolly mammoths have fueled many hypotheses by both evolutionists and creationists. Advocates of the creation-Flood model have drawn up several competing hypotheses because the information on the woolly mammoths is confusing and most of the research is published in Russian. Some creationists explain the mammoth demise by the Flood in the same way as the dinosaurs disappeared. They usually advocate a quick freeze as the mechanism for their extinction and preservation, at least in the permafrost of Siberia. Other creationists have concluded that the mammoths lived during the Ice Age and became extinct at the end of the Ice Age, as uniformitarian scientists also believe. Those who believe the woolly mammoths died at the end of the Ice Age are divided on whether there was a quick freeze or not. The quick freeze hypothesis will be discussed in the next chapter.

Undoubtedly, there were woolly mammoths as well as a great variety of other elephants living before the Flood. We should expect some of these types of elephants, including the mammoths, to have fossilized during the Flood. So, it is possible that mammoths could have been fossilized either during the Flood or after the Flood or both. The woolly mammoths that are the focus of this book are nearly all found in unconsolidated or frozen surficial sediments, indicating they lived during the Ice Age following the Flood (see appendix 4). This would include the frozen mammoth remains in Siberia, Alaska, and the Yukon.

Why Were the Lowlands of Siberia, Alaska, and the Yukon Unglaciated?

Since the woolly mammoths lived by the millions in Siberia, Alaska, and the Yukon, the question naturally comes up of how they could have lived there during the Ice Age. They actually inhabited unglaciated areas, which is a major mystery of the uniformitarian view of the Ice Age (see figure 2.3 on page 28). Climate simulations, using uniformitarian assumptions, often show these areas to be the *first to glaciate*.

In the post-Flood Ice Age model presented in this book, the lowlands would not glaciate because of the warm Arctic and Pacific Oceans. The Arctic Ocean, because of its polar latitude, would rapidly lose heat and moisture to the atmosphere, which would help warm the surrounding lands in the winter.

Newson (1973) demonstrated the dramatic climatic consequences of a warm Arctic Ocean by an atmospheric circulation simulation. He used a climate model to study the effects of removing the sea ice from the higher latitudes, but keeping the surface temperature of the Arctic Ocean at the freezing point of seawater. He ran the climate model with and without sea ice, leaving every other variable in the climate model the same. By comparing the two model runs, he discovered that winter atmospheric temperatures over the Arctic Ocean warmed 40 to 70°F (20 to 40°C)! Furthermore, the warmer temperatures spread to the adjacent lands (figure 14.1). The winter air temperatures over Siberia and Canada warmed 20 to 50°F (12 to 28°C).

If the temperature of the Arctic Ocean were much warmer than the freezing point of sea water, as in the post-Flood Ice Age model, the warmth of the air would have been significantly warmer than in Newson's simulation. Figure 14.2 shows how Siberia, Alaska, and the Yukon would have been warmed by the onshore flow of relatively warm air that was heated by warm water from the Arctic and North Pacific Oceans. The warm air would have kept the lowlands of Siberia, Alaska, and the Yukon from developing glaciers while the mountains of the area rapidly glaciated.

Mammoths Spread over Northern Hemisphere Early in the Ice Age

Since there was no ice to stop the mammoths spreading into Siberia, how did they spread to the rest of the Northern Hemisphere where we find their remains today?

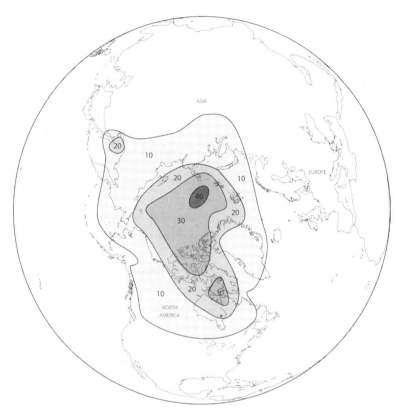

Figure 14.1. Winter temperature changes in centigrade at polar latitudes with just the removal of the Arctic sea ice cap, leaving the temperature of the ocean at freezing.

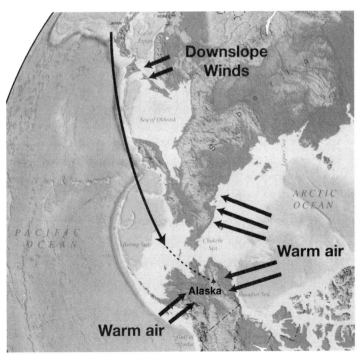

Figure 14.2. The main storm track is well off eastern Asia, with warm onshore flow from the air heated by the warm Arctic and North Pacific Ocean.

The woolly mammoth appears to have descended from one Genesis kind (see appendix 3 for an explanation of the elephant kind, including mammoths, within the new creationist subfield of baraminology). Whether two woolly mammoths descended from the ark, or whether the woolly mammoths developed from the genes of two elephants that had a large gene pool, they would have multiplied slowly after the Flood — at first. As the Ice Age progressed, their numbers would have increased rapidly due to the power of geometric progression. There was plenty of time for their population to increase to many tens of millions during a 700-year Ice Age (see boxed section later in this chapter). It would be no trouble for them to migrate into Europe and western Asia from the *mountains of Ararat*. The migration of the mammoths into the United States is the main challenge.

Once they made it to Siberia, they could eventually spread into Alaska. The Bering Sea and the Bering Strait, as well as the continental shelves around Siberia and Alaska, are very shallow. As ice collected on the land, the sea level dropped enough to provide a land bridge between Siberia and Alaska. The mammoths and many other animals spread from Siberia into Alaska and the Yukon over the Bering Land Bridge (Oard, 1990, p. 84–86). Accompanying them were the small mammals, like the shrew and the meadow mouse. Animals that cannot tolerate very cold conditions could have made it to North America by this route early in the Ice Age when the winter temperatures were much warmer than today.

From the Yukon Territory, the animals spread southeast through an ice-free corridor along the east slopes of the Rocky Mountains. Once into the state of Montana, the animals were free to multiply and spread all across the United States and points south. Figure 1.6 (page 19) shows the distribution of the woolly mammoth in the Northern Hemisphere during the Ice Age. The Columbian mammoth generally occupied the territory just south of the woolly mammoth distribution, as far south as the Central American country of Costa Rica (Agenbroad and Nelson, 2002, p. 22).

During this time of migration and dispersal, the climate of the entire Northern Hemisphere was characterized by mild winters and cool summers. Figure 14.3 is a schematic of postulated winter and summer temperatures for Siberia since the Flood. The small change in seasonal temperatures allowed the animals and plants that preferred a cold climate to mix with those that preferred a mild climate. These disharmonious associations are frequently found in Ice Age deposits, and explain another mystery of the Ice Age (see chapter 1).

THE ICE AGE ENVIRONMENT OF SIBERIA

In chapter 2, we established that the current environment of Siberia is very inhospitable to woolly mammoths and other mammals. How would the post-Flood Ice Age have been different to allow the mammoths to spread into Siberia and beyond?

After leaving the ark, the mammoths would have gradually grazed their way northeast, eventually reaching Siberia. When they arrived, the Ice Age likely had

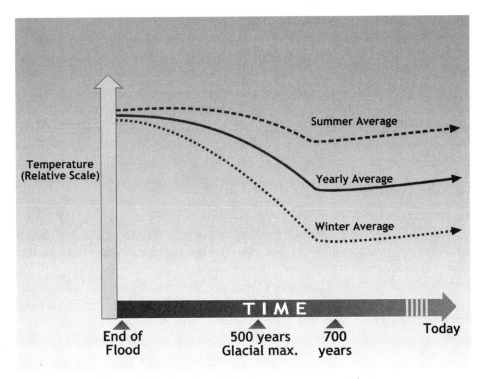

Figure 14.3. Postulated Siberian temperature with time.
(Drawn by Dan Lietha of AIG)

just begun. The Siberian winters would have been mild and the summers cool with little contrast between the seasons. The environment would have been much different than today, allowing the woolly mammoths to migrate in and through Siberia.

The deduction of mild winters is supported not only by the carcasses and abundant bones found in Siberia (see chapter 2), but also other data. The evidence is somewhat obscured by the tendency of scientists to simply pigeonhole evidence of warmth into supposed "interglacial" and "interstadial" periods (for example in Ukraintseva, 1981). Sher (1991, p. 215) states that an element of circular reasoning occurs in simply placing warmth indicators into interglacials:

> *This increases the danger of circular reasoning. For instance, it hardly would be correct to conclude that the last interglacial was the warmest in the region when such a conclusion was based on the sites where deposits are assigned to this age because they appear to represent the warmest climate in regional sequence.*

The indications of warmer winters includes: (1) large trees found in growth position within the permafrost of the far north (Quackenbush, 1909, p. 126; Kaplina and Lozhkin, 1984), (2) some plants associated with carcasses that grow more than

600 miles (1,000 km) to the south (Guthrie, 1990a, p. 185; Ukraintseva, 1981, 1993), (3) insects that belong in a significantly warmer climate (Matthews, 1974, p. 1364–1365; Kiselev and Nazarov, 1984; Berman et al., 1994), (4) many of the Siberian and Alaskan animals that survive today but live much farther south (Guthrie, 1990a, p. 310–311), and (5) the marine sediments in northern Siberia and Alaska below the mammoth steppe that contain a warmer fauna indicating water temperatures 7–14°F (4–8°C) warmer than today (Larsen, Funder, and Thiede, 1999, p. 6; Mangerud, Svendsen, and Astakhov, 1999). The vegetation in the stomach of the Beresovka mammoth was at first claimed to support the current tundra climate, but a re-analysis indicated some of it grew much farther south (Ukraintseva, 1993, p. 18). The vegetation that grows in Siberia today, such as buttercups, do also grow in a warmer climate.

The animals and environment of Siberia indicate the Ice Age climate began with mild winters (figure 14.3). A wetter climate would also occur immediately after the Flood due to the onshore flow of moist air from the Arctic and North Pacific Oceans (see figure 14.2). Since warm air holds more water vapor, and because copious evaporation would occur from the warm Arctic Ocean, the precipitation following the Flood would have been heavy in Siberia, Alaska, and the Yukon. This greater precipitation probably caused these regions to have been generally forested early in the Ice Age, a situation that apparently is verified by the finding of trees and *in situ* stumps within the surficial sediments.

As the Ice Age progressed, the Arctic Ocean would gradually cool off, resulting in significantly less evaporation. The cooling winter and summer temperatures would also result in a gradually drying atmosphere. Since summers would have been cooler than normal due to volcanic dust and gases, summer showers and thunderstorms would have been mostly suppressed. Usually, large-scale cool-season storms weaken in the summer, and since summer showers would be less than today, summers would by generally dry during the mid and late Ice Age period. Thus, the climate of Siberia would gradually dry with time since the start of the Ice Age (figure 14.4). The environment would change from a generally forested landscape to a vast grassland or steppe environment about midway into the Ice Age. A grassland is favored by relatively mild winter temperatures, abundant cool season precipitation, and dry summers, such as occurs on the high plains of North America today. Grass from a steppe environment is vegetation the mammals could eat, unlike the bog vegetation that grows there today. The mammals would have plenty of grass to eat over the wide expanse of Siberia. This scenario would solve what uniformitarian scientists call "the productivity paradox," a condition where way too many animals thrived for the amount of food thought to be available.

Even after the Arctic Ocean surface cooled to the freezing point of seawater, it would still not freeze over. (At the freezing point, Newson's simulation would be the most applicable.) There are a number of reasons for this, but this would largely be due to the difficulty of freezing salt water and because of the water circulation in the

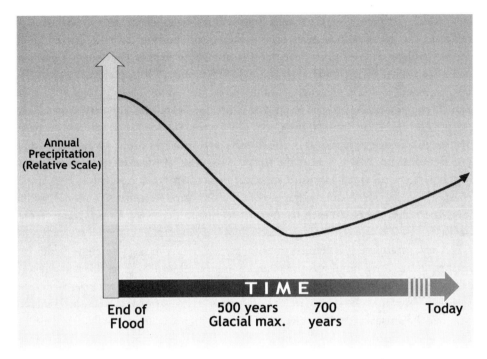

Figure 14.4. Postulated Siberian annual precipitation with time.
(Drawn by Dan Lietha of AIG.)

Arctic Ocean. The Arctic Ocean would most likely remain ice free throughout the Ice Age — until deglaciation when meltwater floated over the saltwater and froze.

No Permafrost at the Beginning

It is the permafrost, which is permanently frozen ground, in Siberia today that causes the bogs and keeps mammals from migrating into Siberia in the summer. With so many mammals in Siberia during the Ice Age, the winters must have been warm enough to inhibit the growth of permafrost.

Permafrost today is divided up into discontinuous and continuous zones. Discontinuous permafrost forms when the annual average temperature is around 30°F (-1°C), while continuous permafrost forms when the annual average temperature has fallen to 20°F (-7°C) or below (Washburn, 1980, p. 26). Continuous permafrost over the non-glaciated areas of Siberia probably did not occur until late in the Ice Age (figure 14.5).

Little or no permafrost during the early and mid Ice Age is unthinkable to uniformitarian scientists. However, there is substantial evidence that this was indeed the case. Many of the mammals that lived in Siberia would have had great difficulty walking on a boggy substrate, especially the woolly mammoth and saiga antelope (see chapter 2).

The saiga antelope with its small hooves is strong evidence for the lack of permafrost. The antelope now lives on the steppes of southern Siberia. Their highly specialized hooves favor open, level terrain and cannot navigate on boggy substrate or in deep snow (Sher, 1968; Harington, 1981). Sher (1968, p. 1252) notes: "*In the Pleistocene, as today, the saiga could not move over mushy, boggy ground or in deep snow.*" And yet, Ice Age fossils of saiga antelope are found throughout Siberia, even on the New Siberian Islands, in Alaska and in the Yukon (see figure 2.4 on page 30). In Alaska, they are found in the interior and near the Arctic Ocean. The only one found in the Yukon is near the Arctic coast, east of MacKenzie delta, indicating that the northwest Laurentide ice sheet delayed in developing along the Arctic coast. This delay seems anomalous within the uniformitarian Ice Age model, while it is expected in the post-Flood Ice Age model due to the warm Arctic Ocean to the north.

A few evolutionary scientists attempt to reconcile the saiga antelope fossils by reasoning that the ground was permanently frozen (Sher, 1968). In this way the antelope could run all over Siberia during the Ice Age. If the ground were permanently frozen, what would the saiga antelope and other animals eat? It is also questionable whether the animals could survive such a cold climate. Many animals that lived in the far north during the Ice Age now live much farther south in a more temperate climate.

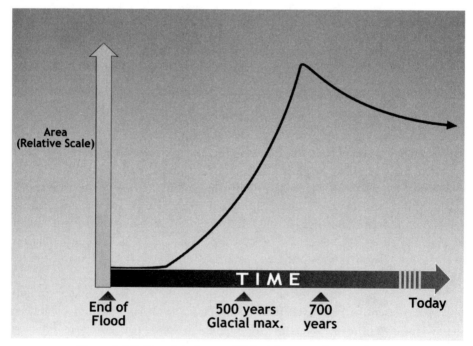

Figure 14.5. Postulated area of Siberian permafrost with time.
(Drawn by Dan Lietha of AIG.)

Beaver fossils and beaver-cut wood also indicate a lack of permafrost in Siberia, Alaska, and the Yukon during part of the Ice Age. (This assumes that the interpretation of beaver-cut wood is correct.) Quackenbush (1909) believes he discovered the frozen remains of a beaver dam in northwest Alaska. Beavers do not like permafrost, because only the top two feet melt during the summer and refreeze in the winter. Deep-burrowing animals, such as the badger and ferret, lived in Siberia during the Ice Age, providing further evidence that for a period of time there was no permafrost.

The most straightforward interpretation of the animal data is that the Ice Age winters were much warmer, and the permafrost did not developed until late in the Ice Age.

HIPPOS ASSOCIATED WITH WOOLLY MAMMOTHS AND REINDEER

Hippopotami are found together with reindeer and woolly mammoth fossils in northwest Europe (see chapter 1). This is probably the most dramatic example of a disharmonious association, but such associations were common during the Ice Age. The unique climate — mild winters and cool summers — during the post-Flood rapid Ice Age resulted in disharmonious associations.

Specifically, the situation of the hippos associated with cold climate animals can be explained by realizing that northwest Europe would have been bathed in warm onshore flow early in the Ice Age. The hippos would find an agreeable environment from which to spread across Europe and into southern England. As the Ice Age progressed and the ocean water cooled, the climate of northwest Europe would cool with time. Toward the end of the Ice Age the mountains and lowlands of the British Isles finally glaciated. During this time, the animals that preferred the cold migrated across another land bridge over the shallow southern North Sea and into southern England. There they mixed with the climatically stressed hippos occupying the area. This would explain how some of the cold-tolerant animals lived temporarily with the hippos and ended up being buried together.

Disharmonious associations still remain almost a complete mystery to uniformitarian scientists, but are anticipated in the post-Flood Ice Age model. However, uniformitarian scientists are not without hypotheses. Appendix 2 critiques the four main uniformitarian explanations for Ice Age disharmonious associations.

MAMMOTH POPULATION EXPLOSION

Around 10 million woolly mammoths lie buried in Siberia alone. With an Ice Age of only 700 years, people question whether that was enough time for them to have grown to such a large population. We can estimate the mammoth population explosion after the Flood by examining the reproductive habits of the African elephant.

Modern elephants are good analogs for woolly mammoths since it is likely that the mammoth is just one member of the elephant kind (see appendix 3).

The mammoth has a profile and size similar to the modern elephant, especially the Asian elephant (G. Haynes, 1991). The specialized tusks, trunk, and pillar-like legs are similar in both. Recently, a variety of the Asian elephant has been observed in Nepal with a massive hump behind its head and the characteristic sloping back typical of mammoths (Sarfati, 2000). The bones of mammoths have a comparable length to modern elephants but are more massive (G. Haynes, 1991, p. 22–24). Mammoth DNA is similar to elephant DNA (Höss, Pääbo and Vereshchagin, 1994). Preserved mammoth dung in caves and alcoves of the Colorado Plateau (Agenbroad and Mead, 1989) and stomach contents of Siberian mammoths indicate that elephants and mammoths had identical post-gastric digestion (G. Haynes, 1991, p. 59). It is therefore likely that the mammoth displayed similar social characteristics, reproductive strategy, growth pattern, and feeding styles as modern elephants (G. Haynes, 1991, p. 106).

The elephant reproductive rate can vary a fair amount (Laws, Parker, and Johnstone, 1975, p. 204–227). Elephants do not reach sexual maturity until they are 10 to 23 years old (Pilgram and Western, 1986). They live 50 to 60 years. McDonald (1984, p. 421,428) states that modern elephants usually have one calf per litter and give birth every 5 years, although the time can be shorter. Haynes (G. Haynes, 1991, p. 65) recorded that an elephant female can give birth from 3 to 9 years apart in Hwange National Park, Zimbabwa, resulting in 5 to 15 calves in a lifetime. Eltringham (1982) states that elephants generally produce a calf at intervals of 4 to 5 years with twins 1.35 percent of the time. However, some have suggested that elephants can give birth every 2 to 3 years, and there is a case of a zoo elephant giving birth 2 years and 5 months after its first birth (Eltringham, 1982, p. 86). If an elephant does not become pregnant right away, she has another cycle in 2 months. So she does not have to wait another 2 to 5 years, but can become pregnant soon after a failed pregnancy. Once pregnant, the gestation period is 21 to 22 months and the calf suckles for about 2 years. Based on tusk growth rate, Fisher (1996, p. 310) determined that mastodons can reach sexual maturity at 10 years old and give birth every 2 to 6 years.

The reproductive rate is especially enhanced in a favorable environment and when the population is low or the animals are being hunted regularly (Laws, Parker, and Johnstone, 1975; Eltringham, 1982, p. 84–88; Lee and Moss, 1986, p. 358; G. Haynes, 1991, p. 65; Ward, 1997, p. 219). There are no natural enemies for a mature elephant, except man (Ward, 1997, p. 132), but calves are subject to predation. Calf mortality rises during drought years, especially for males (Lee and Moss, 1986, p. 353). When a calf dies, the mother elephant conceives sooner than expected — around 20 months later (Lee and Moss, 1986, p. 358; Fisher, 1996, p. 310). Elephants are fairly adaptable to various environments (Ward, 1997, p. 133) and migrate short distances during the dry season in Africa. They are mostly grazers but can also browse leaves from trees

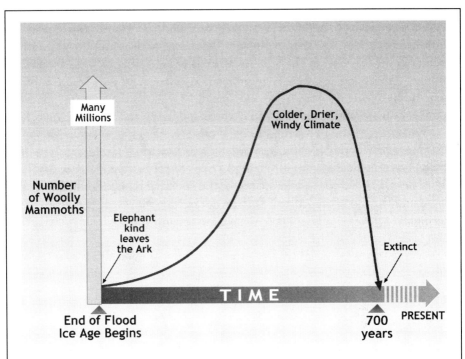

Figure 14.6. Flood to present woolly mammoth timeline.
(Drawn by Dan Lietha of AIG.)

and bushes (Eltringham, 1982, p. 92–96). So, the elephant is quite hardy and can potentially reproduce fairly quickly in a favorable environment.

Based on these variables, it would be difficult to estimate the growth of the woolly mammoth population during the Ice Age. A short cut is to estimate woolly mammoth doubling rate by comparing them to the reproductive rates for various herds of African elephants for which there is data. Haynes (G. Haynes, 1991) reports that in Hwange National Park, the elephant population increased from 13,000 to 22,000 in 20 years. This a doubling rate of about 25 years. This reproductive rate is in spite of poaching and drought. If mammoths increased at this rate, there would be eight million living mammoths within 550 years after the Flood (Sarfati, 1999). However, the elephant reproductive rate can be significantly faster. Mithen (1993, p. 170) states that population increases of 3 to 5 percent per year are commonly reported for African elephants. At a 4 percent rate, doubling about every 18 years, there would be 657 million mammoths in 500 years. Mithen (1993, p. 170) also reports that in Addo National Park, South Africa, the population increased 7 percent per year for 27 years, which is likely the maximum possible growth rate in Africa today. This is a doubling time of about 10 years, which is the estimate I had previously used for mammoths (Oard, 1990, p. 83). At this doubling rate there would be 1.3

billion mammoths living three hundred years after the Flood! This estimate probably is close to the mammoth reproduction rate, especially in the early years after the Flood when the number of predators was still small and the environment more ideal. So, there is no problem accounting for millions of woolly mammoths during a 700-year Ice Age. Figure 14.6 shows the time-line for the number of mammoths from the end of the Flood to the end of the Ice Age.

From the remains of mammoths in Siberia and Alaska, the mammoth population was apparently healthy with little sign of predation. Guthrie (1990a, p. 25) reports that most mammoths lived to a ripe old age based on teeth wear. The above reproduction rates are estimates for the potential number of mammoths living near the end of the Ice Age. They do not include the many more that lived during the Ice Age that could potentially have become fossils.

CHAPTER FIFTEEN

WERE SIBERIAN MAMMOTHS QUICK FROZEN?

The complete disappearance of the woolly mammoths and other animals that thrived during the Ice Age is a major mystery of paleontology. Based on the carcasses and the state of preservation of the stomach food, a quick freeze appears reasonable.

Many theorists have advocated a quick freeze to account for the frozen mammoths and other animals in Siberia, as well as the lowlands of Alaska and the Yukon. The quick-freeze hypothesis is an old idea, developed by scientists in the late 19th century (Digby, 1926, p. 51–55). Birds Eye Frozen Foods Company ran an experiment based on heat conduction and the state of preservation of the stomach contents. They concluded that the atmospheric temperature had to quickly fall below –150°F (–100°C) (Dillow, 1981, p. 383–396).

EVIDENCE AGAINST THE QUICK FREEZE

Despite its appeal, there is much evidence against the quick-freeze hypothesis (Oard, 2000b). One of the more obvious is the woolly mammoths of Siberia and elsewhere are associated with the Ice Age and not the Genesis flood (see appendix

Figure 15.1. A helicopter removes a block of permafrost believed to contain the Jarkov mammoth.

4). Most creationists who advocate a quick freeze (Dillow, 1981; Brown, 2001) believe it occurred at the onset of the Flood.

A second problem with the quick-freeze hypothesis is the very small number of carcasses compared to the number of decomposed mammoths that are entombed in the permafrost. In 1929, there were only 39 known carcasses of woolly mammoths and rhinoceroses (Tolmachoff, 1929, p. 20). Of these, only about a *half dozen* were fairly complete; most of the 39 animals consisted of only a few small remnants of soft tissue attached to the bones (Tolmachoff, 1929, p. 41). Since 1929, a few dozen new carcasses have been discovered, including the baby mammoth, Dima, found in 1977 (Stewart, 1977, 1979; Dubrovo et al., 1982; Guthrie, 1990a; Ukraintseva, 1993). Walter Brown (2001, p. 160–161) lists 58 carcasses as of 2001.

The Jarkov mammoth was excavated in north central Siberia in 1999 (Stone, 1999) and was widely publicized as a carcass encased in a block of permafrost in two Discovery Channel documentaries in 2000 and 2001. Figure 15.1 shows a helicopter pulling out a block of permafrost believed to contain the Jarkov mammoth. Unfortunately, upon thawing out the block, they found only a skeleton with a small strip of flesh.

Advocates of the quick-freeze hypothesis estimate that probably thousands of woolly mammoth carcasses are buried in the permafrost (Dillow, 1981, p. 328–334).

However, it is hard to determine how many carcasses still lie hidden in the permafrost. The ones that have been found represent rare finds that are usually discovered after a river has eroded its banks. Many more than Tolmachoff's figures have been found by the native Siberians, who are reluctant to report a carcass to the authorities or scientists because of their superstitions. These have been left to rot or are eaten by wolves or Arctic foxes. On the other hand, ivory hunters have *not* been afraid to report a mammoth carcass and have combed Siberia for several hundred years, reporting thousands of mammoth tusks but very few carcasses. Furthermore, even if a carcass is reported, until recently it was very hard to mount an expedition to retrieve it in the barren, almost impassible terrain of Siberia. Tolmachoff (1929, p. 41) estimated that the number of carcasses with some remaining soft parts is probably hundreds or possibly thousands of times more than was known in 1929. This would bring the possible number of carcasses up to about 50,000. This is still a small number, compared to the many millions that have been entombed in the permafrost. Thus, even if Tolmachoff's estimate is correct, the number of carcasses is still rare.

The scarcity of mammoth carcasses indicates that most died a normal death and decayed. Therefore, it is reasonable to conclude that nearly all of the mammoths and other animals died and decayed normally before, or while becoming interred in the permafrost (Sutcliffe, 1985, p. 113). This suggests that the rare intact carcasses are the result of unique circumstances.

Third, the carcasses often show evidence of partial decay (Sutcliffe, 1985, p. 113). The meat is not fresh as some people have asserted. For instance, the internal organs of the Beresovka mammoth had rotted away and the stomach was badly decayed when it was found (Lister and Bahn, 1994, p. 44). The Shandrin carcass found in 1972 was composed of a complete mammoth skeleton with some preserved internal organs and over 600 pounds (275 kg) of plant matter from the gastrointestinal tract (Ukraintseva, 1993, p. 67–80). The remainder of this mammoth had decomposed. Some of the abdominal parts of the Selerikan horse, found on the upper Indigirka River in 1977, were quite decayed by enzyme action (Guthrie, 1990a, p. 30). Much of the muscle tissue of the Yuribei mammoth, found in 1979, on the Yuribei River near the Arctic coast of northwest Siberia, was decomposed (Ukraintseva, 1993, p. 108, 134). If they had been quick frozen and rapidly buried, there should have been much less decay.

Fourth, fly pupae are often found associated with bones and carcasses (Péwé and Hopkins, 1967, p. 268–269; Sutcliffe, 1985, p. 113; Thorson and Guthrie, 1992, p. 221). This is a sign of an unsensational death and decay. Guthrie (1990a, p. 86) states that fly pupae are common in Alaskan Ice Age bones; some have been found wedged into the brain case. More than 1,000 blowfly pupae cases were found within the nasal cavity of one of the mammoth partial carcasses found at Colorado Creek, Alaska, in 1983 (Elias, 1992). It is unlikely these fly pupae were laid after modern exposure. Fly pupae should not be associated with bones and carcasses if death and burial were by a quick freeze.

Fifth, signs of scavenging are occasionally found on the newly retrieved carcasses. Guthrie (1990a) has discovered numerous signs of the scavenging of Blue Babe, the partial bison carcass found in the muck near Fairbanks, Alaska. The signs included bite and claw marks, probably from lions; pieces of bone and flesh scattered about the carcass; and a large tooth fragment embedded in the neck. Evidence of scavenging was also discovered on two partial mammoth carcasses from Alaska (Thorson and Guthrie, 1992). The Selerikan horse had no head, suggesting scavenging after death. Since the horse was in a general standing position with its hind legs lower than its front legs, Guthrie (1990a, p. 32) speculates the horse sank up to its neck in a bog and a carnivore ate its head (figure 15.2). The last frame in figure 15.2 shows how the horse was discovered by gold miners, who used the horse's hooves hanging from the ceiling to hold their lantern. The idea of a carnivore eating its head while stuck up to its neck is a reasonable conclusion. However, the surrounding sediments are not bog sediments, and besides, why didn't the predator also sink in the bog? An alternate possibility will be provided in the next chapter. How could the quick freeze hypothesis explain such scavenged carcasses?

Sixth, the animals preserved as carcasses appear to have died at different times of the year (Guthrie, 1990a, p. 1–44; Ukraintseva, 1993). A quick freeze would

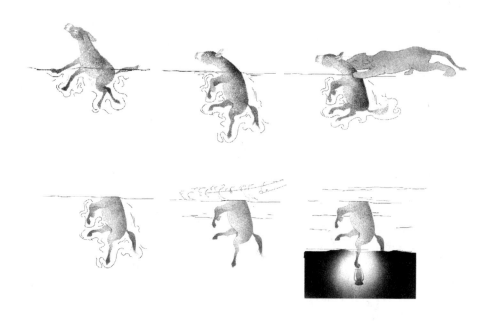

Figure 15.2. This series of illustrations demonstrates how Guthrie believes the Selerikan horse died and lost its head. Note that the carcass is in a general standing position.
(From Guthrie, 1990a)

be instant and in the same season. Indications as to the time of death include the type and seasonal development of its stomach vegetation, the condition of its pelt, the presence of insects, and the characteristics of the teeth and tusks. The famous Beresovka mammoth is believed to have died in late summer or early fall. Although somewhat controversial, numerous Alaskan mammoth teeth indicate most deaths happened during the winter (Guthrie, 1990a, p. 247). But the abundant fly pupae associated with one of the Colorado Creek, Alaska, mammoths, along with dung beetles in the mammoth dung from the site (dung beetles are only attracted to fresh dung), points to a summer death for this mammoth (Elias, 1992, p. 47).

The Selerikan horse died when herbaceous plants were in blossom, in late July or early August (Ukraintseva, 1993, p. 86). However, Guthrie (1990a, p. 31) thinks the horse died in late fall, based on its full winter coat and mature seeds found in its stomach. These differing opinions demonstrate the uncertain nature of some of this evidence or possibly the special environmental conditions of the area that are not according to uniformitarian expectations. The Mylakhchin bison, found in 1971, in the middle Indigirka River valley, probably died in early summer, deduced from the low amount of grass and herb fruits found in its gastrointestinal tract (Ukraintseva, 1993, p. 98–108). Ukraintseva (1993, p. 115) thinks the Yuribei mammoth died in early spring or late autumn when vegetation and flowering was not occurring. She also believes the evidence points to an early spring death for the Shandrin mammoth (Ukraintseva, 1993, p. 74). Based on its hair and fat, Guthrie (1990a, p. 81–82) concludes the bison carcass named Blue Babe died sometime during the autumn or early winter. A sectioned tooth from Blue Babe showed its summer growth was complete and that the winter annulus had not yet fully developed. Although Blue Babe had numerous signs of scavenging, there were no fly pupae or scavenging beetles, confirming it died in a cooler time of year (Guthrie, 1990a, p. 84, 86). Table 15.1 lists the probable seasons of death for many Ice Age mammals. Although

TABLE 15.1. ESTIMATED SEASONS OF DEATH FOR VARIOUS FROZEN CARCASSES

1) Beresovka mammoth — late summer or early autumn

2) Colorado Creek mammoth — summer

3) Selerikan horse — summer or autumn

4) Mylakhchin bison — early summer

5) Yuribei mammoth — early spring or late autumn

6) Blue Babe bison — autumn or early winter

7) Alaskan deaths — mostly winter

8) Shandrin mammoth — early spring

some of these conclusions are controversial, the bulk of evidence indicates different seasons of death for the carcasses, contrary to what would be expected in an instantaneous quick freeze.

A seventh piece of evidence against a quick freeze is most of the remains in Siberia are mammoths (Ukraintseva, 1993, p. 24). Many other types of animals that were fleeter of foot lived with the woolly mammoth, yet, many of these animals managed to escape. The most likely explanation is they migrated out of the area as the climate changed. This would have taken some time. A sudden drop in the temperature to below –150°F (–100°C) would freeze *all the animals in their tracks*. There should be a large number of other animals buried with the mammoths, if the quick freeze really happened. These seven pieces of evidence against a quick freeze are summarized in table 15.2. Taken together they add up to a strong case against the quick-freeze hypothesis (Oard, 2000b).

HOW ARE THE STOMACH CONTENTS EXPLAINED?

If all the above evidence suggests the mammoths were not quick frozen, then how can we explain the state of their gastrointestinal contents, the main evidence for a quick freeze?

Birds Eye Frozen Foods Company made their calculations based solely on heat conduction. Back in 1990, I suggested we examine other variables that may account for the state of preservation of the stomach contents (Oard, 1990, p. 131). The only evidence that another mechanism could have been involved was the discovery of preserved wood fragments from the stomach of a mastodon excavated in the warm country of Venezuela (Sutcliffe, 1985, p. 37). I should have followed up on my research at the time, since the likely solution to the question of the half-digested food in the stomach of a few woolly mammoth carcasses was already available.

The key, I believe, lies in the digestive physiology of the elephant, which can be used as an analog for the mammoth. Until the 1970s, little was known about their

---

TABLE 15.2. SUMMARY OF THE EVIDENCE AGAINST A QUICK FREEZE

1) Mammals associated with the Ice Age

2) Carcasses rare

3) Carcasses partially decayed

4) Fly pupae associated with bones and carcasses

5) Signs of scavenging

6) Different seasons of death

7) Remains mostly woolly mammoths

digestive system, and virtually nothing about the microbial aspects of digestion (van Hoven, Prins, and Lankhorst, 1981). This situation soon changed during elephant-culling operations in Kruger National Park in South Africa. Based on 50 freshly killed elephants, it was discovered that the main digestive process of elephants occurs *after* the food passes through the stomach, primarily in the cecum and colon (van Hoven, Prins, and Lankhorst, 1981; van Hoven and Boomker, 1985). Digestion is caused mainly by bacteria and protozoa, which each new-born elephant must ingest from the outside environment to start the process. The researchers found *no* protozoa and *no* fermentation in the stomachs of the culled elephants. Furthermore, very little hydrolysis of the cellulose was taking place in the stomach, although it had a very acidic pH of about 2. This high acidity is expected to partially degrade the stomach contents. Therefore, they found the *stomach is mainly a storage area before digestion* (Eltringham, 1982, p. 17). Gary Haynes (1991, p. 58) explains:

> *The digestive system is based on postgastric (hindgut) fermentation (Van Hoven and Boomker, 1985; van Hoven, Prins, and Lankhorst 1981). The stomach is large, but serves mainly to store ingested food. Enzymes within the stomach partly break down vegetation, but most nutrients are extracted in the huge cecum and large intestine, where microbes ferment the food remaining after gastric processing* (Van Hoven et al., 1981).

Horses and rhinoceroses, but not bison, are also hindgut fermenters. The bison is a ruminant. It is interesting that the plant remains in the Selerikan horse carcass were also partly decayed (Ukraintseva, 1993, p. 83), while the stomach contents of the Mylakhchin bison carcass were digested with the plant macro remains difficult to identify (Ukraintseva, 1993, p. 100). This difference is what would be expected based on the different digestive processes of these animals.

Partially Preserved Stomach Vegetation in the American Mastodon

Further evidence that a quick freeze is not needed to partially preserve stomach vegetation in animals with hind-gut digestion comes from the American mastodon (figure 15.3). Ice Age mastodon fossils are relatively common in the northeast United States. They are sometimes found in old bogs that are mainly composed of peat. Preserved vegetation from the gastrointestinal tracks of mastodons has been reported occasionally from these bogged mastodons in the northeast United States (Howorth, 1887, p. 289–303; Hapgood, 1958, p. 257–265; Lepper et al., 1991, p. 120). Recently the skeleton of a mastodon was discovered in peat on top of an Ice Age end moraine in Ohio (Lepper et al., 1991). The remains yielded a discrete, cylindrical mass of plant material found in association with the intact vertebrae and ribs. The gastrointestinal contents had a pungent odor with a floral content markedly different from the peat. Most of the macro remains could not be identified. However, seeds in

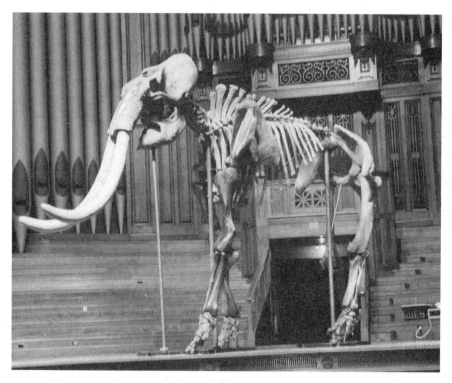

Figure 15.3. Mastodon skeleton.

the material indicated an early autumn death, which was reinforced by an analysis of the tusk dentin. Pollen analysis indicated 62 percent herbaceous types (i.e., grazing vegetation), which is interesting since the mastodon is thought to be predominantly a browser that eats leaves and small shoots from trees and bushes.

The discoveries of plant material associated with mastodons indicate that given the right conditions (in permafrost for Siberian mammoths and peat for mastodons), the stomach contents can be preserved in various states of decay. A quick freeze is an unnecessary hypothesis.

CHAPTER SIXTEEN

EXTINCTION OF THE WOOLLY MAMMOTH

Millions of woolly mammoths roamed the grassy steppes of Siberia, Alaska, and the Yukon by the middle of the Ice Age. They also spread into Europe and southern North America. Then suddenly, at the end of the Ice Age, they all disappeared. Dozens of other large mammals and birds also disappeared from continents or the whole earth. Why? I will focus mainly on Siberia and then discuss end Ice Age extinctions in other parts of the world.

HOW DID THE WOOLLY MAMMOTH DIE IN SIBERIA?

Many of the Siberian mammals likely died from the cold, wind, and drought that came during the deglaciation phase (Oard, 1990, p. 132). Only the most hardy and resourceful animals could survive for long. It is possible that the mammoth's woolly coat and plenty of dried grass gave them enough warmth and calories that they were able to slake their thirst by eating snow. Most of the available water was frozen. I tend to think that only the largest mammoths would have enough body mass to make this work. It helps a little that the woolly mammoths were able to handle some cold.

There is a question about how cold-adapted the woolly mammoths actually were, since a few scientists have claimed the mammoths lacked oil glands in their skin that would repel the water on their woolly coat. A wet woolly coat would be a powerful cooling mechanism to the animal. However, Russian scientists have shown that the woolly mammoth did possess oil glands to waterproof its wool (Stone, 2001, p. 100). The woolly mammoth did posses other features that are adaptations to a cold climate, such as long hair, small ears, a small tail, and a flap of skin over its anus. So, the woolly mammoth likely could take more cold than most other animals.

It is true that the climate tolerance of some animals is high. Horses live today in central Siberia, but ranchers help them to survive the winter. The reintroduced musk ox lives as far north as the northern Taimyr Peninsula and Wrangel Island, northern Siberia, which is a little warmer in winter than interior Siberia. But, there are limits to cold tolerance, even for the woolly mammoth. During the deglaciation period, the Siberian winter temperatures probably dropped about 20°F (12°C) colder than today. This bone-chilling cold would have even stressed animals that were well dressed for it.

Cold, wind, flooding, and drought can account for many of the mammoth deaths, but there is still the question as to how most of them became interred in the permafrost. There are several possibilities. The most-mentioned possibility is that the mammoths were trapped in bogs. Some undoubtedly were trapped in bogs (Coffin and Brown, 1983, p. 256–267). The position of the Selerikan horse suggests entrapment in a bog to Guthrie (1990a, p. 30–34). Bogs would have been caused by the summer melting of the permafrost. When the top foot or two (about half a meter) of permafrost melts in the summer, the water would pool since the permafrost below remains frozen. The large animals inexperienced with bogs could possibly have fallen into one. However, a bog may form year after year, and the animal trapped in the bog may never end up in the permafrost below the bog. Furthermore, large animals likely are strong enough to pull themselves out of a shallow bog (Guthrie, 1990a, p. 15). Since the bogs of Siberia would be shallow, a trapped mammoth would very likely not suffocate and end up in a standing position. Moreover, if the Siberian mammoths commonly died in bogs, there should be evidence in the form of peat or bog vegetation surrounding the bones. However, it seems that the vast majority of mammal remains are not surrounded by peat or bog vegetation.

During deglaciation, some of the animals would have been trapped by flooding rivers. Those that were trapped would have ended up in river terraces or flood plains that would be incorporated into the permafrost. Some animals lie buried in river deltas where they emptied into the Arctic Ocean. Ukraintseva (1993) provides evidence that the Khatanga and Shandrin mammoth carcasses were buried fluvially. Currently, there is evidence of catastrophic flooding in the upper Ob River basin of western Siberia on the scale of the glacial Lake Missoula flood (Oard, 2004a). The Ob River flood originated from a burst proglacial lake from the Altai Mountains of southwest Siberia (Baker, Benito, and Rudoy, 1993; Carling, 1996). Some animals surely must have been buried in this gigantic flood. The Berelekh mammoth cemetery in north-central Siberia contains the remains of more than 156 woolly mammoths and a few other types of animals. The cemetery is very likely a fluvial concentration, possibly a post-Ice Age lag from mammoths washed out of the nearby permafrost hills (Vereshchagin and Tomirdiaro, 1999, p. 193; Agenbroad and Nelson, 2002, p. 57–58).

Some mammoths appear to have perished in lakes (Mangerud, Svendsen, and Astakhov, 1999, p. 66). Abundant shorelines up to and around 300 feet (90 m) above sea level (Baker, 1997, p. 100; Svendsen et al., 1999) indicate there was a ponded Ice Age lake in the middle and lower reaches of the Ob River valley of western Siberia.

I believe the key to the majority of the well-preserved bones, tusks, and carcasses in the permafrost can be found in the *type of sediment* surrounding the woolly mammoths.

MAMMOTHS MOSTLY BURIED IN WIND-BLOWN SILT

According to those who have studied the deposits that contain most of the mammoth remains in Siberia, the vast majority of the animals are found in what are called "yedomas" (or "edomas") (Vereshchagin, 1974). The yedomas, a Yakut name, are hills with a high proportion of ground ice. They generally stand about 30–60 feet (10 to 20 m) high, but sometimes up to 200 feet (60 m) high (Vereshchagin, 1974, p. 5; Kaplina and Lozhkin, 1984). In Alaska, the material is called "muck" (Guthrie, 1990a). Muck is organic-rich deposits named by gold miners for the material above auriferous gravels in Alaska and the Yukon (Fraser and Burn, 1997, p. 1333). Vereshchagin (1974, p. 6) states that the yedomas contain a great profusion of mammal bones:

> *The great abundance of bones of large herbivores in the Yedoma is convincing evidence of the rich pasturage offered by this region during the Pleistocene. . . .*

Tomirdiaro (1982, p. 34) also states that there is a large number of mammoth, horse, bison, and even saiga antelope bones in yedomas. Hamilton, Craig, and Sellmann (1988, p. 950) write in regard to the muck of Alaska that is commonly found in the bottom of valleys:

> *Bones of large, extinct vertebrates, such as bison and mammoth, are common in the valley-bottom deposits, which generally contain abundant plant and animal remains.*

What type of sediment makes up the yedomas and muck? There has been a great deal of controversy and a number of hypotheses on the origin of yedomas and muck. Until fairly recently, the Siberian plains were considered regions of alluvial or lacustrine deposition (Tomirdiaro, 1982). Now it is accepted that the yedomas and

*Figure 16.1. Gold miners washing out muck (reworked loess)
to find gold in the gravel below.*

muck are composed of *loess* (Péwé, Journaux, and Stuckenrath, 1977; Tomirdiaro, 1982; Péwé and Journaux, 1983; Pielou, 1991, p. 151; Sher, 1995; Fraser and Burn, 1997). Loess is wind-blown silt mixed with a little clay and fine sand (figure 16.1). Vereshchagin and Tomirdiaro (1999, p. 190–191) state:

> *Of particular interest for paleozoologists is the "edoma."* . . . *This is actually a loess layer, as a rule containing the largest amount of remains of Late Pleistocene animals.*

Guthrie (1990a, p. 53) reinforces this observation:

> *Like most of the Soviet Far East, large expanses of Alaska and the Yukon Territory were not glaciated during the Pleistocene. Because these areas were bounded on several sides by enormous glaciers and glacial outwash streams, today much of Beringia [eastern Siberia, Alaska and the Yukon] is mantled with a thick deposit of eolian (wind-blown) silt called loess.* . . .

So, the vast majority of Ice Age animals are buried in wind-blown silt.

There is much support for a wind-blown origin for the sediments in yedomas. The lack of channels or channel deposits in the yedomas and vertical roots of herbaceous plants that often penetrate the entire thickness of the yedoma rules out a fluvial or lacustrine origin (Tomirdiaro, 1982). Loess in north central Siberia is about 30 to 115 feet (10 to 35 m) thick, but around 160 feet (50 m) thick near the Lena and Aldan Rivers of central Siberia (Péwé, Journaux, and Stuckenrath, 1977; Péwé and Journaux, 1983, p. 20). Loess is thickest near the rivers and thins in the uplands, typical of loess deposits elsewhere (Péwé and Journaux, 1983). Arkhipov (1997, p. 56) states:

> In eastern Siberia the aeolian loess cover containing ice veins is called "edo-ma" (loess-ice formation; Tomirdiaro, 1980; Bolikhovsky, 1987). The wind-blown sediments locally reach significant thicknesses (15–20 m) [45–65 ft.] and cover marine sediments of terraces III and alluvial deposits of terrace II. Similar loess deposits occur south of the permafrost zone (south of 60°N) in the inner regions of Siberia.

Alaskan and Siberian loess is similar (Péwé and Journaux, 1983). Stephen Taber (1943, p. 1473) says that the thickness of the silt in Alaska varies from a few inches to over 200 feet (60 m), but in some river valleys it is considerably thicker, probably due to downslope mass transport (Guthrie, 1990a, p. 53–58; Fraser and Burn, 1997, p. 1333). In unglaciated Alaska, the loess is as thin as an inch on the upper slopes, about 65 feet (20 m) thick on middle slopes, and as much as 115 feet (35 m) or more thick in the valley bottoms (Péwé, 1975, p. 34–43; Preece et al., 1999, p. 71). At least some of the loess apparently was deposited from unglaciated river valleys that were choked full of glacial silt during deglaciation. Today, loess is deposited downwind from braided rivers that drain glaciers (Walker and Everett, 1991).

However, there does not seem to be enough sources for the abundant loess in Siberia and Alaska. Besides glacial outwash deposits in river valleys, another possible source for loess is the wide, exposed continental shelves, at least until the shelves were flooded late in the deglaciation phase. The loess closest to the coast has a high salt content, giving credence to this prospect (Hopkins, 1982, p. 18–19). It is also possible that much mud was left on the land after the Genesis flood receded. This mud could have been reworked into wind-blown deposits at the end of the Ice Age.

The loess in Siberia has a fairly high organic content. It is composed of buried vegetation and peat layers, as well as animals (Fraser and Burn, 1997). Some trees were buried in loess and remain "in situ" as stumps (Taber, 1943, p. 1483–1484; Hamilton, Craig, and Sellman, 1988), while other trees and vegetation have slid downslope forming reworked loess, particularly in Alaska. Fraser and Burn (1997, p. 1342) state in regard to the peat layers within the loess:

> Numerous peat beds are horizontally continuous, with some containing tree stumps in growth position. Retransportation of some organic material is suggested by the unsorted nature of several portions of the unit. Commonly, such organic material is twisted and broken and has random orientations.

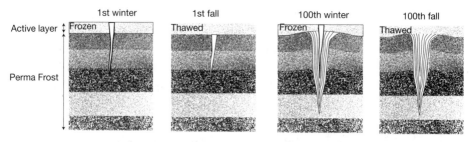

Figure 16.2 The development and enlargement of an ice wedge, if ice is still present, or an ice wedge cast, if the ice is melted.

This reworked loess that slid down hills in Alaska is what is called muck. The twisted, broken, and randomly orientated vegetation in the Alaskan muck probably is responsible for some of the exaggerations of some writers, such as Velikovsky. Upon thawing, the decaying vegetation in the loess gives off a stench.

HOW DID ICE DEVELOP IN THE LOESS?

The loess is rich in ground ice and ice wedges (see figure 16.2). The ground ice most likely developed within the silt through a segregation processes in which layers of ice and ice lenses formed (Taber, 1943; Guthrie, 1990a, p. 19–22; Michel, 1998). Silt has a porosity of greater than 50 percent (Washburn, 1980, p. 263), so silt is especially favorable for the formation of ground ice. Water flows too slowly in clay and too fast in sand for significant ice lenses and wedges to form. With silt, the water flow would be absorbed at the right pace to freeze against a barrier and build layers and lenses, as well as ice wedges. Walker and Everett (1991, p. 459) describe segregated ice in modern loess near Prudhoe Bay:

> *Silty deposits can develop large volumes of segregated ice, largely due to the platey structure common to these wind-blown deposits. Interstitial water moves by capillary action along moisture tension gradients to freeze into lens-shaped bodies of segregated ice ranging in thickness from a few millimetres to several metres. . . . Segregations of nearly pure ice in 1 m thick loess at Prudhoe Bay can account for between 10 and 70% of a given volume.*

The amount of segregated ice in Siberian loess can be quite large, up to 90 percent, with vertical ice veins about 30 feet (10 m) wide (Wright and Barnosky, 1984, p. xvii). Usually, the average amount of ice in the muck of Alaska is more like 50 percent (Taber, 1943, p. 61). Segregated ice is believed to have formed at the same time as the loess was deposited as a result of summer precipitation (Michel, 1998). The timing within the uniformitarian paradigm is late in the last glacial period. They judge the climate as being colder than it is today based on C-14 dating and oxygen isotope ratios (Mahaney et al., 1995).

It is likely the segregated ice and ice wedges gave vent to the myth that the mammoths are encased in ice. Otto Herz, one of the excavators of the Beresovka mammoth, was convinced that the animal had fallen into a crevasse within an ice sheet. The mammoths are entombed in silt, not ice (Guthrie, 1990a, p. 71), although segregated ice and ice wedges commonly surround their bones and carcasses.

How Does the Post-Flood Ice Age Explain
the Animals Buried in Loess?

As the climate cooled and dried, the animals likely were forced to move north to the warmer coastal regions where it was warmer in the winter. The Arctic coast was warmer because the ocean had not yet frozen over. This is because saltwater is difficult to freeze. Once deglaciation was well underway, fresh meltwater from the ice sheets and mountain ice caps poured over the denser saltwater. This started the rapid formation of sea ice. Sea ice would reinforce atmospheric cooling and drying by reflecting more sunlight to space and decreasing oceanic evaporation from the Arctic Ocean. As more of the ocean surface froze, the atmosphere would cool more, producing even more sea ice, just like a chain reaction. The amount of water poured out over the Arctic Ocean during glaciation would have been huge, since these rivers today are quite large. In fact, 10 percent of all water discharged from continental rivers into the oceans today occurs in the Arctic Ocean (Thiede, Kassens, and Timokhov, 2000, p. 366). During deglaciation, much more water than today would have poured out into the Arctic Ocean and frozen due to all the meltwater from mountain ice caps. The formation of sea ice over the entire Arctic Ocean could have probably taken only a few years. The freezing would be enhanced by a significantly smaller ocean early in deglaciation. At glacial maximum, the very wide continental shelf off Siberia and Alaska was not covered by water.

By the end of deglaciation, the coast would have been inhospitable. The weather had become so cold and dry that many animals had to either flee or die. The mammoths being less able to travel long distances over the developing permafrost and snow were unable to make it out of Siberia. Since most of the continental shelf was exposed early in deglaciation, animals would be able to herd to the relatively high points of the New Siberian Islands. At this time, these islands were connected to the mainland. Deglaciation would have been fast, even catastrophic. Sea level would have risen, sometimes catastrophically. It is likely that the large amount of animals on the Arctic continental shelf took refuge on the New Siberian Islands during rising sea level. They were eventually cut off from the mainland with little food. Massive amounts of mammoth bones are found on these islands as well as the coastal areas.

In the post-Flood Ice Age model, strong winds would have characterized deglaciation, especially during winter and spring (Oard, 1990, p. 109–119). Synoptic or large-scale wind is generally proportional to the subtropical-to-polar temperature difference, using the thermal wind equation (Oard, 1990, p. 46–49). Since the polar latitudes were much colder, the mid latitude westerly winds and the polar northeasterly winds would have been significantly stronger than today. In a dry environment, this would have caused an extraordinary amount of blowing silt and local sand. (Clay can be difficult to pick up by the wind, since it often forms a crust.) Large quantities of wind-blown material are observed as relic features of the Ice Age in many areas of the Northern Hemisphere and in the Ice Age portion of the Greenland and Antarctica ice cores. An extraordinary amount of blowing silt would be deposited from the combination of strong winds, dry climate, glacial silt particles from outwash areas, and probably the exposed continental shelves. It is known that mammoths and other mammals are entombed in loess in other areas of the Northern Hemisphere (Howorth, 1887, p. 102; Schultz, 1968; Vereshchagin, 1974, p. 6; Sutcliffe, 1985, p. 43). Table 16.1 is a summary of all the factors that would contribute to dry windy storms at the end of the Ice Age.

The wind deposition of mineral-rich loess would also reinforce the diverse grassland environment and hold off bog vegetation for a time (Zimov et al., 1995, p. 775). It would cover the thickening permafrost and allow the surface to drain during the summer. The areas of loess deposition today in northern Alaska show a greater variety of plants and tend to inhibit bog vegetation (Walker and Everett, 1987, 1991). Blowing silt would make the winter snow dirty, reduce the albedo, and contribute to rapid spring melting. This quick melting has been observed along the edge of roads in the Alaskan taiga and tundra that are covered by dust deposition from the road (Walker and Everett, 1987). It is also possible that the existence of so many mammals in Siberia helped reinforce the grassland environment by trampling the bog vegetation (Zimov et al., 1995). Plenty of grass would continue to keep the animals relatively healthy. However, the loess could hold off the bogs only for so long in a cooling climate. Eventually, the bogs would take over and the environment would change from a steppe to tundra. It is well known that in the wind-blown silts of Siberia, steppe vegetation occurs along with the mammal remains (Sher, 1991, p. 219; Zimov et al., 1995, p. 767; Fraser and Burn, 1997, p. 1342).

TABLE 16.1. REASONS FOR DRY, WINDY DUST STORMS AT THE END OF THE ICE AGE

1) Colder winters
2) Colder ocean
3) More sea ice
4) Drier atmosphere
5) Stronger N-S temperature difference

This changing environment probably accounts for the finding of a mixture of steppe and tundra vegetation in the stomachs of some of the carcasses and for the mixed pollen assemblage in the sediments around the carcasses (Ukraintseva, 1993).

After deglaciation, the summers and the winters became warmer (the post-glaciation climate could be what uniformitarian scientists call the Holocene hypsothermal). Deglaciation would account for the thawing that is widely recognized not only in Siberia and Alaska, but elsewhere south of the former ice sheets (Selby, 1985, p. 541–542). It is well known that there are relic permafrost features, such as ice wedge casts, south of where the Laurentide and Scandinavian ice sheets once existed. The permafrost in Siberia and Alaska according to Guthrie has melted northward (Guthrie, 1990a, p. 221). Melting reveals why the yedomas are now hills. The top of the permafrost melted in spots forming hollows, called alases. They are thermokarst features (Selby, 1985, p. 412–415), which Soffer (1985, p. 22) believes were caused by the melting of the Scandinavian ice sheet, while Sher (1997, p. 327) describes them as a catastrophic event after the Ice Age. Bones of mammals are concentrated at the bottom of the alases (Vereshchagin and Tomirdiaro, 1999, p. 188). This is known to occur during a thaw.

In Alaska, the situation would have been different because of the higher relief. Either while the loess was being deposited or during the great post-glacial thaw, much of the loess would have slid into the valleys and formed the "muck."

Gigantic Dust Storms Explain the Carcass Puzzles

How would dust storms explain the rare carcasses and the other carcass puzzles? As discussed in chapter 1, there are a number of puzzles associated with the carcasses that have precipitated a multitude of disputable conclusions. The carcass puzzles are: (1) some carcasses and skeletons found in a general standing position, (2) three woolly mammoths and two woolly rhinos suffocated, (3) millions of animals became entombed in rock hard permafrost, and (4) some mammals have broken bones. The strong, cold winds during deglaciation whipped up multiple dust storms that blew across Siberia. The dust storms varied in intensity throughout the deglaciation phase, but regardless, the dead mammals would have been buried fairly quickly. Quick burial explains the preservation of the many millions of bones and tusks of the woolly mammoths and other mammals, the third carcass puzzle.

I believe the preservation of carcasses and the explanation of the other carcass puzzles can be explained by the most fierce dust storms. The Dust Bowl era in the Midwest United States in the 1930s provides an excellent analog for conditions in Siberia at the end of the Ice Age (figure 16.3). Many dust storms of variable intensity occurred during the dust bowl era. An intense dust storm can produced drifts many feet (a meter or more) high, just like drifts in a blizzard. During the dust bowl, several accumulating storms partially buried houses and barns and covered machinery and fences (figure 16.4). Some cattle caught in dust storms breathed in so much dust that they suffocated, and newborn calves smothered in a matter of hours (Worster, 1979, p. 22).

It is possible that the dust storms at the end of the Ice Age in Siberia were so intense that some woolly mammoths may have suffocated from blowing dust before they were buried. Another possibility is that silt would have been deposited around the animal caught out in the storm in much the same way blowing and drifting

Figure 16.3. Approaching dust storm.

*Figure 16.4. Large dust drift to the top of a house
during the dust bowl era in the Midwest.*

snow gathers against a snow fence. It is possible that a woolly mammoth could have been completely buried and suffocated in one gigantic dust storm. As a result, some of these animals could have been left in a general standing position, braced by the dust around them, as well as suffocated, which seems to be the case with the Beresovka mammoth.

Is there any proof from the carcasses that they died in dust storms? Other than the sediment surrounding the mammoths, there is little evidence from the carcasses, themselves. This lack of evidence is probably because the researchers have not looked for dust in the lungs area, or the evidence could have been obscured because of the surrounding loess. However, the baby mammoth, Dima, does provide possible evidence of suffocation in a dust storm. Guthrie (1990a, p. 14) states:

> *Mud in the gastrointestinal tract, silt in the respiratory system, and skeletal parts of Coleopteran beetles are incongruent with death in winter.*

Although uniformitarian scientists are blind to the possibility of death during a dust storm, they do consider the observation of silt and mud within the carcass a puzzle.

Burial in loess would also account for how the animals were interred in the developing permafrost. An animal covered by silt could be frozen fairly quickly, if the dust storm were caused by a cold front. Once a carcass was covered, the freezing temperatures from the permafrost below would move *upward* and the cold air would cool the carcass *from above*. A carcass would not have to be forced downward into rock-hard permafrost, as Howorth thought, but the permafrost would have formed around it.

The preservation of the mammoths and other animals would vary, depending upon the exact conditions and speed of the process. The preserved carcasses could simply be those rare carcasses that were rapidly buried by the most fierce dust storms and frozen quickly enough to preserve the flesh and stomach contents. The cold would also slow decay by keeping bacteria counts low (Farrand, 1962). Taber (1943, p. 1489) states:

> *Decomposition of organic matter is brought about almost entirely by bacteria which are relatively scarce in cold climates.*

So the freezing of the carcasses could take several days and still leave the stomach contents only partially decayed.

Since the top foot or two (about half a meter) of the ground melted each year, a number of buried animals close to the surface would have thawed out and rotted, especially if the yearly deposit of loess was thin. This probably is what happened to the Shandrin mammoth, which is composed of bones and the stomach area but no muscle tissue. The muscle tissue could have thawed one or several times and decayed before the final burial in silt. Either because of thawing or by not being buried deep enough in loess, the vast majority of the animals would have decayed naturally, leaving only bones and tusks. Since bones and tusks are more durable, they could have undergone several freeze-thaw cycles before their final deep burial in loess. Since the number of cycles varied, the preservation of the tusks would vary as well. Predictably, the number of carcasses and the preservation of tusks increases northward (Taber, 1943, p. 1490).

Burial in dust storms instead of bogs, explains why the Selerikan horse was missing its head. Instead of having only its head exposed from a bog, as Guthrie surmises, the animal could have been buried in a dust storm with only its head showing. Then, a carnivore came and ate what was exposed. An analysis of the surrounding sediments and vegetation favors entrapment in wind-blown silt and not a bog (Ukraintseva, 1993, p. 89).

Time Is Not a Side Issue

Uniformitarian scientists do not recognize the significance of this wind-blown silt as a solution of the many mammoth mysteries. This is because they stretch the deposition of the loess over thousands of years bringing it to the point of insignificance. Guthrie (1990a, p. 78) states:

> *These [large bones] could not be preserved by a few millimeters of annual eolian loess-fall; their preservation required large quantities of reworked silt.*

Vereshchagin (1974, p. 6) corroborates with a much more generous, but still inadequate, annual loess deposition:

> *One important factor was the fall of loess on the cold wet ground. However, this deposition could hardly have exceeded 2–3 cm [one inch] a year and, at that rate, it would have taken 20–30 years to cover a mammoth, during which time the bones and tusks would have been almost entirely destroyed by atmospheric processes.*

In the creation-Flood Ice Age model, the total loess deposition is compressed into *a few hundred years or less*, making loess deposition much more significant for the burial of mammoths. Time is not a side issue in creationist explanations for major mysteries of the past. I have often found that a short time scale is *the key* in providing reasonable solutions to long-standing mysteries of the past. Uniformitarian scientists will continue in their struggle to solve the riddles of the Ice Age and the woolly mammoths because of their dedication to present process over long ages.

The Explanation for the Broken Bones

The fourth puzzle is the broken bones found in the Beresovka mammoth and the Selerikan horse.

The bones could easily have been broken by shifting of ground ice and frozen sediments, either during formation or afterward (Guthrie, 1990a, p. 4). In other words, the breaks could be a post-mortem effect caused by shifting permafrost. Vereshchagin and Tomirdiaro (1999, p. 188) state:

> *After burial in the permafrost the organic remains could have shifted vertically within a wide range owing to their physical properties and the features of the permafrost environment. . . . It is now known that in frozen ground bones and pieces of wood are sometimes shifted vertically(!) by 10–15 m [30–50 feet] along the boundary of the frozen ground and ice veins.*

Sher (1995, p. 39) points out that the yedoma ice complex is known to be prone to plastic deformation.

Although some researchers lean toward such a post-mortem explanation, which makes sense, there was considerable blood near the wound of the foreleg in the Beresovka mammoth (Pfizenmayer, 1939, p. 104). Bleeding had occurred between the muscles and the fatty connective tissues, indicating the leg was broken *while the animal was still alive or right after death.* For an explanation of the broken foreleg, we can refer to another mammoth graveyard as an analog. This graveyard is at Hot Springs, South Dakota, where 52 mammoths have been excavated from an ancient sinkhole. Some of these mammoths also had broken forelimbs. Note the two reasons given by mammoth expert Larry Agenbroad and colleague (Agenbroad and Laury, 1975, p. 24) for the broken limb bones:

> *The processes that would provide such breakage are limited to only two, exclusive of human activity: (1) torsional stress, as provided by trying to extricate a limb mired in mud, muck, quicksand, etc., probably even enhanced by an accompanying accidental fall; or (2) the possibility of trampling of recently deceased animals by newly entrapped individuals.*

We can safely eliminate man and trampling in a Siberian dust storm. That leaves the first explanation. Mammoths standing against an unusually severe dust storm would find themselves mired in very deep loess. If they had not yet suffocated they would try valiantly to extricate themselves. The torsional stress could break limbs, especially the more mobile front limbs.

In summary, Figure 16.5 presents a series of illustrations summarizing the carcass puzzles.

Mass Extinctions at the End of the Ice Age

By the end of the Ice Age, the woolly mammoths had disappeared from Siberia. The woolly mammoth also went extinct over the whole Northern Hemisphere (see figure 14.6 on page 147 for a time-line of the woolly mammoths from the end of

Figure 16.5. The mammoth is completely buried by a dust storm and breaks its front leg while trying to free itself, A to I. Further dust storms smooth the surface of the dust drift, J. Then water moves upward in the silt, J through N. The water and silt become permafrost, O, and then the permafrost faults, P, further breaking bones in the mammoth.

(Drawn by Dan Leitha of AIG.)

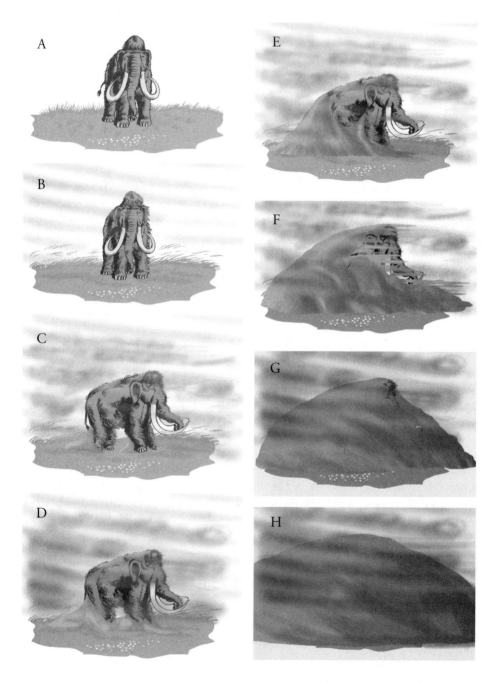

the Flood to the end of the Ice Age). Agenbroad and Nelson (2002, p. 87) state: "Why did mammoths disappear from Earth? This question remains one of the great unsolved mysteries of all time."

Most of the other large mammals also became extinct or died off on whole continents at the end of the Ice Age. For instance, horses and camels of Ice Age North America disappeared, but survived on other continents. Horses were introduced in recent times by Europeans. Such mass extinctions are especially perplexing to uniformitarian scientists, and there is much controversy over the cause, as outlined in chapter 5.

A multitude of remains prove woolly mammoths and other animals had thrived and migrated over the entire Northern Hemisphere at the beginning of the Ice Age. The climate was equable (little change between winter and summer) and the plants and animals represented a mix of different climatic types. The post-Flood Ice Age model can not only explain the disharmonious mixing of animals, but can also explain the dramatic climate changes that brought their demise.

The animals were accustomed to mild winters for most of the Ice Age. When the cold came at the end, they likely were not prepared. They would have required extra food to keep themselves warm. In addition to suffering from the cold, the ice sheets were melting and causing occasional superfloods. They also had to contend with gigantic dust storms, boggy ground from permafrost at the edge of the ice sheets, drought, grass fires, etc. The woolly mammoth and other large herbivores would be especially hard hit, partly because they required so much more food and water. They would be tottering on the edge of extinction within a short time. Carnivores and carrion birds would have their fill for a time, but as their food source died, it would be their turn to go extinct. The end Ice Age mass extinctions were selective in that mainly large animals went extinct. The mass extinctions should really be called the extinction of the massive (Stone, 2001, p. 102).

There is abundant evidence of severe drought and giant dust storms after the zenith of the Ice Age. The severe dust storms were probably the major cause for all the extinctions in the Northern Hemisphere. (Drought likely was the major climatic culprit in the Southern Hemisphere.) Loess is rather common south of and within the periphery of the former ice sheets in the Northern Hemisphere. It forms a thick blanket in parts of central China (Williams et al., 1998, p. 179). This was probably desert loess that blew in from the west. Unfortunately, it has not been recognized, yet, that large parts of Siberia are also covered with a layer of loess (Williams et al., 1998, p. 179). In North America, we find large areas of stabilized sand dunes, for instance extensive sand dunes cover areas of the Great Plains (Muhs and Holliday, 1995). The Nebraska sand hills blanket a large portion of western Nebraska and are up to 400 feet deep! Similar dunes are found north of the Cypress Hills in southeast Alberta and southwest Saskatchewan. Dunes are common in northern Europe and northwest Asia (Zeeberg, 1998). Today, all of these dunes are mostly stabilized by vegetation. The dunes attest to the severity of the drought and dust storms during deglaciation. The climate in North America was so terrible that even camels and horses were driven to extinction! But other large mammals, such as elk, deer, and bison survived. It is not known why they survived while others went extinct. Could it be that elk, deer, and bison can live in more variable habitats, such as mountainous terrain with more moisture, while those that went extinct lived mainly on the plains?

Man, who had spread over the earth by this time (see chapter 13), was also stressed. Earlier he had found abundant game, but the climate change made hunting more difficult. Some have suggested that man caused the extinctions. It is questionable whether a hunting party could have taken down a large healthy mammoth with spears. Driving them off cliffs or into bogs would make more sense. When the animals were in a weakened state, they would have been easier to kill. Mammoths and other animals often were forced to congregate around scarce watering holes during end Ice Age drought, as C. Vance Haynes (1991) and others believe. These watering holes would be ideal spots for man to hunt the mammoths.

So, man contributed a *little* to the extinction of the mammals. The climate change was the real culprit, by far. The minor role of man is supported by the relatively scarce association of mammoth remains with spear points, indicating there was no mass slaughter. Most researchers are unconvinced that man could have caused the extinctions in Siberia. There were far too many woolly mammoths, woolly rhinoceroses, horses, bison, and other animals for them to have had a significant effect.

Uniformitarian scientists do not see a unique climate at the end of the Ice Age as being the cause of multiple extinctions. This is primarily because of their stretched out time scale. This has kept the mystery of end Ice Age mass extinctions unsolved for over 200 years! By compressing the time scale into a 100- to 200-year period, the extensive sand and loess deposits over many areas of the world indicate a major disaster, far worse than the storms of the Dust Bowl era in the 1930s.

In conclusion, climate change at the end of the Ice Age was the main cause of late Ice Age extinctions. A post-Flood Ice Age explains why the large animals did not go extinct at the end of previous glaciations. *There were no previous glaciations or interglacials.* There was only one Ice Age, brought on by the unique conditions that followed the global Flood.

When we apply the Genesis flood and the biblical timetable to objective scientific evidence, confusion clears, mysteries are solved, and God is glorified.

THE CONFUSION OF ELEPHANT AND MAMMOTH CLASSIFICATION

Mammoths are part of the order Proboscidea, or elephant order. The order was named from the word *proboscis*, meaning "long, flexible snout" or trunk. There are only two living representatives of Proboscidea, the African and Asian elephants. Many other types of elephants are found as fossils, including mastodons and gomphotheres (Shoshani and Tassy, 1996). A particular type of mastodon, *Mammut americanum*, accompanied the mammoth into North America during the Ice Age. However, it is believed the mammoths and mastodons in North America lived in different habitats — mammoths preferring open grassland and mastodons favoring forested areas.

PROBOSCIDEA CLASSIFICATION

All of the animals in the order Proboscidea in general look like types of elephants. They mostly vary on the shape of the tusks, the details of the teeth, and the number and location of their tusks (Shoshani and Tassy, 1996). The gomphothere is an interesting elephant type. It has *four* tusks, two small ones extending out from the upper jaw, typical of nearly all Proboscidea, and two that spread downward from the lower jaw. One type of gomphothere has two broad lower tusks that are *shovel shaped*.

Ever since the beginning of the science of biology, scientists have attempted to group animals into categories. The groups were based generally on the way the animals looked or by their morphology. Carolus Linnaeus was the first to provide a major classification of living animals about 250 years ago, starting with the kingdom and ending with the variety (table A1.1). The second lowest level, the species, is supposed to be an interbreeding unit in nature that produces viable offspring.

TABLE A1.1
CLASSIFICATION SYSTEM

1) Kingdom
2) Phylum
3) Class
4) Order
5) Family
6) Genus
7) Species
8) Variety

There are problems defining a species for several reasons. For many organisms, sex is irrelevant; there are no males and no females. Furthermore, biologists do not know how most living things reproduce in the wild (Tangley, 1997). Some types of organisms may look similar, but do not breed. There have been a number of surprises when supposedly separate species that do not normally breed in the wild, have mated and produced offspring in zoos. This brings up the question of what really is an interbreeding unit. Biologists have learned over the years that animals that can potentially breed do not normally mate because of various non-genetic factors, including physical appearance, social behavior, and different habitats.

When scientists applied Linnaeus's system to fossils, they encountered many problems. Sometimes a fossil is only a scrap, such as a piece of jaw or teeth, and secondly, there appears to be much more variety with fossils than there is in living animals. The worst problem is that the test of interbreeding to determine the boundaries of a species can never be applied with fossils. The resulting classification criteria become quite nebulous and subjective. There are biologists who favor making any variation in teeth or bone a different species. These are called the splitters, who multiply the number of species. Then there are the lumpers, who accept a fair amount of variety for their definitions of species, genus, family, etc. These two groups have battled for years.

There are several methods now employed for classifying organisms. Since any one organism has hundreds of characteristics that can potentially be used to compare with other organisms, the biologists must decide which characteristics are important. This can be rather arbitrary. Those characteristics that are not important, but similar in organisms that are classified far apart, are attributed to parallel or convergent evolution. Such a similarity in organisms classified far apart is attributed to animals living in similar environments. These animals supposedly develop similar structures in similar environments. This concept is questionable because there is an abundance of different variables on both the regional scale and the microscale that make up any one environment, and it is doubtful that any two environments would be close enough over millions of years to produce similar structures.

Scientists who classify animals, called taxonomists, have run into numerous problems in attempting to group the various elephants (Shoshani and Tassy, 1996). It seems that the splitters have had a "hey-day" with the multiplication of species within the order Proboscidea (Maglio, 1996). Fox and Smith (1992, p. 3) state:

> In all, Webb clarifies the often cumbersome elephant taxonomy, with its long "splitting" tradition in nomenclature. . . .

Many subjective elements are inherent within the classification system, as indicated by the recognition that *parallel evolution* and intra-taxon variability are widespread phenomena (Todd and Roth, 1996). So, the art of classifying the elephants is difficult. Tassy and Shoshani (1996, p. 3) state their frustration over the whole

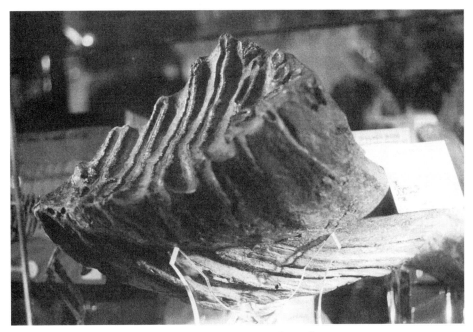

Figure A1.1. Mammoth tooth.

enterprise: *"The classification and phylogeny of proboscideans is a never-ending academic game. . . ."*

The main classification criterion for Proboscidea, as well as other animals, is the shape of the teeth (G. Haynes, 1991, p. 3; Tassy and Shoshani, 1996, p. 6). As stated in a recent conference that Foronova and Zudin (1999, p. 104) attended:

> *The wide dispersal of elephants into the vast territories of Eurasia and North America in the Pliocene and Pleistocene led to the appearance of a large variety of forms. The group systematics, based partly on cranial features and mainly on molar structure, are complicated and often confused.*

How well do teeth serve as a classification scheme? The literature indicates that the answer is *not very well*. The crowns of African elephant molars are diamond shaped, while in the Asian elephant they are composed of thin parallel ridges, called lamellae, that are similar to mammoths (figure A1.1) (Redmond, 1993, p. 22). There is also a fair amount of variability within the two types of modern elephant teeth (Todd and Roth, 1996, p. 201–202). To indicate how arbitrary and subjective the use of teeth can be in classifying Proboscidea, there is a case reported in the literature of one fossil mastodon from Spain that exhibited teeth from two different "families" of Proboscidea:

> *If these teeth had not been found in the same mandible, it is more than*
> *probable that they would not only have been attributed to two different genera,*
> *but to two different families* (Mazo, 1996, p. 142).

What does this say about employing teeth to classify species, especially when taxonomists argue over fine details of teeth morphology?

Obvious evidence that the splitters have gone wild is that the two types of living elephants, the African elephant, *Loxodonta africana*, and the Asian elephant, *Elephas maximus*, are classified into *two different genera*. There is even talk of adding a second species within the African elephant genus, based on mitochondrial DNA (Day, 2000). However, it is known that the two genera of modern elephants can *interbreed successfully*, which is normally one of the tests for determining varieties within one species.

This successful mating occurred only once (Lowenstein and Shoshani, 1996). It happened in the Chester Zoo in England between a male African elephant and a female Asian elephant. The male offspring, named Motty, died 10 days later of a disease (necrotic enterocolitis). Hybrid offspring do not occur in the wild because the range of the African and Asian elephants does not overlap in nature. Hybrids are more likely to occur in zoos, but generally, a zoo that owns both genera of elephants would not house them together. Based on the definition of species, the two living genera of elephants should probably be classified as *one* species.

The example of the successful mating of the two living genera of elephants indicates that many other elephants should be classified into the same species. The diamond shape of the African elephant teeth resembles the teeth of the Ice Age American mastodon, commonly found in surficial sediments in the northeastern United States. There are not many other differences between these two animals. The thin parallel ridges of the Asian elephant resemble the teeth of mammoths (G. Haynes, 1991, p. 3–9). Besides more hair, the differences between the woolly mammoth and the Asian elephant are minor. This suggests the likelihood of interbreeding capabilities of American mastodons and mammoths.

Mammoth Classification

Mammoths are a genus within the order Proboscidea and have the same classification problems as with other elephants. It is believed by geologists and paleontologists, who study fossils, that the order Proboscidea evolved about 50 million years ago from northern Africa (G. Haynes, 1991, p. 3–9). The first mammoths are thought to have appeared in Africa four million years ago and spread northward and evolved in Eurasia and North America. Evolutionists believe the woolly mammoth is one of the last species to have evolved from other types of mammoths in Siberia as a result of the extreme cold (Lister and Bahn, 1994).

The taxonomy of mammoths is usually split geographically into a Eurasian and a North American group. The classification scheme is based mainly on such variables as molar hypsodonty (height of a crown), number of lamellae (ridges on the crown), and enamel thickness. History shows there are a multiplication of mammoth names, and when similar types are discovered in Eurasia and North America, the similarity is attributed to the vague and seemingly unreasonable concept of "parallel evolution" (Dudley, 1996, p. 290; Lister, 1996).

True to form, there is significant within-species variability to explain similarities between two supposedly different species, applying such adjectives as *an advanced or primitive character* (G. Haynes, 1991, p. 6; Lister and Bahn, 1994; Lister, 1996; van Essen and Mol, 1996, p. 219; Roth, 1996, p. 252; Dudley, 1996). Harington and Shackleton (1978, p. 1282) point out some of the problems with the mammoth classification scheme:

> *Finally, we wish to point out problems concerning the relationship of North American and Eurasian mammoths. In North America, how can Columbian mammoths be separated adequately from imperial mammoths, and how can "advanced" states of the Columbian mammoth (e.g.,* Mammuthus columbi jeffersoni*) be separated from woolly mammoths? How can imperial and Columbian mammoths of North America be differentiated from the steppe mammoths of Eurasia* (Mammuthus armeniacus)?

It is likely that all mammoths should be classified as one species, or at least within one biblical kind. Furthermore, I would include all the member of the order Proboscidea within one Genesis kind (see appendix 3). In general, there seems to be two main varieties, or subspecies, of mammoths on both continents. The woolly mammoth, *Mammuthus primigenius*, is one variety that is relatively small, about 9 to 11 feet (about 3 meters) tall and weighing about 12,000 pounds (5,500 kilograms). It is found in both Eurasia and North America. The second variety, for simplification, will be lumped together from both Eurasia and North America and referred to as the Columbian mammoth, *Mammuthus columbi*, which is about 13 feet (4 meters) tall and weighs 20,000 pounds (9,100 kilograms). The woolly mammoth generally favored the north, and the Columbian mammoth ranged mostly across the southern part of the mammoth range. There was overlap at the north-south boundary of the ranges, and there seems to be a continuum between the two varieties of mammoths. Haynes (G. Haynes, 1991, p. 6) sums it up:

> *However, there may be a gradient [continuum] based on body size and tooth morphology that could indicate that* M. columbi *and* M. primigenius *were not descendants of two entirely separate dispersals. . . . No clear differences in postcranial morphology distinguish the two species; enamel thickness is considered partially diagnostic, but individual teeth and even parts of a given tooth have variable enamel thickness.*

APPENDIX 2

POSSIBLE EXPLANATIONS FOR DISHARMONIOUS ASSOCIATIONS

There are four possible explanations for the unique mix of cold- and heat-loving animals that were common during the Ice Age: 1) seasonal migration, 2) increased climatic tolerances, 3) the mixing of glacial and interglacial fossils, and 4) an equable climate with cool summers and mild winters (Grayson, 1984a, p. 17–20).

SEASONAL MIGRATION

A few scientists have opted for seasonal migration, but this hypothesis has never made it very far. Scientists have pointed out that the hippopotamus could not have migrated very far during the summer, even if the temperatures were warm enough to lure the animals to England (Grayson, 1984a, p. 17). Many of the disharmonious animals are small and are not expected to have migrated. Problems have already been noted for the suggestion that woolly mammoths migrated into Siberia during the summer (see chapter 2). Plants and insects do not migrate but can spread into new territory over time.

INCREASED CLIMATIC TOLERANCE

One difficulty with using extinct, or even living, animals to infer disharmonious associations is that the climatic tolerances of most animals are rarely known (Cole, 1995, p. 132). It is recognized that most animals are more climatically elastic than their current habitats would suggest (Howorth, 1887, p. 132). Tigers, for example, can live in cold as well as warm climates. The Siberian tiger lives in east central Asia (Howorth, 1887, p. 133). Vereshchagin and Baryshnikov (1984, p. 510) state:

> At the beginning of the twentieth century in the USSR the tiger occurred in Transbaikal [south central Siberia], along the courses of central Asiatic rivers, in the Far East, and the Amur Valley. Occasional individuals were encountered in the southern part of western Siberia and Yakutia [north central Siberia].

Some had argued that the hippo, found in northwest Europe during the Ice Age, was cold adapted, but this has been dismissed by most (Grayson, 1984a, p. 16), although the hippo is known to handle cool weather for short periods of time in English zoos (Howorth, 1887, p. 133).

Despite the wider range of climatic tolerances for animals, one cannot use this unknown factor to dismiss too many disharmonious associations. Disharmonious associations are so common that they cannot all be attributed to a greater tolerance to cold or heat. Furthermore, some of the fossils have living representatives whose climate tolerance is well known, such as holly, ivy, and water chestnuts. Fossils of these plants occurred in the British Isles during the Ice Age, while today they are normally found farther south (Stuart, 1982, p. 15).

MIXING

Mixing of glacial and interglacial deposits is a common explanation for the hippopotamus fossils alongside of cold-adapted animals in northwest Europe (Stuart, 1982, p. 90; Sutcliffe, 1985, p. 24). Interglacials are the periods between ice ages according to the standard uniformitarian understanding of the Pleistocene epoch. Each ice age is believed to have lasted 100,000 years and repeated cyclically over the past one million years. Between 1 million and 2.4 million, the ice ages are believed to have cycled every 40,000 years. During the 100,000-year cycle, an interglacial is supposed to last only 10,000 years, while the glacial phase is 90,000 years. According to their theory, since the last ice age ended somewhere between 10,000 and 20,000 years ago, the next ice age is due soon. The interglacial climate we now enjoy is supposed to be waning. Previous interglacials can be thought of as having a similar climate to today (Stuart, 1991, p. 546). So, animals that prefer the cold would live in England during glacial time and animals that prefer the warmth would spread up to England during interglacials. Then, because of landsliding or other mixing processes, glacial and interglacial animals would be mixed together. This is what Nilsson (1983, p. 227) suggests:

> *The occurrences of such taxa as hippopotamuses that are closely adapted to warmth, may result from the reworking of older, interglacial deposits.*

There are several problems with the mixing hypothesis. First, there should be evidence for the mixing of *sediments*, not just a mixing of animals with contrary climatic tolerances. There does not appear to be much mixing of sediments. Grayson (1984a, p. 16) informs us:

> *In the valley of the Thames [southern England], for instance, woolly mammoth, woolly rhinoceros, musk ox, reindeer* (Rangifer tarandus), *hippopotamus* (Hippopotamus amphibius), *and cave lion* (Felis leo spelaea) *had all been found by 1855 in stratigraphic contexts that seemed to indicate contemporaneity.*

Grayson does not believe the hippopotamus fossils were mixed with the cold-tolerant animals. In an example of disharmonious fossils from eastern Washington, Rensberger and Barnosky (1993, p. 331) see little evidence of significant mixing:

> *Although we cannot rule out minor stratigraphic mixing . . . the observed amounts of bioturbation at most of the collecting sites are insufficient to support a contention that stratigraphic mixing by itself produced the no-analogue [disharmonious] species associations.*

Mixing is possible in cases where the stratigraphic units have been poorly distinguished. Graham and Lundelius (1984, p. 224) discount mixing because disharmonious associations are much too common to be spurious in all cases.

Second, the mixing hypothesis assumes that warmth-loving animals could have migrated far to the north and, therefore, beyond their climatic limits of today. Old-age theorists believe the earth currently enjoys a "warm interglacial," called the Holocene. Today's "interglacial" climate has not motivated the hippo to journey from Africa up to England, nor has the climate inspired any other warmth-loving animal to migrate to the colder climes. It is likely too cold in today's northern climate, as well as in previous postulated interglacials in northwest Europe, for the hippopotamus.

Third, if mixing is the cause, it should have carried over into the current interglacial, the Holocene epoch. Why would the supposed frequent mixing of sediments suddenly stop at the end of the Ice Age? Disharmonious associations, however, are rare in the Holocene (Graham and Lundelius, 1984, p. 224).

Fourth, disharmonious associations are found in all previous interglacials in the standard sequence as well as in glacial times. Guthrie (1984, p. 264) states: *"Earlier interglacials and glacials reveal a fauna and flora more like that of a heterogeneous savanna."* Guilday (1984, p. 255) reinforces this statement:

> *Pleistocene local faunas assigned to both pre-Wisconsinan glacial and interglacial periods are equally diverse in composition and their taxonomic makeup, especially of the reptiles and amphibians, suggests climate equability (Holmon 1980) without a hint of Holocene polarity [separation].*

Guilday is essentially saying that no matter whether a particular layer is assigned a glacial or an interglacial age, the fauna is still equally diverse and disharmonious. In referring to the last interglacial, called the Sangamon in North America, Alroy (1999, p. 113) discovered:

> *If the Sangamonian faunas are correctly categorized, then disharmony was nearly as common during the Wisconsinan [last Ice Age] as during an earlier interglacial that was every bit as warm as the Holocene. The climate equability hypothesis would be hard pressed to explain such a pattern.*

Although Alroy rightly points out that such interglacial disharmonious associations are evidence against an equable climate, they are also evidence against the second option of mixing. Mixing would have to be common in these interglacial sediments — a situation that rarely occurs in the interglacial of today. This brings up the question of why interglacials also show disharmonious associations. Maybe there were no interglacials but all the animals represent life in one Ice Age.

AN EQUABLE ICE AGE CLIMATE

Despite the objection of Alroy, many scientists prefer the explanation of an equable climate with cool summers and mild winters during the Ice Age (Graham and Semken, 1987; Stuart, 1991; Cole, 1995, p. 131). Ernest Lundelius (1992, p. 37) writes:

> These associations are very common in Pleistocene faunas in all parts of the world where there is adequate data. They have been termed "disharmonious." . . . They have been interpreted as indicating more-equable climates in the past.

Grayson (1984a, p. 18) reinforces this conclusion in regard to the hippopotamuses living alongside musk ox and reindeer:

> If the musk ox required cold, and the hippopotamus required warmth, and the stratigraphic evidence implied that they had coexisted, then a straightforward reading of all this information could imply that glacial climates had not, as most felt, been marked by severe winters, but had instead been equable.

It is interesting that as long ago as 1867 Lartet argued that an equable climate can account for the surprising distribution of warm- and cold-tolerant animals:

> There must have been cooler summers for the reindeer and musk-ox; and, on the other hand, warmer winters for the hippopotamus and other species whose analogs are today found withdrawn toward the tropical regions (Grayson, 1984a, p. 18).

An equable climate is also reinforced by the high diversity of animals in the Ice Age sediments:

> In modern floras and faunas there is a positive correlation between increased species diversity and decreased climatic variability as measured by winter-summer differences in mean temperature . . . thus the degree of diversity in late Pleistocene disharmonious biotas suggests that they existed during times when the climate was equable and seasonal extremes in temperature and effective moisture were reduced . . . (Graham and Lundelius, 1984, p. 224).

An equable climate would also explain the mix of warm- and cold-tolerant plants during the Ice Age, for instance in France:

> *The implications of the botanical co-occurrences seemed clear to Saporta: only a humid, equable climate would have allowed such an association* (Grayson, 1984a, p. 19).

Although an equable climate enjoys much support from the fossils, it still cannot be explained by uniformitarian Ice Age simulations. It certainly is not expected from standard ideas of what an ice age should be like. There are of course a few wild guesses. For instance, Stuart (1991, p. 517–518) states:

> *The apparently paradoxical situation where Wisconsinan [late Ice Age] winters were less severe than today is thought to have resulted from the vast ice sheet preventing arctic air from sweeping across the Plains.*

From a meteorological point of view, the ice sheets could not have blocked Arctic air. They would have *created* Arctic air that would have no trouble spilling southward away from the ice sheets. Nevertheless, Stuart does admit that disharmonious associations are paradoxical because winters would have to have been *warmer*, even at the peak of the Ice Age. This leaves him and other scientists with the question: How can there be warmer winters during an ice age?

APPENDIX 3

THE ELEPHANT KIND

Creationists understand that the classification category of species is *not* the same as the Genesis kind. Species is a man-made classification that is generally defined as an interbreeding unit that is reproductively isolated from other units. It is well known, however, that individuals from different species or even different genera can potentially interbreed, but do not normally do so. There are factors that can cause "reproductive isolation" within a large group of animals. Animal behavior, size, environmental separation, or complex reproductive strategies can deter reproduction. Animals that can reproduce, but normally do not, would be included within one Genesis kind. In the classification system, however, the splitters have dominated (see appendix 1), so animals have been split up into different species within a genus. The original Genesis kind was undoubtedly a much broader classification than a species.

Then what are the boundaries of the Genesis kind and do all the types of elephants, living and fossil, fit into one kind? There is a fair amount of research into the definition of the various Genesis kinds, called baramins (Marsh, 1976, Frair, 2000). This subfield of study within creationism is called baraminology. It is obvious that the human species is one Genesis kind or baramin, but when it comes to animals and plants, it is often difficult to classify them into baramins. Sometimes, the kind may be at the species level, as in modern humans, or at the genus level or sometimes at the family level. It should be rare that the kind is at the level of the order or class. This is why John Woodmorappe (1996, p. 5–7) in his book on the reasonableness of Noah's ark used the genus level as the *average* for the Genesis kinds. He ended up with only 16,000 animals that needed to be on Noah's ark (Woodmorappe, 1996, p. 8–13). So, there would have been plenty of room on the ark for all the animals that would have repopulated the earth after the Flood.

Defining the Genesis kinds is very difficult because we do not know enough about genetics, and it is at the genetic level that the kinds need to be defined. Even the test of interbreeding is not a foolproof determination because we do not know how genetic defects (mutations, etc.) have built up over time to interfere with the reproductive process. We also have come to realize that animals that appear to be one kind do not interbreed (at least normally) because of different ingrained behaviors (a scientific subfield called ethology), mating practices, and other such complications.

When it comes to elephants, do all the members of the order Proboscidea belong to one Genesis kind? We do not know for sure, since nearly all of the recognized species are extinct. One thing we do know is that each species within Proboscidea, and there were once over 500 (Maglio, 1996), is *not* a separate kind. The example presented in appendix 1 about elephant teeth from two different families found in the same animal should alert us to the probability that many of these defined species and genera are within the "elephant kind."

Based on the amount of splitting and the poor classification system of the order Proboscidea, as well as the unique and many similar aspects of their morphology, I lean toward Jonathan Sarfati's view (2000). He thinks the order Proboscidea is probably one created kind — the elephant kind. It is known that the two living genera of elephant can interbreed successfully. The mammoths and mastodons that lived after the Flood may have diverged from two elephants that contained genes for all of the elephant kind. Mammoths are fairly close in anatomy to the Asian elephant. It is likely that if the woolly mammoth lived today that it could interbreed with the Asian elephant. In fact, mammoth researchers are even hoping to fertilize mammoth cells by placing a frozen mammoth sperm from a Siberian mammoth carcass into the womb of an Asian elephant.

WOOLLY MAMMOTHS —

FLOOD OR ICE AGE?

Some creationists believe the mammoths died during the Flood (Dillow, 1981; Brown, 1995, 2001), while others believe the evidence points to a post-Flood demise. Since there was much more variety within each type of animal before the Flood, mammoths very likely lived before the Flood. Therefore, fossils of these pre-Flood mammoths should exist in sedimentary rocks in some areas. However, there is plenty of evidence that the woolly mammoths in Siberia, Alaska, and the Yukon and almost all other surficial sites in the Northern Hemisphere died *after* the Flood.

The first argument against the mammoth death-in-the-Flood hypothesis is that mammoths are *buried in unconsolidated surficial sediments* that indicate the action of *post-Flood processes*.

This is certainly true for the mammoths found outside of Siberia, Alaska, and the Yukon. This evidence includes spear points associated with or embedded in the remains of mammoths at a dozen localities in North America (Saunders, 1992, p. 128). One mammoth at Naco, Arizona, had eight spear points, presumably from Clovis man, associated with the skeleton (Saunders, 1992, p. 129). Mammoths are commonly found buried in glacial till, river flood plain debris, river terraces, tar pits, caves, rock shelters, wind-blown loess, sinkholes, and peat bogs (Oard, 1990, p. 87–88; Stuart, 1991, p. 517). There are an estimated 100 predominantly male mammoths in a sinkhole at Hot Springs, South Dakota, of which about half have been excavated (Agenbroad, 1998, p. 27). These are all geological features that likely could not form in the Flood but must have developed in the post-Flood time due to surficial geological processes.

The woolly mammoths in Siberia, Alaska, and the Yukon are also found in unconsolidated surficial sediments that are now permanently frozen. For instance, woolly mammoths in northwest Siberia are found in sediments *above* glacial till, a post-Flood surficial sediment (Sher, 1997, p. 323).

If the animals were killed by an ice or hail dump from space during the early Flood, as some creationists postulate, the animals should be found in the lower portion of the sedimentary rocks, a little above crystalline rocks. Furthermore, this surficial sediment lies *upon hundreds to thousands of feet* of consolidated sedimentary rocks that practically all advocates of the creation-Flood paradigm would attribute to the Flood. Most of Siberia is composed of sedimentary rocks of all ages within the uniformitarian geological time scale (Knystautas, 1987, p. 17). "Mesozoic" sedimentary rocks underlie the Selerikan horse carcass, which was found in frozen loam between layers of peat (Ukraintseva, 1993, p. 80–98). Peat is a result of post-Flood processes. The baby mammoth, Dima, was discovered within slope wash on the ten-meter terrace of the Kirgilyakh River, which was carved out of Jurassic shales and sandstones (Dubrovo et al., 1982; Guthrie, 1990a, p. 7–24). The bedrock below the Cape Deceit fauna of Kotzebue Sound, Alaska, mostly consists of Paleozoic metalimestone and schist (Guthrie and Matthews, 1971, p. 474). There is a large concentration of mammoths within the surficial deposits of the New Siberian Islands. This surficial sediment lies upon thousands of feet of carbonates with marine fossils, coal layers, and other sedimentary rocks (Fujita and Cook, 1990). Some of these sedimentary layers were once as deep as 50,000 feet (15,200 m) before deformation. These are not unlike sedimentary rocks found in the western United States. Practically all creationists would consider that such rocks were deposited during the Flood. The mammoths are found on top of these lithified sedimentary rocks within unconsolidated frozen sediments.

The second piece of evidence is that the woolly mammoths were part of a vast mammoth steppe, and they mingled with a wide variety of other mammals on this steppe during the Ice Age. This community of mammals ranged from western Europe through Russia, Siberia, Alaska, and the Yukon (Guthrie, 1990a). The mammoth steppe continued just south of the ice sheet in the United States. To *isolate* the frozen woolly mammoth remains in Siberia, Alaska, and the Yukon for a special catastrophic extinction scenario during the Flood, while ignoring the remainder of the Ice Age mammoth steppe does not make sense.

A third indication is that the woolly mammoths are rarely found in glaciated areas, especially near the centers of former ice sheets. When found with glacial deposits, it is practically always at the periphery of the ice sheets. If the remains are discovered on top of the glacial till, mammoths simply migrated into areas formerly glaciated. If the remains are underneath or within till, a dead mammoth that formerly lived next to the ice sheet could have been covered by glacial debris during a readvance or surge of the periphery. Either one of these can explain the bones and tusks of mammoths in deep valleys of south Norway (Bergersen and Garnes, 1983). Another seemingly anomalous occurrence of mammoths and other mammals is the discovery of their bones in central British Columbia about 60 miles (95 km) east of Smithers underneath glacial till (Harrington, Tipper, and Mott, 1974). These mammals can be explained by the fact the Ice Age in British Columbia would have started in the mountains and with time spread to the lowlands because of the onshore flow from the warm North Pacific Ocean. Furthermore, there is a gap in the Rocky Mountains where the Peace River flows from central British Columbia to the high plains. Mammoths and other animals could have easily migrated from the ice-free corridor west through the gap in the mountains and into central British Columbia where they were trapped and eventually covered by the expanding Cordilleran ice sheet.

A fourth indication of the post-Flood nature of Siberian mammoths is that mammoths and other Ice Age animals are the objects of post-Flood activity by man. Mammoths and other Ice Age animals are depicted in cave art from Europe to the Russian Plain and Siberia (Stuart, 1991, p. 489). These animals are especially common on cave walls of Europe. They are even found on cave walls in the southern Ural Mountains of Russia (Lister and Bahn, 1994, p. 103). These appear to be the same animals as found in the muck of Alaska (Guthrie, 1982, p. 308). Ivory carvings are rather common in early man sites in southern Siberia (Lister and Bahn, 1994, p. 113). More than 70 mammoth bone huts have been discovered on the central Russian Plain (Soffer, 1985; Ward, 1997, p. 144). Bones of 149 mammoths make up the bone hut at Mezhirich (Soffer, 1985, p. 75).

Fifth, very few of the mammoth bones found in Siberia, Alaska, and the Yukon surficial deposits are permineralized, as would be expected if they were Flood fossils. Permineralized fossils have most of their organic matter replaced by inorganic chemicals. The frozen mammoth bones still contain 90 percent of their collagen and many have some bone marrow (Guthrie, 1990a, p. 245). The ivory tusks can still be carved like normal ivory from living elephants. That is why tusks are considered valuable and have fueled an extensive ivory trade for several centuries.

Advocates of a Flood demise for the Siberian mammoths have made several mistaken deductions on the data from the woolly mammoth and its environment. One such deduction is that there are 4,000 or more feet (more than 1,200 m) of muck in Siberia and Alaska with animal and vegetable remains scattered uniformly throughout it (Dillow, 1981, p. 351–353; Brown, 1995, p. 111). This is based on a short 1969 article in the obscure journal *Pursuit*, a journal of the society for the investigation of the unexplained (Anonymous, 1969). The article discusses the discovery of frozen trees about 1,000 feet (300 m) deep by an oil company drilling on the North Slope of Alaska. The vegetation was tropical to subtropical (Williams, 1980, p. 54). In Siberia, the Russians are said to have drilled in places 4,000 feet (1,200 m) into "muck," which they considered a mysterious frozen earth. The anonymous author implied that this muck was widespread and deep. No references were provided. This muck has been identified and is not only shallow but also not all that mysterious.

Vegetation from a much warmer climate is not unusual in strata in Asia and Canada (Oard, 1995a, b). This frozen stratum may be from the Flood. After weighing the available evidence, I concluded that nearly all of this vegetation was deposited during the Flood, especially if it is dated by uniformitarians as Cretaceous and Tertiary. One of the most compelling pieces of evidence is multiple leaf and twig layers in early Tertiary deposits on Axel Heiberg Island. They are just as well preserved at the *bottom* of each bed as at the top (Oard, 1995b, p. 138). There is no evidence of bacterial or fungal decay of the leaf litter. If this was an in situ leaf layer, even in an anaerobic swamp, the bottom vegetation should show some evidence of decay. Besides, much of the vegetation is of the kind that would not normally grow in a swamp. It is likely the vegetation, some of which is frozen and not permineralized, was rafted into the area during the Flood.

In table A4.1, I summarize the five main evidences that the woolly mammoths in Siberia, Alaska, and the Yukon died at the end of the Ice Age.

TABLE A4.1. EVIDENCES OF POST-FLOOD EXTINCTION OF WOOLLY MAMMOTHS IN SIBERIA, ALASKA, AND THE YUKON

1) Buried in unconsolidated surficial sediments, not deep in the sedimentary rocks

2) Part of a post-Flood surficial mammal steppe community across the Northern Hemisphere

3) Rarely found in glaciated areas

4) Objects of post-Flood activity of man

5) Not permineralized as expected for most animals that died in the Flood

---

REFERENCES

Agenbroad, L.D. 1998. *Pygmy (dwarf) mammoths of the Channel Islands of California*. Hot Springs, SD: Mammoth Site of Hot Springs, SD, Inc.

Agenbroad, L.D., and R.L. Laury. 1975. Geology, paleontology, paleohydrology, and sedimentology of a Quaternary mammoth site, Hot Springs, South Dakota: 1974–1979 excavations. *National Geographic Society Reports* 16:1–32.

Agenbroad, L.D., and J.I. Mead. 1989. Quaternary geochronology and distribution of *Mammuthus* on the Colorado Plateau. *Geology* 17:861–864.

Agenbroad, L.D. and L. Nelson. 2002. *Mammoths: Ice Age giants*. Minneapolis, MN: Lerner Publications Company.

Alley, R.B., et al. 1997. Visual-stratigraphic dating of the GISP2 ice core: Basis, reproducibililty, and application. *Journal of Geophysical Research* 102(C12):26,367-26,381.

Alroy, J. 1999. Putting North America's end-Pleistocene megafaunal extinction in context. In *Extinctions in near time — Causes, contexts, and consequences*. D.E. MacPhee, editor. New York: Kluwar Academic/Plenum Publishers, p. 105–143.

Alt, D. 2001. *Glacial Lake Missoula and its humongous floods*. Missoula, MT: Mountain Press Publishing Company.

Anderson, P.M. 1985. Late Quaternary vegetational change in the Kotzebue Sound area, Northwestern Alaska, *Quaternary Research* 24:307–321.

Anonymous. 1969. Much about muck, *Pursuit* 2(4):68–69.

Arkhipov, S.A. 1997. Environment and climate of Sartan maximum and late glacial in Siberia. In *Late glacial and postglacial environmental changes — Quaternary, Carboniferous-Permian, and Proterozoic*. I.P. Martini, editor. New York: Oxford University Press, p. 53–60.

Baker, V.R. 1997. Megafloods and glaciation. In *Late glacial and postglacial environmental changes — Quaternary, Carboniferous-Permian, and Proterozoic*. I.P. Martini, editor. New York: Oxford University Press, p. 98–108.

Baker, V.R., G. Benito, and A.N. Rudoy. 1993. Paleohydrology of late Pleistocene superflooding Altay Mountains, Siberia, *Science* 259:348–350.

Bales, R.C., J.R. McConnell, E. Mosley-Thompson, and B. Csatho. 2001. Accumulation over the Greenland ice sheet from historical and recent records. *Journal of Geophysical Research* 106 (D4):33, 813–833.

Bamber, J.L., and P. Huybrechts. 1996. Geometric boundary conditions for modeling the velocity field of the Antarctic ice sheet. *Annals of Glaciology* 23:364–373.

Bamber, J.L., R.L. Layberry, and S.P. Gogineni. 2001. A new ice thickness and bed set for the Greenland ice sheet 1, measurements, data reduction, and errors. *Journal of Geophysical Research* 106 (D24):33, 773-33, 780.

Baryshnikov, G., G. Haynes, and J. Klimowicz. 1999. Mammoths and the mammoth fauna: Introduction to the studies of an extinct ecosystem. In *Mammoths and the mammoth fauna: Studies of an extinct ecosystem.* G. Haynes, J. Klimowicz, and J.W.F. Reumer, editors. Proceedings of the First International Mammoth Conference. Rotterdam: Jaarbericht Van Het Natuurmuseum, p. 3–8.

Batten, D., editor. 2004. *The revised & expanded answers book.* Green Forest, AR: Master Books.

Beaney, C.L., and J. Shaw. 2000. The subglacial geomorphology of southeast Alberta: Evidence for subglacial meltwater erosion. *Canadian Journal of Earth Sciences* 37:51–61.

Beck, M.W. 1996. On discerning the cause of late Pleistocene megafaunal extinctions. *Paleobiology* 22(1):91–103.

Beget, J.E. 1986. Modeling the influence of till rheology on the flow and profile of the Lake Michigan lobe, southern Laurentide ice sheet, U.S.A. *Journal of Glaciology* 32(111):235–241.

Beget, J. 1987. Low profile of the northwest Laurentide ice sheet. *Arctic and Alpine Research* 19:81–88.

Bell, A., and W. Strieber. 2000. *The coming global superstorm.* New York: Pocket Books.

Berger, W.H. 1991. On the extinction of the mammoth: Science and myth. In *Controversies in modern geology — Evolution of geological theories in sedimentology, earth history, and tectonics.* D.W. Müller, J.A. McKenzie, and H. Weissert, editors. New York: Academic Press, p. 115–132, .

Bergersen, O.R. and K. Garnes. 1983. Glacial deposits in the culmination zone of the Scandinavian ice sheet. In *Glacial deposits in north-west Europe*. J. Ehlers, editor. Rotterdam: A.A. Balkema, p. 29–40.

Berman, D., S. Armbruster, A. Alfimov, and M. Edwards. 1994. Subarctic steppe communities in Beringia. In *Bridges of the science between North America and the Russian Far East, 45th Arctic science conference, section 2 — Beringia revisited: Recent discoveries and interpretations*, p. 10.

Birkeland, P.W. 1984. *Soils and geomorphology*. New York: Oxford University Press.

Bloom, A.L. 1971. Glacial-eustatic and isostatic controls of sea level. In *The late Cenozoic glacial ages*. K.K. Turekian, editor. New Haven, CT: Yale University Press, p. 355–379.

Bloomberg, R. 1989. WW II planes to be deiced. *Engineering Report*, March 9, 1989.

Bocherens, H., G. Pacaud, P.A. Lazarev, and A. Mariotti. 1996. Stable isotope abundances (^{13}C, ^{15}N) in collagen and soft tissues from Pleistocene mammals from Yakutia: Implications for the palaeobiology of the mammoth steppe. *Palaeogeography, Palaeoclimatology, Palaeoecology* 126:31–44.

Bowen, D.Q. 1978. *Quaternary geology: A stratigraphic framework for multidisciplinary work*. New York: Pergamon Press.

Bower, B. 1987. Extinctions on ice. *Science News* 132:284–285.

Bower, B. 1988. Marine scene expands for early Amercans. *Science News* 133:164.

Bray, J.R. 1976. Volcanic triggering of glaciation. *Nature* 260:414–415.

Brennand, T.A., J. Shaw, and D.R. Sharpe. 1996. Regional-scale meltwater erosion and deposition patterns, northern Quebec, Canada. *Annals of Glaciology* 22:85–92.

Brown, W. 1995. *In the beginning: Compelling evidence for creation and the flood*, 6th edition. Phoenix, AZ: Center for Scientific Creation.

Brown, W. 2001. *In the beginning: Compelling evidence for creation and the flood*, 7th edition. Phoenix, AZ: Center for Scientific Creation.

Burney, D.A. 1999. Rates, patterns, and processes of landscape transformation and extinction in Madagascar. In *Extinctions in near time — Causes, contexts, and consequences*. D.E. MacPhee, editor. New York: Kluwar Academic/Plenum Publishers, p. 145–164.

Carling, P.A. 1996. Morphology, sedimentology, and palaeohydraulic significance of large gravel dunes, Altai Mountains, Siberia. *Sedimentology* 43:647–664.

Chapin, III, F.S., G.R. Shaver, A.E. Giblin, K.J. Nadelhoffer, and J.A. Laundre. 1995. Responses of Arctic tundra to experimental and observed changes in climate. *Ecology* 76(3):694–711.

Charlesworth, J.K. 1957. *The Quaternary era*. London: Edward Arnold.

Chorley, R.J., A.J. Dunn, and R.P. Beckinsale. 1964. *The history of the study of landforms or the development of geomorphology — Volume one: Geomorphology before Davis*. New York: John Wiley & Sons.

Chorowicz, J., and J. Fabre. 1997. Organization of drainage networks from space imagery in the Tanezrouft plateau (Western Sahara): Implications for recent intracratonic deformations. *Geomorphology* 21:139–151.

Clayton, L., J.T. Teller, and J.W. Attig. 1985. Surging of the southwestern part of the Laurentide ice sheet. *Boreas* 14:235–241.

Coffin, H.G., with R.H. Brown. 1983. *Origin by design*. Washington, DC: Review and Herald Publishing Association.

Cole, K.L. 1995. Equable climates, mixed assemblages, and the regression fallacy. In *Late Quaternary environments and deep history: A tribute to Paul S. Martin*. D.W. Steadman and J.I. Mead, editors. Hot Springs, SD: The Mammoth Site of Hot Springs, South Dakota, Inc., p. 131–138.

Collard, M., and L.C. Aiello. 2000. From forelimbs to two legs. *Nature* 404:339–340.

Coulson, D. 1999. Preserving Sahara's prehistoric art. *National Geographic* 196(3):82–89.

Crickmay, C.H. 1975. The hypothesis of unequal activity. In *Theories of landform development*. W.N. Melhorn and R.C. Flemal, editors. London: George Allen & Unwin, p. 103–109.

Damon, P.E. 1968. The relationship between terrestrial factors and climate. In *The causes of climatic change*. J.M. Mitchell Jr., editor. Meteorological Monographs, 8(30). Boston, MA: American Meteorological Society, p. 106–111.

Day, M. 2000. Jumbo history — Africa is home to not one but two species of elephants. *New Scientist* 166(2232):15.

De Angelis, M., J.P. Steffensen, M. Legrand, H. Clausen, and C. Hammer. 1997. Primary aerosol (sea salt and soil dust) deposited in Greenland ice during the last climatic cycle: Comparison with east Antarctic records. *Journal of Geophysical Research* 102(C12):26,681-26,698.

Dennell, R.W. 1992. The origins of crop agriculture in Europe. In *The origins of agriculture — An international perspective*. C.W. Cowan and P.J. Watson, editors. Washington, DC: Smithsonian Institution Press, p. 71–94.

Derbyshire, E. 1979. Glaciers and environment. In *Winters of the world*. B.S. John, editor. New York: John Wiley and Sons, p. 58–106.

Digby, B. 1926. *The mammoth and mammoth-hunting in north-east Siberia*. London: H.F. & G. Witherby.

Dillow, J.C. 1981. *The waters above: Earth's pre-Flood vapor canopy*. Chicago, IL: Moody Press.

Dong, B., and P.J. Valdes. 1995. Sensitivity studies of Northern Hemisphere glaciation using an atmospheric general circulation model. *Journal of Climate* 8:2471–2496.

Donn, W.L., and M. Ewing. 1968. The theory of an ice-free Arctic Ocean. In *The causes of climatic change*. J.M. Mitchell Jr., editor. Meteorological Monographs, 8(30). Boston, MA: American Meteorological Society, p. 100–105.

Dubrovo, I. 1990. The Pleistocene elephants of Siberia. In *Megafauna and man — Discovery of America's heartland*. Hot Springs, SD: The Mammoth Site of Hot Springs, South Dakota, Inc., scientific papers, volume 1, p. 1–8.

Dubrovo, N.A., R.Y. Giterman, R.N. Gorlova, and N.V. Rengarten. 1982. Upper Quaternary deposits and paleogeography of the region inhabited by the young Kirgilyakh mammoth. *International Geology Review* 24(6):621–634.

Dudley, J.P. 1996. Mammoths, gomphotheres, and the great American faunal interchange. In *The Proboscidea — Evolution and palaeoecology of elephants and their relatives*. J. Shoshani and P. Tassy, editors. New York: Oxford University Press, p. 289–295.

Ehlers, J. 1996. *Quaternary and glacial geology*. New York: John Wiley & Sons.

Elias, S.A. 1992. Late Wisconsin insects and plant macrofossils associated with the Colorado Creek mammoth, southwestern Alaska: Taphonomic and paleoenvironmental implications. In *International Workshop on Classification of Circumpolar Arctic Vegetation*. Boulder, CO: Institute of Arctic and Alpine Research, University of Colorado, p. 45–47.

Eltringham, S.K. 1982. *Elephants*. Dorset, England: Blandford Press.

Ericson, D.B., and G. Wollin. 1967. *The ever-changing sea*. New York: Albert A. Knopf.

Eyles, N. 1983. Glacial geology: A landsystems approach. In *Glacial geology: An introduction for engineers and earth scientists*. N. Eyles, editor. New York: Pergamon Press, p. 1–18.

Eyles, N., W.R. Dearman, and T.D. Douglas. 1983. The distribution of glacial landsystems in Britain and North America. In *Glacial geology: An introduction for engineers and earth scientists*. N. Eyles, editor. New York: Pergamon Press, p. 213–228.

Fagen, B.M. 1987. *The great journey — The peopling of ancient America*. London: Thames and Hudson.

Farrand, W.R. 1961. Frozen mammoths and modern geology. *Science* 133:729–735.

Farrand, W.R. 1962. Frozen mammoths. *Science* 137:450–452.

Feininger, T. 1971. Chemical weather and glacial erosion of crystalline rocks and the origin of till. *U.S. Geological Survey Professional Paper 750-C*. Washington, DC: U.S. Government Printing Office, p. C65–C81.

Fisher, D.C. 1996. Extinction of proboscideans in North America. In *The Proboscidea — Evolution and palaeoecology of elephants and their relatives*. J. Shoshani and P. Tassy, editors. New York: Oxford University Press, p. 296–315.

Foronova, I.V., and A.N. Zudin. 1999. In *Mammoths and the mammoth fauna: Studies of an extinct ecosystem*. G. Haynes, J. Klimowicz, and J.W.F. Reumer, editors. Proceedings of the First International Mammoth Conference. Rotterdam: Jaarbericht Van Het Natuurmuseum, p. 103–118.

Fouts, D.M., and K.P. Wise. 1998. Blotting out and breaking up: Miscellaneous Hebrew studies in geocatastrophism. In *Proceedings of the Fourth International*

Conference on Creationism. R.E. Walsh, editor. Pittsburgh, PA: Creation Science Fellowship, p. 217–228.

Fox, J.W., and C.B. Smith. 1992. Introduction: Historical background, theoretical approaches, and proboscideans. In *Proboscidean and Paleoindian interactions.* J.W. Fox, C.B. Smith, and K.T. Wilkins, editors. Waco, TX: Baylor University Press, p. 1–14.

Frair, W. 2000. Baraminology — Classification of created organisms. *Creation Research Society Quarterly* 37(2):82–91.

Fraser, T.A., and C.R. Burn. 1997. On the nature and origin of "muck" deposits in the Klondike area, Yukon Territory. *Canadian Journal of Earth Sciences* 34:1333–1344.

Fujita, K., and D.B. Cook. 1990. The Arctic continental margin of eastern Siberia. In *The geology of North America: Volume L — The Arctic Ocean region.* A. Grantz, L. Johnson, and J.F. Sweeney, editors. Boulder, CO: Geological Society of America, p. 289–304.

Geist, V. 1987. Bergmann's rule is invalid. *Canadian Journal of Zoology* 65:1035–1038.

Gilbert, R., and J. Shaw. 1994. Inferred subglacial meltwater origin of lakes on the southern border of the Canadian shield. *Canadian Journal of Earth Sciences* 31:1630–1637.

Ginenthal, C. 1997. *The extinction of the mammoth.* Forest Hills, NY: Ivy Press Books.

Graham, R.W., and E.L. Lundelius Jr. 1984. Coevolutionary disequilibrium and Pleistocene extinctions. In *Quaternary extinctions: A prehistoric revolution.* P.S. Martin and R.G. Klein, editors. Tuscon, AZ: University of Arizona Press, p. 223–249.

Graham, R.W., and H.A. Semken Jr. 1987. Philosophy and procedures for paleoenvironmental studies of Quaternary mammalian faunas. In *Late Quaternary mammalian biogeography and environments of the Great Plains and prairies,* Illinois State Museum scientific papers 22. Springfield, IL: Illinois State Museum, p. 1–17.

Grayson, D.K. 1977. Pleistocene avifaunas and the overkill hypothesis. *Science* 195:691–693.

Grayson, D.K. 1984a. Nineteenth-century explanations of Pleistocene extinctions: A review. In *Quaternary extinctions: A prehistoric revolution*. P.S. Martin and R.G. Klein, editors. Tuscon, AZ: University of Arizona Press, p. 5–39.

Grayson, D.K. 1984b. Explaining Pleistocene extinctions — Thoughts on the structure of a debate. In *Quaternary extinctions: A prehistoric revolution*. P.S. Martin and R.G. Klein, editors. Tuscon, AZ: University of Arizona Press, p. 807–823.

Grossman, D. 2003. Drilling through ice in search of history. *New York Times* July 22, 2003.

Guthrie, R.D. 1982. Mammals of the mammoth steppe as paleoenvironmental indicators. In *Paleoecology of Beringia*. D.M. Hopkins, J.V. Matthews Jr., C.E. Schweger, and S.B. Young, editors. New York: Academic Press, p. 307–326.

Guthrie, R.D. 1984. Mosaics, allelochemics and nutrients — An ecological theory of late Pleistocene megafaunal extinctions. In *Quaternary extinctions: A prehistoric revolution*. P.S. Martin and R.G. Klein, editors. Tuscon, AZ: University of Arizona Press, p. 259–297.

Guthrie, R.D. 1990a. *Frozen fauna of the mammoth steppe — The story of Blue Babe*. Chicago, IL: University of Chicago Press.

Guthrie, R.D. 1990b. Late Pleistocene faunal revolution: A new perspective on the extinction debate. In *Megafauna and man — Discovery of America's heartland*, scientific papers, volume 1, Hot Springs, SD: The Mammoth Site of Hot Springs, South Dakota, Inc., p. 42–53.

Guthrie, R.D., and M.L. Guthrie. 1990. On the mammoth's dusty trail. *Natural History* 99(7):34–41.

Guthrie, R.D., and J.V. Matthews Jr. 1971. The Cape Deceit fauna/early Pleistocene mammalian assemblage from the Alaskan Arctic. *Quaternary Research* 1:474–510.

Hamilton, T.D., J.L. Craig, and P.V. Sellman. 1988. The Fox permafrost tunnel: A late Quaternary geologic record in central Alaska. *Geological Society of America Bulletin* 100:948–969.

Hammer, C., P.A. Mayewski, D. Peel, and M. Stuiver. 1997. Preface to special volume on ice cores. *Journal of Geophysical Research* 102(C12):26,315–26,316.

Hapgood, C.H. 1958. *Earth's shifting crust — A key to some basic problems of earth science.* New York: Pantheon Books.

Hapgood, C.H. 1970. *The path of the pole.* New York: Chilton Book Co.

Harington, C.R. 1981. Pleistocene saiga antelopes in North America and their paleoenvironmental implications. In *Quaternary Paleoclimate.* W.C. Mahaney, editor. Norwich, England: Geo Abstracts, p. 193–225.

Harington, C.R., and D.M. Shackleton. 1978. A tooth of *Mammuthus primigenius* from Chestermere lake near Calgary, Alberta, and the distribution of mammoths in southwestern Canada. *Canadian Journal of Earth Sciences* 15:1272–1283.

Harington, C.R., H.W. Tipper, and R.J. Mott. 1974. Mammoth from Babine Lake, British Columbia. *Canadian Journal of Earth Sciences* 11:285–303.

Haynes Jr., C.V. 1991. Geoarchaeological and paleohydrological evidence for a Clovis-age drought in North America and its bearing on extinction. *Quaternary Research* 35:438–450.

Haynes, G. 1990. The mountains that fell down: Life and death of heartland mammoths. In *Megafauna and man — Discovery of America's heartland.* L. Agenbroad, J.I. Mead, and L.W. Nelson, editors. Hot Springs, SD: The Mammoth Site of Hot Springs, South Dakota, Inc., scientific papers, vol. 1, p. 22–31.

Haynes, G. 1991. *Mammoths, mastodonts, and elephants.* Cambridge, NY: Cambridge University Press.

Haynes, G. 1999. The role of mammoths in rapid Clovis dispersal. In *Mammoths and the mammoth fauna: Studies of an extinct ecosystem.* G. Haynes, J. Klimowicz, and J.W.F. Reumer, editors. Proceedings of the First International Mammoth Conference. Rotterdam: Jaarbericht Van Het Natuurmuseum, p. 9–38.

Hibben, F.C. 1943. Evidence of early man in Alaska. *American Antiquity* 8:254–259.

Hobbs, H. 1999. Origin of the driftless area by subglacial drainage — A new hypothesis. *Geological Society of America Special Paper 337.* Boulder, CO: Geological Society of America, p. 93–102.

Hooke, R.L. 1999. Lake Manly shorelines in the eastern Mojave Desert, California. *Quaternary Research* 52:328–336.

Hopkins, D.M. 1982. Aspects of the paleogeography of Beringia during the Late Pleistocene. In *Paleoecology of Beringia.* D.M. Hopkins, J.V. Matthews Jr., C.E. Schweger, and S.B. Young, editors. New York: Academic Press, p. 3–28.

Hopkins, D.M., J.V. Matthews Jr., C.E. Schweger, and S.B. Young, editors. 1982. *Paleoecology of Beringia.* New York: Academic Press.

Höss, M., S. Pääbo, and N.K. Vereshchagin. 1994. Mammoth DNA sequences. *Nature* 370:333.

Howorth, H.H. 1880. The mammoths in Siberia. *Geological Magazine* 7:550–561.

Howorth, H.H. 1887. *The Mammoth and the flood — An attempt to confront the theory of uniformity with the facts of recent geology.* London: Sampson Low, Marston, Searle, & Rivington. Reproduced by The Sourcebook Project, Glen Arm, Maryland.

Hoyle, F. 1981. *Ice, the ultimate human catastrophe.* New York: Continuum.

Huybrechts, P., D. Steinhage, F. Wilhelms, and J. Bamber. 2000. Balance velocity and measured properties of the Antarctic ice sheet from a new compilation of gridded data for modeling. *Annals of Glaciology* 30:52–60.

Imbrie, J., and K.P. Imbrie. 1979. *Ice ages: Solving the mystery.* Short Hills, NJ: Enslow Publishers.

Johanson, D.C., and M.A. Edey. 1981. *Lucy: The beginning of humankind.* New York: Simon and Schuster.

Johanson, D., and J. Shreeve. 1989. *Lucy's child: The discovery of a human ancestor.* New York: William Morrow and Company.

John, B. 1979. Ice ages: A search for reasons. In *Winters of the world.* B.S. John, editor. New York: John Wiley & Sons, p. 29–57.

Kahlke, R.D. 1999. *The history of the origin, evolution and dispersal of the Late Pleistocene* Mammuthus-Coelodonta *faunal complex in Eurasia (large mammals).* Hot Springs, SD: Mammoth Site of Hot Springs South Dakota, Inc.

Kaplina, T.N., and A.V. Lozhkin. 1984. Age and history of accumulation of the "ice complex" of the maritime lowlands of Yakutia. In *Late Quaternary environments of the Soviet Union.* A.A. Velichko, editor. Minneapolis, MN: University of Minnesota Press, p. 147–151.

Kennett, J.P. 1982. *Marine geology*. Englewood Cliffs, NJ: Prentice-Hall.

Keys, D. 1999. *Catastrophe: An investigation into the origins of the modern world*. New York: Ballantine Books.

Kiger, P.J. 2000. Great mammoth discoveries, Discovery Channel online.

Kirschvink, J.L., E.J. Gaidos, L.E. Bertani, N.J. Beukes, J. Gutzmer, L.N. Maepa, and R.E. Steinberger. 2000. Paleoproterozoic snowball earth: Extreme climatic and geochemical global change and its biological consequences. *Proceedings of the National Academy of Science* 97(4):1400–1405.

Kiselev, S.V., and V.I. Nazarov. 1984. Late Pleistocene insects. In *Late Quaternary environments of the Soviet Union*. A.A. Velichko, editor. Minneapolis, MN: University of Minnesota Press, p. 223–226.

Klassen, R.W. 1994. Late Wisconsinan and Holocene history of southwestern Saskatchewan. *Canadian Journal of Earth Sciences* 31:1822–1837.

Knystautas, A. 1987. *The natural history of the USSR*. New York: McGraw-Hill.

Kor, P.S.G., and D.W. Cowell. 1998. Evidence for catastrophic subglacial meltwater sheetflood events on the Bruce Peninsula, Ontario. *Canadian Journal of Earth Sciences* 35:1180–1202.

Krishtalka, L. 1984. The Pleistocene ways of death. Book review of *Quaternary extinctions: A prehistoric revolution*, P.S. Martin and R.G. Klein, editors. *Nature* 312:225–226.

Kröpelin, S., and I. Soulié-Märsche. 1991. Charophyte remains from Wadi Howar as evidence for deep Mid-Holocene freshwater lakes in the Eastern Sahara of Northwest Sudan. *Quaternary Research* 36:210–223.

Kurtén, B. 1986. *How to deep-freeze a mammoth*. New York: Columbia University Press.

Larsen, E., S. Funder, and J. Thiede. 1999. Late Quaternary history of northern Russia and adjacent shelves — A synopsis. *Boreas* 28:6–11.

Laub, R.S. 1992. On disassembling an elephant: Anatomical observations bearing on paleoindian exploitation of Proboscidea. In *Proboscidean and paleoindian interactions*. J.W., Fox, C.B. Smith, and K.T. Wilkins, editors. Waco, TX: Baylor University Press, p. 99–109.

Laws, R.M., I.S.C. Parker, and R.C.B. Johnstone. 1975. *Elephants and their habitats — The ecology of elephants in North Bunyoro, Uganda.* Oxford: Clarendon Press.

Lee, P.C., and C.J. Moss. 1986. Early maternal investment in male and female African elephant calves. *Behavioral Ecology and Sociobiology* 18:353–361.

Lepper, B.T., T.A. Frolking, D.C. Fisher, G. Goldstein, J.E. Sanger, D.A. Wymer, J.G. Ogden III, and P.E. Hooge. 1991. Intestinal contents of a Late Pleistocene mastodont from midcontinental North America. *Quaternary Research* 36:120–125.

Lister, A.M. 1993. Mammoths in miniature. *Nature* 362:288–289.

Lister, A.M. 1996. Evolution and taxonomy of Eurasian mammoths. In *The Proboscidea — Evolution and palaeoecology of elephants and their relatives.* J. Shoshani and P. Tassy, editors. New York: Oxford University Press, p. 203–213.

Lister, A., and P. Bahn. 1994. *Mammoths.* New York: Macmillan.

Long, A., A. Sher, and S. Vartanyan. 1994. Holocene mammoth dates. *Nature* 369:364.

Lowenstein, J.M., and J. Shoshani. 1996. Proboscidean relationships based on immunological data. In *The Proboscidea — Evolution and palaeoecology of elephants and their relatives.* J. Shoshani and P. Tassy, editors. New York: Oxford University Press, p. 49–54.

Lubenow, M.L. 2004. *Bones of contention: Creationist assessment of human fossils.* Grand Rapids, MI: Baker Book House.

Lundelius Jr., E.L. 1992. Quaternary paleofaunas of the Southwest. In *Proboscidean and paleoindian interactions.* J.W. Fox, C.B. Smith, and K.T. Wilkins, editors. Waco, TX: Baylor University Press, p. 35–49.

MacPhee, R.D.E., editor. 1999. *Extinctions in near time — Causes, contexts, and consequences.* New York: Kluwer Academic/Plenum Publishers.

Mahaney, W.C., F.A. Michel, V.I. Solomatin, and G. Hütt. 1995. Late Quaternary stratigraphy and soils of Gydan, Yamal and Taz Peninsulas, Northwestern Siberia. *Palaeogeography, Palaeoclimatology, Palaeoecology* 113:249–266.

Maglio, V.J. 1996. Forward. In *The Proboscidea — Evolution and palaeoecology of elephants and their relatives.* J. Shoshani and P. Tassy, editors. New York: Oxford University Press, p. ix.

Manabe, S., and A.J. Broccoli. 1985. The influence of continental ice sheets on the climate of an ice age. *Journal of Geophysical Research* 90(C2):2167–2190.

Mangerud, J., J.I. Svendsen, and V.I. Astakhov. 1999. Age and extent of the Barents and Kara ice sheets in Northern Russia. *Boreas* 28:46–80.

Marsh, F.L. 1976. *Variation and fixity in nature.* Mountain View, CA: Pacific Press Publishing Association.

Marshall, L.G. 1984. Who killed cock robin? In *Quaternary extinctions: A prehistoric revolution.* P.S. Martin and R.G. Klein, editors. Tuscon, AZ: University of Arizona Press, p. 785–806.

Martin, P.S., and R.G. Klein, editors. 1984. *Quaternary extinctions: A prehistoric revolution.* Tuscon, AZ: University of Arizona Press.

Martin, P.S., and D.W. Steadman. 1999. Prehistoric extinctions on islands and continents. In *Extinctions in near time — Causes, contexts, and consequences.* D.E. MacPhee, editor. New York: Kluwar Academic/Plenum Publishers, p. 17–55.

Mathews, W.H. 1974. Surface profiles of the Laurentide ice sheet in its marginal areas. *Journal of Glaciology* 13(67):37–43.

Matthews Jr., J.V. 1974. Quaternary environments at Cape Deceit (Seward Peninsula, Alaska): Evolution of a tundra ecosystem. *Geological Society of America Bulletin* 85:1353–1384.

Mazo, A.V. 1996. Gomphotheres and mammutids from the Iberian Peninsula. In *The Proboscidea — Evolution and palaeoecology of elephants and their relatives.* J. Shoshani and P. Tassy, editors. New York: Oxford University Press, p. 136–142.

McCauley, J.F., et al. 1982. Subsurface valleys and geoarcheology of the eastern Sahara revealed by shuttle radar. *Science* 218:1004–1020.

McDonald, J.N. 1984. The reordered North American selection regime and Late Quaternary megafaunal extinctions. In *Quaternary extinctions: A prehistoric revolution.* P.S. Martin and R.G. Klein, editors. Tucson, AZ: University of Arizona Press, p. 404–439.

Meese, D.A., A.J. Gow, R.B. Alley, G.A. Zielinski, P.M. Grootes, K. Ram, K.C. Taylor, P.A. Mayewski, and J.F. Bolzan. 1997. The Greenland ice sheet project 2 depth-age scale: Methods and results. *Journal of Geophysical Research* 102(C12):26,411-26,423.

Michaels, P.J., and R.C. Balling Jr. 2000. *The satanic gases: Clearing the air about global warming.* Washington, DC: Cato Institute.

Michel, F.A. 1998. The relationship of massive ground ice and the Late Pleistocene history of Northwest Siberia. *Quaternary International* 45/46:43–48.

Mithen, S. 1993. Simulating mammoth hunting and extinction: Implications for the Late Pleistocene of the central Russian plain. In *Hunting and animal exploitation in the Late Palaeolithic and Mesolithic of Eurasia.* G.L. Peterkin, H.M. Bricker, and P. Mellars, editors. The American Anthropological Association, USA, p. 163–178.

Monastersky, R. 1999. The killing fields — What robbed the Americas of their most charismatic mammals? *Science News* 156:360–361.

Muhs, D.R., and V.T. Holliday. 1995. Evidence of active dune sand on the Great Plains in the 19th century from accounts of early explorers. *Quaternary Research* 43:198–208.

Munro-Stasiuk, M.J. 1999. Evidence for water storage and drainage at the base of the Laurentide ice sheet, south-central Alberta, Canada. *Annals of Glaciology* 28:175–180.

Newson, R.L. 1973. Response of a general circulation model of the atmosphere to removal of the Arctic ice-cap. *Nature* 241:39–40.

Nilsson, T. 1983. *The Pleistocene — Geology and life in the Quaternary ice age.* Boston, MA: D. Reidel Publishing Co.

Nordenskiöld, A.E. 1883. *The voyage of the* Vega *round Asia and Europe.* London: MacMillan and Co.

Oard, M.J. 1990. *An ice age caused by the Genesis flood.* El Cajon, CA: Institute for Creation Research.

Oard, M.J. 1995a. Polar dinosaurs and the Genesis flood. *Creation Research Society Quarterly* 32:47–56.

Oard, M.J. 1995b. Mid and high latitude flora deposited in the Genesis flood — Part I: Uniformitarian paradox. *Creation Research Society Quarterly* 32:107–115.

Oard, M.J. 1995c. Mid and high latitude flora deposited in the Genesis flood — Part II: A creationist hypothesis. *Creation Research Society Quarterly* 32:138–141.

Oard, M.J. 1995d. Only one glaciation in southwest Alberta. *Creation Ex Nihilo Technical Journal* 9(1):4.

Oard, M.J. 1997a. *Ancient ice ages or gigantic submarine landslides?* Creation Research Society Monograph Series No. 6. St Joseph, MO: Creation Research Society.

Oard, M.J. 1997b. *The weather book.* Green Forest, AR: Master Books.

Oard, M.J. 2000a. Only one Lake Missoula flood. *Creation Ex Nihilo Technical Journal* 14(2):14–17.

Oard, M.J. 2000b. The extinction of the woolly mammoth: Was it a quick freeze? *Creation Ex Nihilo Technical Journal* 14(3):24–34.

Oard, M.J. 2001a. Vertical tectonics and the drainage of Flood water: A model for the middle and late diluvian period — Part I. *Creation Research Society Quarterly* 38:3–17.

Oard, M.J. 2001b. Vertical tectonics and the drainage of Flood water: A model for the middle and late diluvian period — Part II. *Creation Research Society Quarterly* 38:79–95.

Oard, M.J. 2001c. Do Greenland ice cores show over one hundred thousand years of annual layers? *TJ* 15(3):39–42.

Oard, M.J. 2002. Wild ice-core interpretations by uniformitarian scientists. *TJ* 16(1):45–47.

Oard, M.J. 2003. Are polar ice sheets only 4,500 years old? *Acts and Facts Impact Article #361.* El Cajon, CA: Institute for Creation Research, p. i–iv.

Oard, M.J. 2004a. *The Missoula flood controversy and the Genesis flood.* Monograph No. 13. Chino Valley, AZ: Creation Research Society.

Oard, M.J. 2004b. *The Greenland and Antarctic ice sheets: Old or young?* El Cajon, CA: Institute for Creation Research.

Oard, M.J. 2004c. The greenhouse warming hype of the movie *The Day after Tomorrow, Acts and Facts Impact Article #373,* Institute for Creation Research, El Cajon, CA, p. i–iv.

Oard, M., and B. Oard. 1993. *Life in the great Ice Age.* Green Forest, AR: Master Books.

Occhietti, S. 1983. Laurentide ice sheet: Oceanic and climatic implications. *Palaeo-geography, Palaeoclimatology, Palaeoecology* 44:1–22.

Olivier, R.C.D. 1982. Ecology and behavior of living elephants: Bases for assumptions concerning the extinct woolly mammoths. In *Paleoecology of Beringia*. D.M. Hopkins, J.V. Matthews Jr., C.E. Schweger, and S.B. Young, editors. New York: Academic Press, p. 291–305.

Oxnard, C.E. 1975. *Uniqueness and diversity in human evolution: Morphometric studies of Australopithecines*. Chicago, IL: University of Chicago Press.

Pachur, H.J., and S. Kröpelin. 1987. Wadi Howar: Paleoclimatic evidence from an extinct river system in the southeastern Sahara. *Science* 237:298–300.

Peixoto, J.P., and A.H. Oort. 1992. *Physics of climate*. New York: American Institute of Physics.

Pendick, D. 1996. The dust ages. *Earth* 5(3):22–23,66–67.

Péwé, T.L. 1975. *Quaternary geology of Alaska*. U.S. Geological Survey Professional Paper 835. Washington, DC: U.S. Government Printing Office.

Péwé, T.L., and D.M. Hopkins. 1967. Mammal remains of pre-Wisconsin age in Alaska. In *The Bering land bridge*. D.M. Hopkins, editor. Stanford, CA: Stanford University Press, p. 266–270.

Péwé, T.L., and A. Journaux. 1983. *Origin and character of loess like silt in unglaciated south-central Yakutia, Siberia, U.S.S.R.* Geological Survey Professional Paper 1262. Washington, DC: United States Printing Office.

Péwé, T.L., A. Journaux, and R. Stuckenrath. 1977. Radiocarbon dates and late-Quaternary stratigraphy from Mamontova Gora, unglaciated central Yakutia, Siberia, U.S.S.R. *Quaternary Research* 8:51–63.

Pfizenmayer, E.W. 1939. *Siberian man and mammoth*. London: Blackie & Sons.

Phillips, P.J., and I.M. Held. 1994. The response to orbital perturbations in an atmospheric model coupled to a slab ocean. *Journal of Climate* 7:767–782.

Pickard, J. 1984. Comments on "Wastage of the Klutlan ice-cored moraines, Yukon Territory, Canada" by Driscoll (1980). *Quaternary Research* 22(2):259.

Pielou, E.C. 1991. *After the Ice Age — The return of life to glaciated North America.* Chicago, IL: University of Chicago Press.

Pilgram, T., and D. Western. 1986. Inferring hunting patterns on African elephants from tusks in the international ivory trade. *Journal of Applied Ecology* 23:503–514.

Pitulko, V.V., et al. 2004. The Yana RHS site: Humans in the Arctic before the last glacial maximum. *Science* 303:52–56.

Preece, S.J., J.A. Westgate, B.A. Stemper, and T.L. Péwé. 1999. Tephrochronolgoy of late Cenozoic loess at Fairbanks, central Alaska. *Geological Society of America Bulletin* 111:71–90.

Quackenbush, L.S. 1909. Notes on Alaskan mammoth expedition of 1907 and 1908. *Bulletin of the American Museum of Natural History* 25:87–130.

Rains, B., J. Shaw, R. Skoye, D. Sjogren, and D. Kvill. 1993. Late Wisconsin subglacial megaflood paths in Alberta. *Geology* 21:323–326.

Redmond, I. 1993. *Elephant.* New York: Alfred A. Knopf.

Rensberger, J.M., and A.D. Barnosky. 1993. Short-term fluctuations in small mammals of the late Pleistocene from eastern Washington. In *Morphological change in Quaternary mammals of North America.* R.A. Martin and A.D. Barnosky, editors. Cambridge, NY: Cambridge University Press, p. 299–342.

Richmond, B.G., and D.S. Strait. 2000. Evidence that humans evolved from a knuckle-walking ancestor. *Nature* 404:382–385.

Rind, D., D. Peteet, and G. Kukla. 1989. Can Milankovitch orbital variations initiate the growth of ice sheets in a general circulation model? *Journal of Geophysical Research* 94(D10):12,851–12,871.

Rosqvist, G. 1990. Quaternary glaciations in Africa. *Quaternary Science Reviews* 9:281–297.

Roth, V.L. 1996. Pleistocene dwarf elephants of the California Islands. In *The Proboscidea — Evolution and palaeoecology of elephants and their relatives.* J. Shoshani and P. Tassy, editors. New York: Oxford University Press, p. 249–253.

Sanderson, I.T. 1960. Riddle of the frozen giants. *The Saturday Evening Post*, p. 39, 82, 83, Jan. 16, 1960.

Sarfati, J. 1999. How did millions of mammoth fossils form? *Creation Ex Nihilo* 21(4):56.

Sarfati, J. 2000. Mammoths — Riddle of the Ice Age. *Creation Ex Nihilo* 22(2):10–15.

Saunders, J.J. 1992. Blackwater Draws: Mammoths and mammoth hunters in the terminal Pleistocene. In *Proboscidean and paleoindian interactions.* J.W. Fox, C.B. Smith, and K.T. Wilkins, editors. Waco, TX: Baylor University Press, p. 123–147.

Scarre, C. 1998. *Exploring prehistoric Europe.* New York: Oxford University Press.

Schermerhorn, L.J.G. 1974. Late Precambrian mixtites: Glacial and/or nonglacial? *American Journal of Science* 274:673–824.

Schmidli, R.J. 1991. *Weather Extremes.* NOAA Technical Memorandum NWS WR-28. Rockville, MD: U.S. Department of Commerce.

Schultz, C.B. 1968. The stratigraphic distribution of vertebrate fossils in Quaternary eolian deposits in the midcontinent region of North America. In *Loess and related eolian deposits of the world.* C.B. Schultz and J.C. Frye, editors. Lincoln, NE: University of Nebraska Press, p. 115–138.

Schulz, M. 2002. On the 1,470-year pacing of Dansgaard-Oeschger warm events. *Paleoceanography* 17(4):1–10.

Schweger, C.E. 1982. Primary production and the Pleistocene ungulates — The productivity paradox. In *Paleoecology of Beringia.* D.M. Hopkins, J.V. Matthews Jr., C.E. Schweger, and S.B. Young, editors. New York: Academic Press, p. 219–221.

Selby, M.J. 1985. *Earth's changing environment.* Oxford: Clarendon Press.

Sharpe, D.R., and J. Shaw. 1989. Erosion of bedrock by subglacial meltwater, Cantley, Quebec. *Geological Society of America Bulletin* 101:1011–1020.

Shaw, B.D. 1976. Climate, environment and prehistory in the Sahara. *World Archaeology* 8(2):133–149.

Shaw, J. 1988. Subglacial erosional marks, Wilton Creek, Ontario. *Canadian Journal of Earth Sciences* 25:1256–1267.

Shaw, J. 1996. A meltwater model for Laurentide subglacial landscapes. In *Geomorphology Sans Frontières*. S.B. McCann, editor. New York: John Wiley & Sons, p. 181–236.

Shaw, J., and R. Gilbert. 1990. Evidence for large-scale subglacial meltwater flood events in southern Ontario and northern New York state. *Geology* 18:1169–1172.

Shaw, J., B. Rains, R. Eyton, and L. Weissling. 1996. Laurentide subglacial outburst floods: Landform evidence from digital elevation models. *Canadian Journal of Earth Sciences* 33:1154–1168.

Shaw, J., et al. 1999. The channeled Scabland: Back to Bretz? *Geology* 27(7):605–608.

Sher, A.V. 1968. Fossil saiga in northeastern Siberia and Alaska. *International Geology Review* 10(11):1247–1260.

Sher, A.V. 1991. Problems of the last interglacial in Arctic Siberia, *Quaternary International* 10–12:215–222.

Sher, A.V. 1995. Is there any real evidence for a huge shelf ice sheet in East Siberia? *Quaternary International* 28:39–40.

Sher, A.V. 1997. Late-Quaternary extinction of large mammals in northern Eurasia: A new look at the Siberian contribution. In *Past and future rapid environmental changes: The spatial and evolutionary responses of terrestrial biota*. B. Huntley, W. Cramer, A.V. Morgan, H.C. Prentice, and J.R.M. Allen, editors. New York: Springer, p. 319–339.

Shoemaker, E.M. 1992a. Water sheet outburst floods from the Laurentide ice sheet. *Canadian Journal of Earth Sciences* 29:1250–1264.

Shoemaker, E.M. 1992b. Subglacial floods and the origin of low-relief ice-sheet lobes. *Journal of Glaciology* 38(128):105–112.

Shoshani, J., and P. Tassy, editors. 1996. *The Proboscidea — Evolution and palaeoecology of elephants and their relatives*. New York: Oxford University Press,.

Siebe, C., P. Schaaf, and J. Urrutia-Fucugauchi. 1999. Mammoth bones embedded in a late Pleistocene lahar from Popocatépetl volcano, near Tocuila, central Mexico. *Geological Society of America Bulletin* 111:1550–1562.

Sjogren, D.B., and R.B. Rains. 1995. Glaciofluvial erosional morphology and sediments of the Coronation — Spondin Scabland, east-central Alberta. *Canadian Journal of Earth Sciences* 32:565–578.

Smith, G.I., and F.A. Street-Perrott. 1983. Pluvial lakes in the Western United States. In *Late-Quaternary environments of the United States*. H.E. Wright Jr., editor. Minneapolis, MN: University of Minnesota Press, p. 190–212.

Soffer, O. 1985. *The upper paleolithic of the Central Russian Plain*. New York: Academic Press.

Stalker, A.M. 1977. Indications of Wisconsin and earlier man from the Southwest Canadian prairies. *Annals of the New York Academy of Sciences* 288:119–136.

Steadman, D.W., and P.S. Martin. 1984. Extinction of birds in the Late Pleistocene of North America. In *Quaternary extinctions: A prehistoric revolution*. P.S. Martin and R.G. Klein, editors. Tuscon, AZ: University of Arizona Press, p. 466–477.

Steadman, D.W., and J.I. Mead, editors. 1995. *Late Quaternary environments and deep history: A tribute to Paul S. Martin*. Hot Springs, SD: The Mammoth Site of Hot Springs, South Dakota, Inc..

Stewart, J.M. 1977. Frozen mammoths from Siberia bring the ice ages to vivid life. *Smithsonian* 8:60–69.

Steward, J.M. 1979. A baby that died 40,000 years ago reveals a story. *Smithsonian* 10:125–126.

Stokstad, E. 2000. Hominid ancestors may have knuckle walked. *Science* 287:2131–2132.

Stone, R. 1999. Siberian mammoth find raises hopes, questions. *Science* 286:876–877.

Stone, R. 2001. *Mammoth: The resurrection of an Ice Age giant*. Cambridge, MA: Perseus Publishing.

Stone, R. 2004. A surprising survival story in the Siberian Arctic. *Science* 303:33.

Strahler, A.N. 1987. *Science and earth history: The evolution/creation controversy*. Buffalo, NY: Prometheus Books.

Stuart, A.J. 1982. *Pleistocene vertebrates in the British Isles*. London: Longman.

Stuart, A.J. 1991. Mammalian extinctions in the Late Pleistocene of northern Eurasia and North America. *Review of Biology* 66:453–562.

Sugden, D.E., and B.S. John. 1976. *Glaciers and landscape: A geomorphological approach*. London: Edward Arnold.

Sutcliffe, A.J. 1985. *On the tracks of Ice Age mammals*. Cambridge, MA: Harvard University Press.

Svendsen, J.I., et al. 1999. Maximum extent of the Eurasian ice sheets in the Barents and Kara Sea region during the Weishselian. *Boreas* 28:234–242.

Taber, S. 1943. Perennially frozen ground in Alaska: Its origin and history. *Geological Society of America Bulletin* 54:1433–1548.

Tangley, L. 1997. How many species are there? *U.S. News and World Report* 123(7):78–80.

Tassy, P., and J. Shoshani. 1996. Historical overview of classification and phylogeny of the Proboscidea. In *The Proboscidea — Evolution and palaeoecology of elephants and their relatives*. J. Shoshani and P. Tassy, editors. New York: Oxford University Press, p. 3–8.

Thiede, J., and H.A. Bauch. 1999. The Late Quaternary history of northern Eurasia and the adjacent Arctic Ocean: An introduction to QUEEN. *Boreas* 28:3–5.

Thiede, J., and J. Mangerud. 1999. New map revises extent of last ice sheet over Barents and Kara Seas. *Eos* 80(42):493–494.

Thiede, J., H. Kassens, and L. Timokhov. 2000. Laptev Sea system discussed at Russian-German workshop. *EOS* 81(32):361,366–367.

Thomas, R.H., and PARCA investigators. 2001. Program for Arctic Regional Climate Assessment (PARCA): Goals, key finds, and future directions. *Journal of Geophysical Research* 106(D24):33, 691–33, 705.

Thorson, R.M., and R.D. Guthrie. 1992. Stratigraphy of the Colorado Creek mammoth locality, Alaska. *Quaternary Research* 37:214–228.

Todd, N.E., and V.L. Roth. 1996. Origin and radiation of the Elephantidae. In *The Proboscidea — Evolution and palaeoecology of elephants and their relatives*. J. Shoshani and P. Tassy, editors. New York: Oxford University Press, p. 193–202.

Tolmachoff, I.P. 1929. The carcasses of the mammoth and rhinoceros found in the frozen ground of Siberia. *Transactions of the American Philosophical Society* 23:11–74.

Tomirdiaro, S.V. 1982. Evolution of lowland landscapes in Northeastern Asia during Late Quaternary time. In *Paleoecology of Beringia*. D.M. Hopkins, J.V. Matthews Jr., C.E. Schweger, and S.B. Young, editors. New York: Academic Press, p. 29–37.

Toon, O.B., et al. 1982. Evolution of an impact-generated dust cloud and its effects on the atmosphere. *Geological Society of America Special Paper 190*. Boulder, CO: Geological Society of America, p. 187–200.

Ukraintseva, V.V. 1981. Vegetation of warm Late Pleistocene intervals and the extinction of some large herbivorous mammals. *Polar Geography and Geology* 4:189–203.

Ukraintseva, V.V. 1993. *Vegetation cover and environment of the "Mammoth Epoch" in Siberia*. Hot Springs, SD: Mammoth Site of Hot Springs, South Dakota, Inc..

van Essen, H., and D. Mol. 1996. Plio-Pleistocene Proboscideans from the southern bight of the North Sea and the eastern Scheldt, The Netherlands. In *The Proboscidea — Evolution and palaeoecology of elephants and their relatives*. J. Shoshani and P. Tassy, editors. New York: Oxford University Press, p. 214–224.

van Hoven, W., R.A. Prins, and A. Lankhorst. 1981. Fermentative digestion in the African elephant. *South African Journal of Wildlife Research* 11(3):78–86.

van Hoven, W., and E.A. Boomker. 1985. Digestion. In *Bioenergetics of wild herbivores*. R.J. Hudson and R.G. White, editors. Boca Raton, FL: CRC Press, p. 103–120.

Vardiman, L. 1993. *Ice cores and the age of the earth*. El Cajon, CA: Institute for Creation Research.

Vardiman, L. 2001. *Climates before and after the Genesis flood: Numerical models and their implications*, El Cajon, CA: Institute for Creation Research, p. 81–92.

Vartanyan, S.L., V.E. Garutt, and A.V. Sher. 1993. Holocene dwarf mammoths from Wrangel Island in the Siberian Arctic. *Nature* 362:337–340.

Vaughan, D.G., J.L. Bamber, M. Giovinetto, J. Russell, and A.P. Cooper. 1999. Reassessment of net surface mass balance in Antarctica. *Journal of Climate* 12:933–946.

Velikovsky, I. 1950. *Worlds in collision*. New York: Pocket Books.

Velikovsky, I. 1955. *Earth in upheaval*. New York: Doubleday & Co.

Vereshchagin, N.K. 1974. The mammoth "cemeteries" of north-east Siberia. *Polar Record* 17(106):3–12.

Vereshchagin, N.K. 1995. An experiment in the interpretation (visual assessment) of mammalian bones from sediments of the Quaternary Period, In *Late Quaternary environments and deep history: A tribute to Paul S. Martin*. D.W. Steadman and J.I. Mead, editors. Hot Springs, SD: The Mammoth Site of Hot Springs, South Dakota, Inc., p. 61–64.

Vereshchagin, N.K., and G.F. Baryshnikov. 1982. Paleoecology of the mammoth fauna in the Eurasian Arctic, In *Paleoecology of Beringia*. D.M. Hopkins, J.V. Matthews Jr., C.E. Schweger, and S.B. Young, editors. New York: Academic Press, p. 267–279.

Vereshchagin, N.K., and G.F. Baryshnikov. 1984. Quaternary mammalian extinctions in Northern Eurasia, In *Quaternary extinctions: A prehistoric revolution*. P.S. Martin and R.G. Klein, editors. Tucson, AZ: University of Arizona Press, p. 483–516.

Vereshchagin, N.K., and I. Y. Kuz'mina, I. 1984. Late Pleistocene mammal fauna of Siberia. In *Late Quaternary environments of the Soviet Union*. A.A. Velichko, editor. Minneapolis, MN: University of Minnesota Press, p. 219–222.

Vereshchagin, N.K., and S.V. Tomirdiaro. 1999. Taphonomic research in permafrost regions: A survey of past and present studies in the former Soviet Union. In *Mammoths and the mammoth fauna: Studies of an extinct ecosystem*. G. Haynes, J. Klimowicz, and J.W.F. Reumer, editors. Proceedings of the First International Mammoth Conference. Rotterdam: Jaarbericht van Het Natuurmuseum, p. 187–198.

Vernekar, A.D. 1972. *Long-period global variations of incoming solar radiation*. Meteorological Monographs 12 (34). Boston, MA: American Meteorological Society.

Walker, D.A., and K.R. Everett. 1987. Road dust and its environmental impact on Alaskan taiga and tundra. *Arctic and Alpine Research* 19:479–489.

Walker, D.A., and K.R. Everett. 1991. Loess ecosystems of northern Alaska: Regional gradient and toposequence at Prudhoe Bay. *Ecological Monographs* 61:437–464.

Ward, P.D. 1997. *The call of distant mammoths — Why the Ice Age mammoths disappeared*. New York: Springer-Verlag.

Washburn, A.L. 1980. *Geocryology: A survey of periglacial processes and environments.* New York: John Wiley & Sons.

Watson, T. 1997. What causes ice ages? *U.S. News & World Report*, 123(7):58–60.

Webb, S.D. 1992. A brief history of new world Proboscidea with emphasis on their adaptations and interactions with man. In *Proboscidean and paleoindian interactions.* J.W. Fox, C.B. Smith, and K.T. Wilkins, editors. Waco, TX: Baylor University Press, p. 15–34.

Wellard, J. 1964. *The great Sahara.* New York: E.P. Dutton and Co., p. 33–34.

Williams, L. 1980. *The energy non crisis.* Wheatridge, CO: Worth Publishing Co..

Williams, L.D. 1979. An energy balance model of potential glacierization of northern Canada. *Arctic and Alpine Research* 11:445–456.

Williams, M., D. Dunkerley, P. de Deckker, P. Kershaw, and J. Chappell. 1998. *Quaternary environments*, second edition. New York: Arnold Publishing.

Woodmorappe, J. 1996. *Noah's ark: A feasibility study.* El Cajon, CA: Institute for Creation Research.

Worster, D. 1979. *Dust Bowl: The Southern Plains in the 1930s.* New York: Oxford University Press.

Wright, G.F. 1911. *The Ice Age in North America.* Oberlin, OH: Bibliotheca Sacra Co..

Wright Jr., H.E., and C.W. Barnosky. 1984. Introduction to the English edition. In *Late Quaternary environments of the Soviet Union.* A.A. Velichko, editor. Minneapolis, MN: University of Minnesota Press, p. xiii–xxii.

Young, R.R., J.A. Burns, D.G. Smith, L.D. Arnold, and R.B. Rains. 1994. A single, late Wisconsin, Laurentide glaciation, Edmonton area and southwestern Alberta. *Geology* 22:683–686.

Zeeberg, J. 1998. The European sand belt in eastern Europe — and comparison of Late Glacial dune orientation with GCM simulation results. *Boreas* 27:127–139.

Zimov, S.A., V.I. Chuprynin, A.P. Oreshko, F.S. Chapin III, J.F. Reynolds, and M.C. Chapin. 1995. Steppe-tundra transition: A herbivore-driven biome shift at the end of the Pleistocene. *American Naturalist* 146:765–794.

Zuckerman, S. 1970. *Beyond the ivory tower: The frontiers of public and private science*. New York: Taplinger Publishing Company.